# The Pratt Family: A Genealogical Record of Mathew Pratt of Weymouth, Mass., and His American Descendants, 1623-1889 – Primary Source Edition

## Francis Greenleaf Pratt

# CONTENTS.

# INTRODUCTION.

THERE are known to have been at least ten persons by the name of Pratt who settled in New England between 1621 and 1650. Some of these individuals were doubtless members of the same family, perhaps brothers, or of other relationship near or remote; but from what places in England they came, or who were their immediate ancestors, or in what ship each arrived, is very much a matter of tradition.

There are to-day, doubtless, in the mother country, legal records, and town or family genealogies, which, if examined, would clear up much of the obscurity which surrounds the early history of the Pratt families. It is to be hoped that at some time, not far distant, some one will make the necessary thorough investigations.

The name of Pratt, from a very remote period, has been common in England, especially in the more southern counties. The family is of Norman descent (the name frequently occurs in the Norman records), and had many distinguished representatives even before the Conquest. Much valuable information relating to the various branches of the Pratt families of England may be found in Chapman's Genealogy of the Pratt Families of Connecticut, who were descendants of Lieutenant William Pratt of Saybrook.

The family has embraced many noteworthy members, both in church and state. For example, Charles Pratt, the son of Sir John Pratt, Chief Justice of the Court of King's Bench under George First, who was born in 1713, educated at Cambridge, admitted barrister, distinguished for his professional knowledge and eloquence, and appointed Lord High Chancellor of Great Britain. He sympathized with the American Colonies in their struggle with the mother

country, and thus incurred the royal displeasure and was obliged to
resign his high office — his conscience and not his king supreme — but
was subsequently restored to honor and office. The love of liberty
and loyalty to truth have been strong traits in the family from its
earliest history.

The pages of this book show that there have not been lacking
many in this country who from the very beginning of its history have
honored their descent, and who have been honored for their unin-
terrupted integrity, their unusual success in business, their marked
intelligence, their patriotism, and their noble Christian purpose.

An attempt has been made in these pages to follow out with
a good degree of accuracy the genealogy of the Pratt family, especially as connected with Mathew of Weymouth. He was probably
related to Joshua Pratt, who settled at Plymouth in 1621, coming
over in the second vessel, and to Phineas Pratt, who came over in
1622 and settled at Weymouth, but afterwards at Plymouth and
Charlestown. These three, who were Pilgrims, are spoken of by the
historians as probably brothers, though the relationship cannot be
positively established. Besides these there was John of Dorchester,
who came over later, but was contemporaneous with them.

They were all the heads of large families, patriarchs of their
households; and their earliest descendants, sons and daughters, settled in Plymouth, Weymouth, Middleboro, Bridgewater, Easton,
Taunton, Quincy, Charlestown, and in many other towns and cities
in eastern and central Massachusetts, where to-day many branches
of their families may be found, while others of the same descent,
thousands in number, are scattered through the whole land.

The sources of information from which the facts in this book
have been derived are various, but they are such as cannot be
questioned. Town and city registers, historical memorials, private
family journals, handed down from generation to generation and
religiously preserved, registers of probate in many cities and counties, early recorded wills, ancient church records, and monumental
tablets in old burial places, have all contributed to the information
contained in these pages. This large field of research has been

patiently explored by Mr. Ernest B. Pratt, to whom much credit is due for his long and enthusiastic effort.

In these investigations many individuals have freely given their counsel and co-operation, to whom it is both a duty and a pleasure to refer with special acknowledgments: To Judge E. Granville Pratt, of Quincy, for the use of his very ample and accurate manuscripts, relating more particularly to the Pratts of Weymouth, Quincy, and Braintree, who are chiefly in the line of Mathew; to Eleazer Pratt, of Boston, long noted for his genealogical studies; to Rev. W. L. Chaffin, of North Easton, who has furnished important matter in relation to the Pratts of his vicinity; to Isaac Pratt, of Boston, and to Gerard C. Tobey of Wareham, for manuscripts loaned; to William Pratt, and to Rev. Francis G. Pratt, of Middleboro, for information relating to the Pratts of Bridgewater and Middleboro; and to Hon. Gilbert Nash, of Weymouth. Important aid has also been obtained from the different libraries, especially the Historical and Genealogical Library of Boston.

Nor should the generosity of many members of the family be forgotten, without whose contributions these investigations could not have been undertaken at the outset, nor carried forward to their final completion.

From the very nature of the work, no book of genealogy can be said to be complete. In attempting to arrange and systematize two hundred and fifty years of family history, errors will inevitably creep in, of name, of place, or of date. Many of the early records of families and of towns were imperfectly kept, some have been lost, others, as those of Taunton, were burned. But enough remains to make the present work fairly complete, especially so in the early generations; and probably any person in the Mathew line who examines it will be able to connect his family properly with the preceding generations, even though his own name may possibly not be found in the book.

# THE PRATTS OF WEYMOUTH.

By HON. GILBERT NASH,

HISTORIAN OF THE TOWN OF WEYMOUTH.

THE name of Pratt occurs upon the records of Weymouth more frequently than that of any other name, and the family has had from the early settlement a larger membership than any other family, and at the present day it counts its numbers among the largest.

The original planter Mathew, whose name is sometimes spelled upon the records Macute, Macuth, Micath, and Micareth, but evidently the same individual, was undoubtedly among the earliest settlers of the town, and came, possibly, or rather probably, with the Gorges Company, although there is no positive evidence of the fact. Yet the fact that his name appears upon no subsequent list, and he is found among the list of land-owners in about 1643, the first recorded list, and recognized as "an old resident," makes the probability almost a certainty.

He may have been a near relative of Phinehas Pratt, who was a member of the Weston Colony of 1622, yet the connection does not appear upon any record, nor is any connection traced between him and Aaron Pratt of Cohasset, except by marriage, or any of the many families of the name who were among the earliest settlers of New England. Like many another family of the old town of Weymouth, whose permanent settlement by the Gorges Company dates about the beginning of August, 1623, next after Plymouth in the Massachusetts Bay territory, its origin is lost with the records of that Company.

In the record of "possessions," which dates about 1643, is a description of his property, consisting of twenty acres in "the mill field" and eighteen acres "on Mill River," which would locate it centrally in the present village of East Weymouth; and it might be possible with care to indicate very nearly the identical property. In this list his name is spelled Mathew; and since this spelling follows through many successive generations, it was probably his true name.

The records of the first three generations taken from the town and county books (there are no early church records to be found) are quite full and complete, more so than those of almost any other family in the town, the planter Mathew leaving a will now upon record. His eldest son, Sergeant Thomas, killed by the Indians April 19, 1676, has records in Suffolk Probate Court identifying his family. His second son Matthew also left a will which is recorded, naming his children, who, with his wife Sarah Hunt, were deaf and dumb, as noticed by Cotton Mather. The third son, John, a cooper, left no children, but is identified by his will. His fourth son, Samuel, a carpenter, married a daughter of John Rogers, and had eight children, whose names are recorded in his will (names of the sons). The will of Joseph, the fifth son, names four sons and son-in-law, Aaron Pratt.

Of the grandchildren, several of them removed to other towns. A Matthew is on record as of Braintree, John in Bridgewater; Joseph also removed to the latter town. William[4], who removed to Easton, was undoubtedly son of William[3] (Matthew[2], Mathew[1]), brother of Joshua of Bridgewater and James of Easton, and their descendants are scattered in large numbers — for they have been a prolific race — all over the country, and are so numerous that their different records are very difficult to trace, and even a comparatively good genealogy of them is a work of immense labor and care.

In colonizing other and often distant places they did not thereby show any symptons of diminution at home, for there the family, until the present century, has easily held its station at the head of all the families in town in point of numbers. "Old Spain," the original home, "Back River" (North and East Weymouth), "Mutton Lane" (Lovell's Corner), and South Weymouth are still the residences of large numbers of the family, and what is true of few if any of the families of other names in the town, nearly if not quite all of the name who are living there are descendants of Mathew, the original planter, and his wife Elizabeth.

And naturally the "blood" is not confined to the name, for as is usually the case with all families, the descendants of daughters bearing other surnames are far more numerous than those of the name itself. Probably not an old family in Weymouth but has among its members many who sprung from the original Pratt stock; and could a convention be called of all who can trace a line of ancestry back to Mathew and Elizabeth, not an old name would be missing; and the name has always, as the records show, been a worthy and an honorable one.

# GENEALOGICAL RESEARCHES.

## By JUDGE E. GRANVILLE PRATT.

The record of that portion of the Pratt family originating in Weymouth affords a wide and unusually difficult field of research, several times carefully and patiently attempted, and as often abandoned, by the genealogist.

Its difficulties spring not only from the apparent mist that surrounds the common ancestor, but also from popular errors and falsely preconceived opinions regarding such origin, as well as from the unusual numbers of the family, and more particularly from the frequent recurrence of single and familiar names, common in the various lines diverging rapidly from the parent stock.

With the idea of bringing some "order out of chaos," and thereby doing some service to the family and the public, I began to gather such materials and glean such facts as could be found from all public and private sources at my command; and, with this end in view, made a thorough compilation of all the births, marriages, intentions of marriage, and deaths, from the earliest records (then kept in Boston), and also from those of the towns of Weymouth and Braintree, to the present day.

An exhaustive research was made of the Probate Records of Suffolk and Norfolk counties, and the earlier records of Plymouth county; and also a minute examination of the Records of Deeds of the first two counties; also from all accessible private records, memoranda, and instruments. Even the almost illegible, moss-grown tombstones of Weymouth were forced to yield their unwilling testimony.

All this information was carefully tabulated after a work of five years. Then the usual errors of record became obvious on comparison with authentic private records and documents, and they were corrected in accordance with established facts. All these data were carefully arranged and indexed, as became absolutely indispensable from the frequent repetition of names.

But the crowning difficulty was to arrange and classify these names under their proper branch of the family, which could only be done by the most careful and patient comparison of each record with all the others, and more particularly with private wills and memoranda.

It is a matter of serious doubt whether the same could have been done in all cases with more than approximate accuracy but for the timely and valuable services made in this direction by my aunt, Mrs. ELIZA T. LOUD, of South Weymouth, now in the eighty-sixth year of her age, a member of the family, a native of Weymouth, always resident there, and who, from age, acquaintance, and ability, was peculiarly fitted for this most difficult task. She has spared no pains in this work, and her success is well worthy of public recognition.

With her manuscript cheerfully placed in my hands it was possible to complete the family classification to my own satisfaction, and I believe, with accuracy.

I am also under obligations to SAMUEL A. BATES, town clerk of Braintree, for like services regarding those families settled in Braintree; as also to various members of the Weymouth Historical Society.

That minor errors have crept into the work is highly probable; but in any case where a doubt arose, the matter was at once carefully and patiently traced to its source.

I did not escape the popular error that our common ancestor was Phinehas Pratt, of the Weston Colony, and later of Plymouth; but a serious doubt quite soon arose as to the truth of this theory, — a doubt which grew stronger under careful investigation, until the theory held so long was fully abandoned, and I became convinced that the original ancestor was Mathew Pratt, also known under other given names, which were doubtless corruptions of his own. To deny this conclusion now would require the falsification of all the public records and private wills and documents at our command bearing on the subject.

After having given all the work of years which could be spared from professional labors to this arduous but fascinating work, I was forced by other duties to suspend active work thereon, hoping to renew the same at no distant day. But, finding this book in progress, with prospect of an early publication, I at last concluded to contribute the result of my own labors to the common fund of family knowledge, with the hope that it may give equal pleasure to the family and the public as to the compiler in its preparation.

# GENEALOGICAL MEMOIR

OF

# MATTHEW PRATT

*(Earliest Settler of the Name in Weymouth, Massachusetts),*

AND HIS

## AMERICAN DESCENDANTS.

1888.

# MATHEW PRATT.

MATHEW was the ancestor of nearly all the Pratts of Weymouth, and many of the name in Bridgewater, Middleboro, Taunton, Mansfield, Stoughton, Norton, Easton, Abington, Braintree, Quincy, Randolph, Holbrook and adjacent towns. His descendants can be found in other localities in Massachusetts, and in almost every state of the United States. He is referred to by Cotton Mather in his "Magnalia," as a very religious man (see quotation under his son Matthew). The reference to the early education of his son, coupled with the fact that he married in Weymouth and had a son born before 1028, places him among the earliest settlers, probably with the Gorges Colony, as his land is located with the "old residents."

In the first records of Weymouth he is frequently referred to as Macute Pratt and Mathew Pratt, the names being interchangeable in the same record; but his signature to the will is spelled Mathew.

The will of Mathew Pratt was recently found on file in the Suffolk County Probate Office at Boston. It is dated March 25, 1672, probated April 30, 1673, recorded May 20, 1673, and is as follows: —

MATHEW PRATT of Weymouth, being in health of body and having a competent use of his understanding and memory does make this to be his last will and Testament as folloe & saith —

First, I doe and bequeath my Soul to God that gave it, & after my decease my body to be decently buried and all my Debts honestly paide, and then all my wordly goods I dispose of thus —

I doe give to my loving wife Elizabeth Pratt all my whole Estate reall and personall, which is hereafter exprest, that is for her natural life.

I doe give to my Son Thomas Pratt after my wives decease, these parcells of land as folloe, four acres of land that did belong to Shaw's house & my share of land that I bought of James Nash &

19

that fifteen acres I bought of Deacon John Rogers & I doe give her that little Island in the fresh pond. I doe give him ten acres in the Cedar Swamp plaine which was a part of my great lott; Ad I doe give him my share in the two acres & half of Salt Marsh at Hollie, upon the condition hee shall pay to my Daughter Chard at my wives decease four pounds.

I doe give to my Son Matthew Pratt at my wives decease these parcells of house & land as follow my now dwelling house with all my houseing and all my Orchard & my land adjoining twenty acres bee it more or less. Ad I doe give him ten acres in the Cedar Swamp plaine which is also a part of my great lott provided hee pay to my Daughter Chard or her assignees three pounds at my wives decease.

I doe give to my Son John Pratt an ewe and lamb.

I doe give to my Son Samuel Pratt twelve acres of land neare his house. Four acres of it was William Brandams & eight acres of it was John Gurney's & when hee hath fenct it out as far as it is pasture hee shall have it and not before. & I doe give him one acre of Salt Marsh by John Pratt's house at my decease. And I doe give him that part of my common lott laide out to mee at Smell Brooke: Ad I doe give him my two acres of Swamp lot where it is in the woods. Ad hee shall have one Cow instead of that spot I thought hee should have in my Orchard.

I doe give to my Son Joseph Pratt that lott that was first Edward Bennetts at the pond twenty acres bee it more or less.

I doe give to my Daughter Chard seven pound sterling in good pay at my wives decease, which is to bee paide by Thomas Pratt & Matthew Pratt as above is expressed: Ad I doe give to her Daughter Johannah Chard my best bed & Coverlid at my wives decease.

I doe give to my Daughter White after my wives decease all that parcell of land that I have in land which is of Marsh & upland about three or four acres which is all except that which is above given to my Son Thomas Pratt & I doe give her two Ewes at my decease —

I doe give to my Son Thomas Pratt's Daughter Sarah five pounds at my wives decease.

I doe give to Thomas Pratt's son William Pratt that halfe mare and her increase that is between Thomas Pratt & myself to be decided at my decease.

I doe appoint my loving wife to bee my Sole Executrix to fulfill all this my last will & to have full power improve my whole Estate for her life & at her decease to give what she leaves to my Children & their Children as she shall then please.

I doe desire the Reverend Pastor Mr Samuell Torrey & my Kinsman Elder Edward Bate & my Son Thomas Pratt to bee the OverSeers to see that this my will bee in all points fulfilled; I doe also comit full power into the hands of these OverSeers to sell or dispose of any thing that I have left to my wife; if she shall have need of it for her comfortable livelihood; but not otherwise to dispose of any land but as above expressed, and hereunto I have set my hand & Seal the twenty-fifth of March 1672.

          *Mathew Prat*     (Seal.)

Signed Sealed in the presence of us
     EDWARD BATE
     THOMAS DYER —

An Inventory of the Estate of Mathew Pratt who deceased August 20, 1672, & appraised by us who were called thereunto the 12th of the 10th month 1672, &c. &c.

Here follows a long Inventory amounting in all to    £215   5s   0d

Some of the items are:

Twelve acres near Sam. Pratt's house.      24   0   0

In the possession of Samll Pratt before the decease of his father Mathew Pratt ten year or upward, given in marriage — more ten acres of wood land at Smell Brook      5   0   0

& two acres of Swamp purchased by Samuell Pratt of his father Mathew Pratt about 5 year before the sd Mathew's death —      01   0   0

20 acres above mentioned was halfe of it paide for before the decease of the sd Mathew Pratt by Joseph Pratt his Sonne in & the whole 20 acres was possest by the saide Joseph Pratt about seven yeare before the saide Mathew's decease —      28 10 0

the reason why the saide Mathew Pratt mentioned these lands in his will was because hee gave them noe deeds of gift of the aforesaid lands —

Some of the Weymouth records are as follows:

At "A General Court holden at Boston the 7th day of 10th month, December, A.D. 1636," land was granted to Mathew Pratt as follows: "Twenty acres in the Mill field, twelve of them first given to Edward Bate, and eight acres to himself, all of it bounded on the east with the land of John Gill, on the west with the land of Richard Waling, on the north with the Rocky Hill, on the south with the land of Richard Addames and Thomas Daly. Also eighteen ackers of upland, first given to Edward Bennott, now in the possession of Mathew Pratt, bounded on the east with the Mill River, on the west with John Whitmarsh's lot, on the north with the Mill ground, on the south with the Pond."

*Joseph Pratt, borne June 10, 1637, son of Mathew.*

In February, 1648, he was a "townsman," (selectman.) Lot granted to Mathew Pratt on the east side of Fresh Pond, February 3, 1651.

"January 11, 1657. — At a meeting of the Townsmen it did appear that upon account that Mathew Pratt, and *his son Thomas* Pratt, had entered 22,000 of boards, the Father 15,000 and son 7000, due to the Towne, £1. 9s. 6d." Land granted to Mathew Pratt, 1658, 1660, 1663, etc. Dec. 19, 1659, an Island in the Fresh Pond above the mill, and swamp land granted to Mathew Pratt.

May, 1660. — "The Towne is indebted to several persons for service in and upon account as follows: To Mathew Pratt for a Wolfe and Woodpecker, paid in boards, £1. s6. d8."

*Joseph Pratt, the youngest son, lived with his father until his marriage,* 1662.

Dec. 29, 1709. — "Mathew Pratt and son-in-law, William Chard."

Mathew was frequently a Townsman or Selectman, and appears to have been one of the most prominent men of the Colony.

In Mathew's will, recorded in the Probate Court at Boston, are found the names of all his children and two of his grandchildren. Also the wills or administration papers of each of his sons, in which they refer to each other as brothers.

In the records of marriages appears "JOHN, son of MATHEW Pratt, and Mary, daughter of Ensign Whitman." In John's will he refers to

"*My nephew*, Lieut. John Pratt," "*My nephew*, Deacon Thomas Pratt," "*My nephew*, Ebenezer Pratt. In the records is also found "*Lieut. John*, son of Samuel and Hannah Pratt, died Feb. 8, 1743;" and "Samuel, son of Mathew Pratt," states, "MY BROTHER, JOSEPH PRATT."

The Weymouth Records state: "Information was given against Joseph Pratt and Samuel Pratt for cutting wood on the Towne's Commons, and transported it contrary to Towne order, were fined fower shillings apiece."

Thus will be seen: —

JOHN, "son of Mathew,"
LIEUT. JOHN, son of Samuel and nephew of John,
DEACON THOMAS, son of Thomas and nephew of John,
EBENEZER, son of Samuel and nephew of John,
JOSEPH, brother of Samuel,

and hence it will be seen that Joseph the first of Weymouth was the son of Mathew Pratt.

NOTE. — As there is only one Joseph mentioned in the Weymouth Records up to the time Joseph marries Sarah Judkins, 1622 (and he "borne June 10, 1637, son of Mathew Pratt"), and after that as he is referred to as Joseph, Senior, until 1719, there can be no question that the first Joseph of Weymouth remained there until his death. Joseph, Jr., moved away from Weymouth to Bridgewater with his cousin William, in 1705. Hence the statement made by the historian Mitchell, in his history, and repeated by others, that Joseph the first, of Weymouth, was the son of Phinehas Pratt, is without the slightest foundation. There is no mention of Phinehas Pratt or his family in the Weymouth Town Records, but only of Mathew and his sons and their children, until after the year 1700. As it is absolutely known that Sarah, daughter of Joseph Pratt of Weymouth, married Aaron Pratt, son of Phinehas Pratt, it is not possible that this Joseph could be the son of Phinehas. Other proofs can be found in the Records, but these are given to show the error into which many have been led by those who have not taken pains to thoroughly examine them.

# EXPLANATION.

---

IN the accompanying Genealogy paternal names are printed in ROMAN CAPITALS, the prefix to each, in parentheses, denoting the number of the generation of the individual. Two columns of figures will be found in the left hand margin of each page. To trace succeeding generations in any family line, note the number in the first or left-hand column opposite the name of a son, and then look forward until you find the same number in its regular order in the second column. To trace preceding generations, note the number in the first column, opposite the generation number, and go back until it is found in its regular order in the second column. Only those lines that are numbered have been carried down, and generally only those descendants that bear the family name are recorded.

The following abbreviations are used: b. *born;* d. *died;* m. *married;* dau. *daughter;* (P.) *published;* (1), (2) first and second marriages.

24

# GENEALOGY.

I. MATHEW PRATT, b. ——; d. Aug. 29, 1672.
    (m. Elizabeth Bate?)

        Children:

| | | | |
|---|---|---|---|
| 9 | 1 | 1 | THOMAS, b. before 1628; d. April 19, 1676. |
| 51 | 2 | 2 | MATTHEW, b. 1628; d. Jan. 12, 1713. |
| 50 | 2¹ | 3 | JOHN, b. ——; d. Oct. 3, 1716. |
| | 3 | 4 | SAMUEL, b. ——; d. ——, 1678. |
| | 4 | 5 | JOSEPH, b. June 10, 1637; d. Dec. 24, 1720. |
| 7 | 5 | 6 | ELIZABETH, b. ——; d. Feb. 26, 1726. |
| 8 | 6 | 7 | MARY, b. ——; d. ——. |

5  7  (II.) ELIZABETH PRATT, of Weymouth (dau. of I. Mathew);
        b. ——; d. Feb. 26, 1726; m. Nov. 22, 1656, William Chard,
        Town Clerk of Weymouth. Elizabeth was his second
        wife. Grace, his first, d. Jan. 23, 1655. He was a school-
        master.

        Children:

        1  THOMAS, b. Sept. 27, 1657.
        2  CHILD, b. March 22, 1659.
        3  CALEB, b. Oct. 19, 1660.
        4  MARY, b. Apr. 8, 1663.
        5  SAMUEL, b. Oct. 1, 1665.
        6  JOANNA, b. Aug. 17, 1667.
        7  PATIENCE, b. Apr. 20, 1671.
        8  HUGH, b. Jan. 4, 1674.

8  8  (II.) MARY PRATT (dau. of I. Mathew), b. ——; m. Thomas
        White, of Braintree, son of Thomas, of Weymouth. He
        was freeman, 1681; d. Apr. 11, 1706.

        Children:

        1  THOMAS, m. (1) Mehitable Adams; m. (2) Mary Bowditch.
        2  MARY, m. Thomas Holbrook.
        3  SAMUEL, b. Sept. 19, 1676; m. (1) Deborah Penniman; m.
          (2) Sarah Torrey.
        4  JOSEPH, m. Sarah Bayley.
        5  EBENEZER, b. 1683; m. Lydia.

1  9  (II.) THOMAS PRATT, of Weymouth (son of I. Mathew), b. before 1628; m. Mary ——.

He was styled "Sergent Pratt," and was killed in the "Sudbury Fight" by the Indians, April 19, 1676. He was a large land-owner at Weymouth; held the office of Selectman several years, and occupied many positions of trust in the town. Rev. William Pratt (III.), in his Diary, states: "My father was slaine by the Indians the 19th day of April, in the year 1676." Henry Axtell was slain by the Indians between Sudbury and Marlboro, April 19, 1676." This establishes the date of the great "Sudbury Fight."

Thomas left no will, but his " brother John Pratt and brother-in-law White" (who married Mary, daughter of Mathew) were appointed guardians of his children, not then of age.

Children :

13  10  1  WILLIAM, b. Mar. 6, 1659; d. Jan. 13, 1713.
15  11  2  THOMAS, b. ——.
        3  SARAH, b. ——; " an impotent, helpless child."
        4  HEPZIBAH, b. ——; m. Ephraim Frost.
        5  ABIGAIL, b. May 15, 1662; m. Wm. Tirrell, son of Wm. and Rebecca Tirrell.

---

10  12 (III.) WILLIAM PRATT of Weymouth (son of II. Thomas), b. Mar. 6, 1659; d. Jan 13, 1713; m. Oct. 20, 1680, Elizabeth Baker of Dorchester, Mass. b. 1655; d. Aug. 20, 1728. (Estate valued £429 11s 6d.)

Child :

14  13  1  THANKFUL, b. Oct. 4, 1683.

Elder William Pratt moved from Weymouth to Dorchester in 1690; was prominent in the organization of a church there 1695, also, the "Dorchester Colony, for Carrying the Gospel Ordinances" to South Carolina, accompanying the expedition to Ashley River above Charleston, S.C., where a town was planted, named Dorchester. This religious colony (over which he was ordained Ruling Elder) was in an unbroken wilderness, twenty miles from any whites. Here they built a church, which is now in ruins; but the society that worshipped there still exists, having moved to Medway, Georgia, continuing to use the Congregational form of worship. This society took the lead against British oppression in 1776; and it opposed seces-

sion in 1861. Of this early settlement a writer states:
"A few dilapidated dwellings remain; and of the brick
church the tower alone stands, two courses high, its wood-
work all decayed, its doors and windows shown, but destroyed in their outlines by the bricks having fallen away."
He returned soon after to Weymouth, the climate not
agreeing with him; from thence, 1705, to Bridgewater, Mass.
(probably with his cousin Joseph), and subsequently to
Easton, 1711, where he died, his grave and that of his wife
being in the Old Burying Ground there. During his life
he kept a diary, which is now in the possession of Joshua
E. Crane, Esq. (a descendant), of Bridgewater. This unique
and exceedingly interesting little book, bound in leather
and well preserved (a pocket almanac and diary, printed in
the year 1691, in London), contains many references to his
life, a great portion of the book containing receipts for
various diseases written therein by Mr. Pratt, from which
it would seem that he was somewhat of an apothecary and
town doctor. Among the most peculiar of these remedies
are the following: "To stop bleeding take sum nip &
hold in the left hand, & put sum to the hollow of the left
foot, & lay sum nip in the neck." "When nothing ale
would do to stop the excessive bleeding at the nous, the
powder of a dryed toad mixed with beeswax put to the
nous hath stoped it: the toad for hast was dryed in the
ouven, but it shuld be hung up by the leag until it is dead
& dry." It also contains a complete account of his missionary tour to S. C. This, with a few other extracts from
this truly valuable work are printed below.

"My father was slaino by the Indians the 19th day of
April in the year 1676. I was borne on the 6th of March
in the year 1659. I was married the 29th day of Oct. in
the year 1680. I removed from Waymouth to bridgewater the 19th day of December in the year 1705. — removed from Waymouth to dorchester about the middle of
April in the year 1690. I was taken sick with the smal
pox the 26th day of March in the year 1691 (his wife, May
5). In the year 1697, the 16th day of December I was
ordained Ruling elder of the Church of Christ. Swear-
ing in a religious manner is a duty when called unto it.
Laid out for my brother Thomas pratt. &c. The 3d day
of September or the 14th day 1700, there was a hurri-
cane in South Carolina. The 24th day of feburary (1698)
there was a great fire in Charlestown, which burnt down
a great part of the town; and a few days before the fire
there was an earthquak in Charlestown. I have given

a bond to Captain Rit of Charlestown, to pay for a negro woman twenty and five pounds, at or before the 18th of August the year 1699."

It will thus be seen that Elder William was a slave-owner, the inventory of the estate mentions "two young negroes, £50." Their names were Heber and Hagar; they became the property of Mrs Elizabeth, and lived with her until she gave them their freedom, 1722, and a portion of land, in the deed of which she speaks in high terms of them. Heber was called "Heber Honesty," and was held in good esteem by all. In 1740 he sold his property to Josiah Pratt of Norton. Of Widow Elizabeth it is stated: "She was a person of excelling Piety and uncommon prudence, one of a very strict and religious conversation, a great lover of God's House, one of a Charitable spirit, and knew how to communicate to others and when there was real occasion would do it cheerfully."

### ACCOUNT OF THE FIRST VOYAGE OF THE DORCHESTER COLONY TO SOUTH CAROLINA.

*From William Pratt's Pocket Memoranda.*

On Dec. the 3d, 1695, we the church that was gathered in order to caring the gospel ordinances to South Carolina at this time, sum of us went into a long boat to go on board the Brigantine Friendship of Boston (Cap Hill), in New England in order to our pasing to Carolina, but missing ye vessell at first by reason of and strength of the wind could not come up with her again but were constrained to endure the cold 3 or 4 hours before we could get at any land, till at length we got to Dorchester neck, & from there returned to Boston all in safty.

December the 5th we set sail in ye aforesaid vessel to go on our voyage & having moderate & steady gale on the Sabbath evening which was the 8th day of ye month and ye 4th day of our being upon ye Sea we were in the latitude of the capes of Virginia, this evening the wind began to bluster being at north west, & the day following blew hard continually increasing its strength so that on Munday ye 9th day of the month in ye evening we wer fain to lie by i. e. take in all ye Sails excepting the main courner which being reafed was left to guide us as well as to stedy her, the helm being lashed to leward. So we continued till tuaday night, & about midnight ye wind was risen so high that the vessel had like to have sunk, by reason that the small sail was enough then to run under water, and had like to have done it, but the sailors made way for ye vessel to rise, by furling the mainsail & and bearing up before the wind, & we so kept except sometimes when ye wind abated as by fits for a short time it did at which time we lay by as before, all ye next day & part of the day following either on wednesday or thursday. We agreed to set apart *Friday* to look to y° Lord by fasting & prayer & to beg of him prosperous winds & weather. On Thursday about noon y° wind begun to lull & the Sun to shine out which it had not done so as that there mit be any observation, after our going out, so that on *Friday* we could with sum comfort carry on the work of the day.

On Saturday the 10th day of our voyage, we found we had got almost as far southward as y° latitude 31° and passed much westing for y° northwest wind had driven us southeastward. On sabbath day which was the 15th day of the month we were so favoured with wind as that we went with great spead on our course. On thursday and so forward y° wind often shifted, yet not so much as to hinder our going on in our dezired course, tho we could not go with so much spead as we desired. Thursday morning being the 19th day of y° month we came in sight of the land of Carolina, but were by a disappointment hindered from going in that day but the next day we got in through divine goodness being the 20th day of December — When we came to y° town our vessel fired 3 guns & the people to welcome us to the land fired about 9 guns which was more than us all, & when we came to ancor being in y° evening many of y° people being worthy gentlemen came on board us & bid us welcom to Carolina & invited many of us to their houses. I was among those most kindly entertained that night. I kept in Charleston about a week & then was carried up by water to Mr Normans, Increas Sumner & I were kindly entertained by the lady Axtel & the two other men endevering to get into favour with the Lady & other neighbors & to obtain the land at Ashly river and that we mit not obtain it, yet they could not provail — for as soon as we came the Lady & others of y° neighbors did more highly esteem of us than of the others as they told us they rejoised at our coming, tho there was no more of y° Church than Increase Sumner & I, & after we had discoursed secretly with them, they wer not only very kind to us, but also used all menes & touk great pains to obtain our Settleing upon Ashluy river & that they should endeavour to persuade our pastor & y° church to settle there.

Our minister was at this time up at Landgrave Mortons & some of the church and others at Charlestoun, our minister & church was strongly persuaded by y° Leout Governor blake & many others to go to new london to settle & upon y° account were persuaded to go to Landgrave Mortous w° was near this place.

About a week after we went by land to Charlestoun and was caryed by water up to Landgrave Mortous we, many of us together went to vew the land at new london. After two days we returned to landgrave Mortons. Mr Lord cald me aside & I had much discers with him and when he heard what I had to say consarning Ashly river and consarning new london Mr Lord was wholy of my mind & willing to take up at upon thos condishons that we discoursed about, at Ashly river which con-

dishons was keept privat between to or three (3) of us, when I
Sought arnestly to god for wisdom & counsel. God was gracious
to me for which I have great caus to prais his name as well as
for many other signal marsys. We kept sumthing secrit from
others which was greatly for our benifit. We came from there
to Mr Curtisis from there to Mr Gilbesons we ware very kindly
entertained at every place where we came, but when we came
we herd of som of thos that came from newengland that
had ben gilty of gros miscarriages wᵗ was atribut to us. Mr
Gilbeson culd me aside and had much discourse with me,
afterword he told me he was very glad yᵗ I came to Carolina
& that he had seen me & had oportunity to discors with
me. He told me he was much discouraged to see the ill-
carage of thos yᵗ came from New England, but afterwords he
was better satisfied & told me he did think thar was a great
diferents betwen the parsons that came from new England tho many did manifest their dislik of bad parsons that
came from New England yet they were glad of the coming of
good persons. We tarried there 2 or 3 days, being kindly entertained & when we came away they gave us provisions for our
voyage down to Charlestoun & were very kind to us. From
these we came to Governor Blakes where we were kindly entertained & wedlind with them, and after some discors with governor
blake we came to Mrs Camers where we lodged all night, being
very kindly entertained, next day we had a comfortable voyage
down to Charlestoun — Being the 14th of Janᵞ. The 16th of
Janᵞ was elxsion day in Charlestoun. After this Mr Lord and
some of the Church came up to Ashly river and upon the Sabbath after being the 20th day of Janᵞ Mr Lord preached at Mr
Normons house upon that text in 8th of romans 1 vrᵉ thus was
many that came to hear of the neighbors round about and gave
dilligent atension.

The 2d day of Feb boing sabbath day Mr Lord preach⁴ at
Ashly river upon yᵉ text 1 Peter 3–18 most of yᵉ neighbors came
to hear, all the next neighbors and some persons came about 10
miles to hear.

The Sacrement of yᵉ Lords Supper was administered to days &
2 deacons chosen. at this time there was great joy among the
good people tho I have sometimes been il & afrade of sickness
or some truble or other yᵗ would happen yet God hath been
very gratious to me and hath herd my request from time to
time and helped me & showed me great marcy & whhen I was
rody to be discouraged many times god incouraged me again &
dolivered out of my troubles.

The 1st day of February being the last day of the week & the
Sacrement to be administered & many of were to come away on
second day morning to Charlestoun to come to New England we
sot apart some time in yᵉ afternoon to pray unto God and there
was much of the spirit of god brething in that ordinance and
when we took our leave of our christian friends there was weep-
ing eyes at our departuer. wo had many a blessing from them.

15  14 (IV.) THANKFUL PRATT (dau. of III. Thomas), b. Oct. 4,
1683; m. May 12, 1702, Daniel Axtell, whose first wife was
Lady Axtell. He came to New England and settled in
Taunton (now Berkley), where he died. His posterity are
the Cranes of Berkley and Bridgewater, among whom are
Silas Axtel Crane, D.D.; Mrs. Caroline Marsh, wife of
Hon. Geo. P. Marsh, U. S. Minister to Rome; Dr. Edward
Crane, Editor of the American Register, Paris, France;
Hon. Joshua E. Crane, of Bridgewater.

Children:
1   ELIZABETH, b. 1703.
2   REBECCA, b. 1706.
3   HANNAH, b. 1710.
4   WILLIAM, b. 1713.
5   HENRY, b. 1715.
6   SAMUEL, b. 1717.
7   EBENEZER, b. 1724.
8   THANKFUL, b. 1725.
9   THOMAS, b. 1727.  Also Daniel, b. 1704.

---

11  15 (III.) THOMAS PRATT (son of II. Thomas), b. in Weymouth;
d. Dec. 1, 1744; m. (1) Deborah ———: she d. Jan. 12,
1727; m. (2) Desire Bonney, March 5, 1729, O. S.

He removed from Weymouth to Middleboro about 1695.
By the records, he was an inhabitant of " Bridge Water
Ford Farm," and sold, 1694, his quarter part of " that
swamp or meadowish ground granted by Plymouth Court
to Andrew Ford and James Lovell, which is called by the
name of Stearns Meadow."

He was a landowner in Middleboro, his name appearing
in the early divisions. 1704 he exchanged land lying on
the shore of Samson's Pond with James Barnabee for upland meadow.

Two of his children are recorded as born in Middleboro,
1701, 1705. A selectman, 1704. Town Treasurer, 1705. Soon
after, 1710, he went to Easton and settled there with his
brother (Elder and Rev.) William, where his children married. Thomas is recorded as a Deacon and Selectman in
Easton, and appears to have been a very prominent man in
the early history of the settlement. (See Chaffin's Hist. of
Easton.)

His Uncle John of Weymouth refers to him in his will
as " Deacon Thomas." Hannah, the widow of his cousin
William, son of (II.) Matthew, married Thomas Randall

and moved to Easton with her children. (See III. William, Son of II. Matthew).

His house stood where what is called the "Sever Pratt house" now stands in South Easton, just above the Cemetery on the east side of the road, and it has never passed out of the possession of the family.

Children:

18  16    1   THOMAS, b. about 1690; d. May 23, 1708.
          2   MARY, b. —— 1692; d. Jan. 17, 1761.
          3   JANE, b. ——; m. Nathl. Alger, Oct. 19, 1726.
25  17    4   JAMES, b. —— 1699; d. Oct. 29, 1774.
          5   ABIGAIL, b. June 23, 1701; m. Sept. 1736, Stephen Blanchard.
          6   HEPZIBAH, b. April 23, 1705; d. April 25, 1702.

          ————————————

16  18  (IV.) THOMAS PRATT of Easton (son of III. Thomas), b. about
              1690; d. May 23, 1706; m. Hannah ——, 1721.
              He was the first schoolmaster of Easton, receiving
              forty shillings salary, a surveyor of highways, and held
              other offices in the town.

          Children:

          1   THOMAS, b. July 31, 1722; d. July 14, 1725.
20  19    2   WILLIAM, b. Feb. 14, 1726.
          3   THANKFUL, b. Apr. 12, 1728; m. Joseph Drake, Oct. 2,
              1751.
          4   HANNAH, b. Jan. 11, 1731; m. Ephraim Cole, Aug. 29, 1754.
          5   THOMAS, b. Dec. 20, 1732.
          6   EPHRAIM, b. Sep. 14, 1736.
          7   RACHEL, b. June 25, 1738; d. March 28, 1753.
          8   DAVID, b. July 16, 1740; d. July 21, 1753.
          9   DEBORAH, b. Sept. 19, 1744; d. May 5, 1745.

          ————————————

19  20  (V.) WILLIAM PRATT of Easton (son of IV. Thomas), b. Feb.
              14, 1726; d. Dec. 11, 1806; m. (1) Silence Manley, Oct. 25,
              1748; b. 1730; d. Apr. 10, 1767. He m. (2) Sarah Taylor,
              b. 1738; d. March 25, 1787. He m. (3) Jemima Monk of
              Stoughton, Nov. 15, 1787. She (Jemima) afterwards m.
              Dea. Joseph Drake.

          Children of Silence:

          1   DEBORAH, b. July 11, 1750; m. Jonathan Ames, 1780.
47  21    2   ENOCH, b. Jan. 25, 1753; d. Aug. 28, 1818.
          3   HANNAH, b. March 9, 1755.
24  22    4   WILLIAM, b. Apr. 7, 1757.

5  ELIJAH, b. Sep. 7, 1759.   (In Revolutionary War.)
6  SILENCE, b. March 23, 1762.
7  DAVID, b. Jan. 15, 1765.

Children of Sarah :

8  EPHRAIM, b. Apr. 18, 1771.
9  NEHEMIAH, b. May 4, 1774.
23  10  NATHAN, b. May 22, 1777; d. March 15, 1800.
11  RHODA, b. Aug. 28, 1780; d. Oct. 19, 1814. ·

---

24 (VI.) WILLIAM PRATT of Easton (son of V. William and Silence), b. April 7, 1757; d. before 1819; m. Dec. 16, 1792, Matilda Hayward Winslow.   (He is styled "William 34.)

Children :

1  JAMES, b. March 3, 1798.
2  JOSHUA, b. Sept. 1803; d. Aug. 9, 1861

---

25 (IV.) JAMES PRATT of Easton (son of III. Thomas), b. 1699; d. Oct. 29, 1774; m. Nov. 22, 1733, Martha Willis, b. 1712; d. Feb. 17, 1762.

Children :

1  JOHN, b. Dec. 6, 1734.
26  2  SETH, b. Nov. 21, 1738; d. Aug. 27, 1802.
3  SILENCE, b. ——; bap. March 6, 1747.
4  MEHITABLE, b. ——; bap. July 1, 1750.
5  JONAH, b. ——; d. June 19, 1753.
6  A Child, b. ——; June 21, 1753.

27 (V.) SETH PRATT of Easton (son of IV. James), b. Nov. 21, 1738; d. Aug. 27, 1802; m. Mindwell Stone, b. 1740; d. May 23, 1828.
    In 1780, Seth Pratt, who had served some time as Lieut., took the command, toward the close of the war, of the East Co.  He was in service in several of the Rhode Island Expeditions.

Children :

28  1  JONAH, b. Dec. 16, 1775; m. Sarah Lothrop, May 23, 1797, Dau. of Isaac.
2  MEHITABLE, b. Dec. 29, 1777; m. Timothy Mitchell, Oct. 1, 1797, went to Vt.
29  3  SETH (DR.), b. March 8, 1780; d. Aug. 12, 1816.
30  4  SEVER, b. Apr. 27, 1782; d. Dec. 11, 1843.

29    31 (VI.) SETH PRATT of Easton (son of V. Seth), b. March 8, 1780;
      d. Aug. 21, 1816; m. Apr. 7, 1807, Rebecca Wheelock, b.
      July 12, 1786; d. Oct. 13, 1871, Dau. of Lyman and Mercy
      (Williams).  He was a physician.

      "Dr. Seth Pratt (b. Mar. 8, 1780, son of Seth), studied
      medicine with Dr. Issachar Snell of No. Bridgewater, and
      was a practising physician in Easton until his death.  He
      lived in the house, built about 1745, and used as a residence
      by the Rev. Solomon Prentice.  He is spoken of in terms
      of high praise as a man and a physician by the Rev. Mr.
      Sheldon, who preached his funeral sermon."

      "Seth Pratt, Jr., M.D., studied medicine at the Harvard
      Medical School, and received his diploma Feb. 25, 1832.
      He at once located at Myricksville, Mass., and remained
      there two years.  In 1834, he removed to Assonet village.
      Dr. Pratt was much interested in the temperance cause,
      and delivered lectures upon the subject."

      Children :

      1  SETH (Dn.), b. Jan. 12, 1809; d. Oct. 10, 1836.
      2  SARAH MALVINA, b. Oct. 12, 1810; m. Oct. 17, 1832, Cap.
         Seneca Hills of Franklin.
      3  ERASMUS DARWIN, b. July 22, 1812; d. March 3, 1834, at
         Dayton, O.

      _____

28    32 (VI.) JONAS PRATT of Easton (son of V. Seth), b. Dec. 16,
      1775; m. May 23, 1797, Sarah Lothrop, b. Aug. 6, 1776,
      Dau. of Isaac.

      Children :

      1  RUTH L., b. Apr. 27, 1790.
      2  JULIA.

      _____

30    33 (VI.) SEVER PRATT of Easton (son of V. Seth), b. Apr. 27,
      1782; d. Dec. 11, 1843; m. Jan. 4, 1807, Charity Lothrop,
      b. Aug. 14, 1790; d. Jan. 3, 1850, Dau. of Isaac and Sarah
      (Baily) of Easton.

      Children :

      1  LAURA, b. —— 1807; m. Edw. W. Doan, Jan. 20, 1828.
37  34  2  AMOS, b. Nov. —, 1809.
40  35  3  ISAAC L., b. —— 1817; m. Harriet W. Drake, May 16, 1844.
41  36  4  ABIJAH R., b. —— 1824; m. Mary C. Winter, Dec. 6, 1846.
      5  DAVID L., b. —— 1829; m. Susan Wade, June 1, 1851.

4 37 (VII.) AMOS PRATT of Easton (son of VI. Sever), b. Nov., 1809;
    d. March 25, 1877; m. (P.) July 22, 1838, Lucy M. Sproat
    of Taunton; she d. Dec. 7, 1849. He was for several years
    on the School committee; a manufacturer and land-owner.

    Children:

9 38  1  Amos Granville, b. July 17, 1840.
    2  Sarah R., b. Jan. 7, 1848.
    3  Elizabeth M., b. Jan. 25, 1850; m. Samuel E. Lowry,
      Dec. 7, 1870. He was (1870) a clergyman at Newton.
    4  Jerome B., b. Aug. 4, 1851. Lives at Roseville, Ill.

---

8 39 (VIII.) AMOS GRANVILLE PRATT of Easton (son of VII.
    Amos), b. July 17, 1840; m. July 2, 1863, Susan F. Thayer,
    b. 1844; d. March 3, 1885, Dau. of Ariel and Abigail.

    Children:

    Edith Abbie, b. ——— 1865; m. Oct. 5, 1886, Jesse J. Swan,
      son of Dr. Caleb and Louisa.
    James Erwin, b. April 29, 1867.

---

5 40 (VII.) ISAAC L. PRATT of Easton (son of VI. Sever), b. ———.
    1817; m. May 16, 1844, Harriet W. Drake, dau. of Joel,
    He lives at Roseville, Ill. (1887).

    Child:

    Isaac Sever, b. Aug. 13, 1849, in Swann, Ill.; d. July 14,
      1865. He was accidentally killed with a pistol, in Easton.

---

6 41 (VII.) ABIJAH R. PRATT of Easton (son of VI. Sever), b. ———
    1824; m. Dec. 6, 1846, Mary C. Winter.

    Children:

    1  Sever H., b. Sept. 22, 1849.
    2  Rox, b. Aug. 16, 1852.
    3  Abby L., b. Apr. 23, 1856.

---

3 42 (VI.) NATHAN PRATT of Easton (son of V. William and (2)
    Sarah), b. May 22, 1777; d. March 16, 1860; m. Nov. 25,
    1804, Sally Packard, she d. Aug. 18, 1831.

    In 1804, Nathan Pratt, blacksmith, bought of Jacob
    Leonard a tract of land, he bought also land from George
    Ferguson. He began at once to build the "Hoe Shop
    Dam," and in less than a year he had completed it, and

had also erected a trip-hammer shop, where he began the manufacture of hoes; Lewis Drake being connected with him in the business. Mr. Pratt moved to Plymouth with Oliver Ames, soon after the latter went there, 1807, and returned with him several years later. Mr. Pratt's shop was a favorite resort for children, who felt at home with the good-natured blacksmith.

Children:

1 SYBIL, b. Apr. 22, 1805; d. March 14, 1824.
2 WILLIAM, b. Dec. 27, 1807; d. at sea.
3 CALVIN, b. Oct. 12, 1810; d. Nov. 16, 1858.
4 JANE, b. Apr. 30, 1813; d. Oct. 22, 1834; m. May 30, 1832, Edwin Wait.
5 RHODA, b. Apr. 10, 1815; m. H. A. Fuller; d. 1887.
6 OREN, b. Sept. 1, 1818; d. Aug. 28, 1852.
44 43 7 ALFRED, b. July 15, 1820.
8 BETSEY, b. Jan. 9, 1823; d. Apr. 8, 1823.
9 SARAH, b. March 2, 1827; d. March 25, 1828.

43 44 (VII.) ALFRED PRATT of Easton (son of VI. Nathan), b. July 15, 1820; m. Jan. 20, 1845, Mary Williams Randall, dau. of Martin. He is a prominent member of the Masonic Lodge and other societies.

Children:

1 JANE FRANCIS, b. Jan. 6, 1846; d. Dec. 20, 1847.
46 45 2 ALFRED FRANKLIN, b. Sept. 11, 1847.
3 MARTIN DUNBAR, b. Sept. 29, 1851; d. Aug. 12, 1852.
4 GEORGE, b. Oct. 23, 1856; m. Feb. 25, 1879, Ruth Holbrook. They reside in Mich.

Children:

1 Carl Holbrook, b. March 20, 1881.
2 Dwight Reed, b. Jan. 12, 1887.

45 46 (VIII.) ALFRED FRANKLIN PRATT of Easton (son of VII. Alfred), b. Sept. 11, 1847; m. Nov. 21, 1871, Hypatia Franklin, b. 1848, dau. of John and Mary Franklin.

Children:

1 GEORGE A., b. Sept. 27, 1873; d. Sept. 27, 1873.
2 GUY WHITTIER, b. Nov. 28, 1874.
3 F. ASHTON, b. July 23, 1881.

21  47 (VI.) ENOCH PRATT, of Easton (son of V. William and Silence),
b. Jan. 25, 1753; d. Aug. 28, 1818; m. Salome Packard,
Apr. 20, 1784, of Bridgewater.

Children:

1  ENOCH, b. Dec. 2, 1785; d. Dec. 13, 1785.
2  HANNAH, b. Oct. 27, 1789; d. Jan. 18, 1883; m. Jonathan
Drake, Dec. 25, 1814.

2⁴  50 (II.) JOHN PRATT, of Weymouth (son of I. Mathew), b. ——;
d. Oct. 3, 1716; m. Oct. 9, 1656, Mary Whitman; she d.
July 10, 1716, aged 82, dau. of John Whitman.

He was a prominent man of Weymouth, holding several
offices, and leaving quite a property. His will is dated
July 12, 1714. Having no children, he leaves his property
principally to his nephews, Lieut. John, Deacon Thomas,
and Ebenezer Pratt; some others being mentioned not of
the immediate family.

NOTE. — Some writers have advanced the opinion, that
John Pratt of Dorchester married the above Mary Whitman;
that is an impossibility, as John of Dorchester died before John
of Weymouth. In the record of deaths his wife is mentioned as
the widow Mary of John Pratt, d. July 10, 1716, aged 82; whereas,
the wife of John of Dorchester married a second time. As
John of Dorchester died in 1647, she (Mary) was obviously of a
generation later. Again the record of her marriage to John
Pratt of Weymouth is nine years after the death of John of
Dorchester. This explanation is given to correct one of many
genealogical errors now in print.—E. B. PRATT.

2  51 (II.) MATTHEW PRATT, of Weymouth (son of I. Mathew),
b. 1628; d. June 12, 1712; m. June 1, 1661, Sarah Hunt
(b. July 4, 1640; d. Aug. 3, 1729), dau. of Enoch and Sarah.

In his will, dated June 4, 1712, he mentions his "brother
John Pratt" and "cousin William Pratt."

Cotton Mather, in his "Magnalia," Vol. 1, page 495,
thus refers to him in connection with the ministry of
Thomas Thatcher:

"One Matthew Prat, whose religious parents had well
instructed him in his minority, when he was twelve years
of age became totally *deaf* through sickness, and so hath
over since continued. He was taught after this to *write*,
as he had been before to *read*; and both his reading and
his writing he retaineth perfectly, but he has almost forgotten to *speak*; speaking but *imperfectly*, and scarce *intel-*

ligibly, and very seldom. He is yet a very judicious Christian, and being admitted into the communion of the church, he has therein for many years behaved himself unto the extreme satisfaction of good people in the neighborhood. Sarah Prat, the wife of this man, is one also who was altogether deprived of her hearing by sickness when she was about the third year of her age; but having utterly lost her hearing, she has utterly lost her speech also, and no doubt all remembrance of everything that refers to language. Mr. Thatcher made an essay to teach her the use of letters, but it succeeded not; however, she discourses by signs, whereat some of her friends are so expert as to maintain a conversation with her upon any point whatever, with as much freedom and fullness as if she wanted neither tongue nor ear for conference. Her children do learn her signs from the breast, and speak sooner by her eyes and hands than by their lips. From her infancy she was very sober and modest; but she had no knowledge of a Deity, nor of anything that concerns another life and world. Nevertheless, God, of his infinite mercy, has revealed the Lord Jesus Christ, and the great mysteries of salvation by him, unto her, by a more extraordinary and immediate operation of his own spirit unto her. An account of her experiences was written from her, by her husband; and the elders of the church employing her husband, with two of her sisters who are notably skilled in her way of communication, examined her strictly hereabout; and they found that she understood the unity of the divine essence, and trinity of persons in the Godhead; the personal union in our Lord, the mystical union between our Lord and his church; and that she was acquainted with the impressions of grace upon a regenerate soul. She was under great exercise of mind, about her internal and eternal state; she expressed unto her friends her desire for help; and she made use of the Bible, and other good books, and with tears remarked such passages as were suitable to her own condition. Yea, she once, in her exercise, wrote with a pin upon a trencher, three times over, 'Ah, poor soul!' and therewith, before divers persons, burst into tears. * * * She was admitted into the church with the general approbation of the faithful * * * and her carriage is that of a grave, gracious, holy woman."

Children:

i MATTHEW, b. Sep. 18, 1665.
i SUSANNA, b. Sep., 1684; m. Thomas Porter.

132 53 3 WILLIAM, b. May 5, 1673.
    4 MARY, b. Nov. 27, 1669; m. —— Allen.
    5 DOROTHY, b. ——; m. Aug. 13, 1700, John Whitman.
207 51 6 SAMUEL, b. April 3, 1676.
    7 SARAH, b. ——; 1672; d. Sep. 16, 1788; m. Isaac Ford.
    8 ANN, b. Sep. 14, 1682; m. Samuel White.
    9 HANNAH, b. Nov. 3, 1670; m. Samuel Whitmarsh.

52 55 (III.) MATTHEW PRATT, of Abington (son of II. Matthew), b. Sept. 18, 1666, in Weymouth; m. Mary ——; she b. Jan. 2, 1665; d. 1761.

He moved from Weymouth to Abington about the time of his father's death and died there July 1, 1746. Hobart, in his historical sketch, states:—Mary, widow of Matthew, died 1761, aged 96.

He was a selectman in 1728, and built a mill (with others) on the stream by Benjamin Hobart's, 1731. A man of considerable property, and probably the first of the name in Abington.

Children:
217 48 1 JOHN, b. Oct. 4, 1691. Moved to Bridgewater.
260 49 2 MICAH, b. —— 1692; d. Dec. 31, 1758. He moved to Taunton.
57 56 3 SAMUEL, b. ——; d. Oct. 14, 1744.
    4 MARY, b. Nov. 22, 1699; m. Feb. 11, 1719, Rev. Samuel Brown, of Abington. They had four children. All died young. She m. (2) Josiah Torrey, of Abington.

NOTE.—This family seems to have scattered, and it was only by great labor and much perseverence that the writer was enabled to locate the above son Micah in Taunton. It seems that about this time some of the young men in the several families of Pratts in Weymouth, probably finding the desirable land all occupied, sought new homes in adjacent and not so thickly settled townships—as we find that the brothers Thomas and William went to Easton; Samuel, son of Samuel, and Micah, son of Matthew, located in Taunton; John, son of Matthew, and Joseph, son of Joseph, in Bridgewater. The evidence in each instance is positive.
                    E. B. PRATT.

56 57 (IV.) SAMUEL PRATT, of Weymouth (son of III. Matthew), b. ——; d. Oct. 14, 1744; m. Oct. 22, 1719, Abigail Humphrey, dau. of Nathl. and Elizabeth (b. Jan. 12, 1698). Suffolk Records Deeds 40-260: "Samuel Pratt, son of Mat-

thew (yeoman) and wife Abigail sold to John Pratt, senior, for £50 their right in Nathl. Humphrey's Estate, Dec. 14, 1726." He was a town officer on several occasions.

Children:

1 ABIGAIL, b. Nov. 29, 1720; m. Peter Whitmarsh, Jan. 18, 1739.

60   58   2 SAMUEL, b. Sept. 7, 1722; d. May 12, 1792.

3 TABITHA, b. Jan. 3, 1725; m. Thomas Cushing, Oct. 24, 1745.

63   59   4 MATTHEW, b. Dec. 3, 1726; d. Oct. 5, 1799.

5 SARAH, b. Sept 12, 1729.

6 ELIZABETH, b. Aug. 14, 1732; m. Jas. Humphrey, Dec. 21, 1758.

7 HANNAH, b. Sept. 28, 1736.

---

56   60   (V.) SAMUEL PRATT, of Weymouth (son of IV. Samuel), b. Sept. 7, 1722; d. May 12, 1792; m. April 7, 1746, Alethea Cushing, dau. of Capt. Adam and Hannah (Greenwood). His wife b. Feb. 21, 1726.

Children:

1 LETITIA, b. July 27, 1746; m. July 12, 1766, E. Whitmarsh.

2 OLLA, b. Sept. 22, 1749.

3 HANNAH, b. Apr. 26, 1752; m. June 31, 1773, A. Bates, Jr.

63   61   4 CUSHING, b. Aug. 20, 1759.

5 TIRZAH, b. June 12, 1764; m. (1) Oct. 7, 1784, Joshua Bates; (2) Jan. 3, 1806, Eben Hunt.

6 ZENAS, b. Nov. 3, 1766; m. Jenny White, Sept. 4, 1794.

---

61   62   (VI.) CUSHING PRATT, of Weymouth (son of V. Samuel), b. Aug. 20, 1759; m. Nov. 13, 1783, Jane Dyer, dau. of Asa and Ruth (Whitmarsh), b. Aug. 20, 1764.

Children:

CHARLES, b. March 5, 1784.

ASA, b. —— ; d. —— ;

SUSAN, b. —— ; m. Asa Webb.

JANE, b. —— ; m. Sept. 10, 1818, Harvey Reed.

Children:

1 *Harvey H.*

2 *Jane T.*

3 *George H.*

4 *Ann F.*

59  63  (V.) MATTHEW PRATT, of Weymouth (son of IV. Samuel of
III. Matthew), b. Dec. 3, 1726; d. Oct. 5, 1799; m. Nov.
5, 1749, Mary Lovell, b. Feb. 5, 1730; d. Nov. 9, 1799;
dau. of Joshua and Sarah.

Children :

67  64  1  MATTHEW, b. May 20, 1752; d. Oct. 15, 1835, aged 83.
94  65  2  JAMES, b. July 17, 1754; d. Jan. 3, 1832.
97  66  3  JOSHUA, b. Sept. 26, 1756; d. Sept. 25, 1828.
        4  MARY, b. July 17, 1758.
        5  RUTH, b. Mar. 13, 1763; m. Dec. 3, 1789.  J. Dyer, Jr.
        6  LUCY, b. Sept. 2, 1765; d. Oct. 13, 1837; m. Apr. 14, 1785,
           Laban Pratt.  (See Laban Pratt.)
        7  DEBORAH, b. June 29, 1769.

64  67  (VI.) MATTHEW PRATT, of Weymouth (son of V. Matthew),
b. May 20, 1752; d. Oct. 16, 1835; m. March 19, 1775, Chloe
Pratt, dau. of Benjamin and Susanna; she b. June 8, 1754;
d. May 29, 1838.

Children :

71  68  1  MATTHEW, b. Jan. 26, 1777; d. Feb. 5, 1825.
        2  POLLY, b. Dec. 12, 1778.
        3  ABIGAIL, b. Oct. 25, 1780.
        4  ANNA or NANCY, b. July 16, 1782; d. Aug. 25, 1828.
        5  WARREN, b. Jan. 8, 1784; d. Sept. 10, 1830.
        6  ROYAL, b. May 13, 1786; d. Apr. 2, 1849.
        7  DEBORAH, b. May 2, 1788.
        8  BETSEY or ELIZABETH, b. April 4, 1790.
        9  CHLOE, b. Jan. 28, 1792; d. Jan. 29, 1792.
73  69  10  JOSIAH, b. Dec. 24, 1793; m. Dec. 13, 1818, Hannah Smith,
            of Abington.
78  70  11  SYLVANUS, b. Dec. 11, 1799.  m. Aug. 21, 1820, Betsey
            Savory, of Plymouth.

68  71  (VII.) MATTHEW PRATT, of Weymouth (son of VI. Matthew), b. Jan. 26, 1777; d. Feb. 5, 1825: m. Apr. 25, 1800,
Rachel Thayer, of Hingham.

Children :

        1  CHLOE, b. Sept. 20, 1802, m. Apr. 10, 1824, Hosea D. Pool.
        2  NABBY, b. June 20, 1805; m. April 24, 1839, Wm. Loud.
        3  MARY LOVELL, b. Aug. 9, 1812.
86  72  4  MATTHEW,  { b. Mar. 14, 1814. Rachel m. Apr. 13, 1833,
        5  RACHEL,   {    Peleg Stetson.

71  73 (VII.) JOSIAH PRATT, of Weymouth (son of VI. Matthew),
       b. Dec. 24, 1793; m. (P.) Dec. 13, 1818, Hannah Smith, of
       Abington.  He kept a grocery-store at Lovell's Corner, on
       Queen Ann's Turnpike and Pleasant Street, S. Weymouth.

       Children :

76  71   1  JOSIAH MERRITT, b. Oct. 22, 1819; m. Mary Pratt.
         2  JOHN QUINCY, b. Apr. 15, 1823; d. March 18, 1825.
82  75   3  BENJAMIN F., b. ——, 1818; m. Sept. 11, 1853, Martha W.
            Pember, b. 1824.

---

74  76 (VIII.) JOSIAH M. PRATT, of Weymouth (son of VII. Josiah),
       b. Oct. 21, 1819; d. ——;  m. Dec. 23, 1840, Mary Pratt.
       He was a shoemaker.  He m. (2) Sarah E. Nash, of Scit-
       uate, Jan. 13, 1862.

       Children :

         1  HENRY CLINTON, b. Nov. 27, 1842; d. July 18, 1845.
         2  JOSIAH, b. Jan 12, 1844; d. Sept. 11, 1844.
         3  FRANCIS SUMNER, b. Feb. 22, 1845.
         4  JOSIAH QUINCY, b. April 3, 1847.
         5  HANNAH MARIA, b. Feb. 6, 1849.
85  77   6  WILLIAM HENRY, b. Mar. 13, 1851.
         7  MARY ELLA, b. May 18, 1853.
         8  CORDELIA FRANCES, b. Nov. 1, 1871; d. July 24, 1872.

---

70  78 (VII.) SYLVANUS PRATT, of Weymouth (son of VI. Matthew
       and Chloe), b. Dec. 11, 1799; d. Aug. 7, 1870; m. Aug. 21,
       1820, Elizabeth Savery, of Plymouth, b. 1795, dau. of Mi-
       chael and Anna (Driscoll); she d. Nov. 10, 1871.

       Children :

89  79   1  HENRY SYLVANUS, b. June 24, 1821.
90  80   2  JOHN W., b. Nov. 30, 1826.
93  81   3  EDWIN B., b. ——; m. (P.) Aug. 7, 1851, Abby Ann Tynes.

---

75  82 (VIII.) BENJAMIN F. PRATT, of Weymouth (son of VII. Jo-
       siah), b. 1818; m. Sept. 11, 1853, Martha W. Pember, dau.
       of Daniel B. and Abigail, of Vermont.

       Child :

84  83   Franklin H., b. Feb. 6, 1855.

83 84 (IX.) FRANKLIN HOWARD PRATT, of Weymouth (son of
VIII. Benjamin F.), b. Feb. 6, 1855; m. March 3, 1880,
Annie W. Ford, dau. of Nathan and Almera; she b. 1855.

Child:

FRANKLIN NATHAN, b. Jan. 25, 1885.

---

77 85 (IX.) WILLIAM H. PRATT, of Brockton (son of VIII. Josiah
M.), b. March 13, 1851; m. Marian L. Walker.

Child:

MAUD L., b. April 7, 1880; d. July 30, 1880.

---

72 86 (VIII.) MATTHEW PRATT, of Weymouth (son of VII. Matthew and Rachel), b. March 14, 1814; d. ———; m. (P.) in
Weymouth, April 11, 1840, Catherine S. Webb, of Scituate.

Children:

86 87   1 MATTHEW EVERETT, b. about 1841.
        2 EMMA J., b. Jan. 23, 1851.
        3 LIZZIE SOPHIA, b. Sept. 7, 1854.
        4 ALICE LINWOOD, b. June 19, 1859; m. Levi Marshall Sut-
          ton, May 1, 1880.
        5 WALKER WEBB, b. April 5, 1867.

---

87 88 (IX.) MATTHEW E. PRATT, of Weymouth (son of VIII. Matthew), b. about 1841; m. July 9, 1862, Caroline A. Bishop,
of Cambridge, dau. of Henry H. and Elizabeth.

Children:

        1 EVERETT MATTHEW, b. April 15, 1863.
        2 CAROLINE ELIZABETH, b. Feb. 13, 1870.

---

70 89 (VIII.) HENRY SYLVANUS PRATT, of Randolph (son of VII.
Sylvanus of Weymouth), b. June 24, 1821; d. March 14,
1863; m. (P.) Nov. 22, 1850, Elizabeth Ann Howard.
He was a manufacturer in Randolph.

Children:

        1 ALMIRA, b. July 16, 1851.
        2 HENRY A., b. Sept. 21, 1857.
        3 Child, b. Aug. 30, 1860.

80 90 (VIII.) JOHN WINSOR PRATT, of Randolph (son of VII.
Sylvanus), b. Nov. 30, 1826; m. (1) Olive Jane Thayer, b.
May 4, 1831; d. May 11, 1856. He m. (2), Sept. 14, 1856,
Nancy E. Spear, b. 1837, dau. of Otis and Elizabeth.

He started in business in Randolph with a very small
capital, and by industry and enterprise has accumulated a
large property, and is now (1888) one of the leading men of
the town. His business is the manufacture of leather shoe-
lacings and shoe-findings, principally the former. He
served one term in the State Legislature, is a Director of
the Randolph National Bank, Trustee of the Turner Library, and has held other influential positions, having been
a very active man, not only in business, but in the Baptist
Church. For the past few years he has devoted considerable of his time to travel, his son Herbert managing the
business during his absence.

Children of Olive :
1  MARY JANE, b. Apr. 24, 1851; d. May 4, 1851.
2  ALICE JANE, b. June 25, 1852; m. Dec. 17, 1873, Charles T.
Bainbridge, of New York.
92 91  3  HERBERT WINSOR, b. June 7, 1855.

Children of Nancy :
4  ISABEL, b. Dec. 28, 1856; m. Nov. 2, 1882, W. C. H. Badger, of Boston.
5  MARY EMMA, b. Aug. 23, 1865.
6  JOHN ARTHUR,
7  ARTHUR SPEAR, } b. Feb. 21, 1870; { d. Sept. 14, 1875.


91 92 (IX.) HERBERT W. PRATT, of Randolph (son of VIII. John
W.), b. June 7, 1855; m. Jan. 26, 1881, Helen White Belcher, dau. of Hon. J. White Belcher of Randolph; she
b. 1860.

He is in business with his father, having the entire
charge of the extensive manufactory.


81 93 (VIII.) EDWIN B. PRATT, of Quincy (son of VII. Sylvanus),
b. Apr. 14, 1832; m. Aug. 7, 1851, Abbie M. Tynes, dau.
of William and Maria; she d. Sept. 19, 1885.

"Removing, in childhood, with his parents to Randolph,
he was educated in the public schools of that town. Very
early in life he commenced, in Boston, the sale of leather,

which business, for more than a quarter of a century, he has successfully followed, winning thereby a handsome competency. Soon after commencing business in Boston he took up his residence in Quincy, and now owns and occupies a fine house opposite the birthplace of the patriot, John Hancock, the present site of the Adams Academy. His business tact and financial ability soon promoted his election as a Director of the Mount Wollaston National Bank, of which institution he has for several years been President. He is also a Director of the National Bank of the Commonwealth of Boston.

Though not an active politician, Mr. Pratt was nominated by the Republicans of Quincy, and handsomely elected by the voters of his district as a member of the House of 1879, serving on the committee on Banks and Banking. Having been re-elected to the House of 1880, he served on the same committee, of which his practical experience made him a valuable member." (Marden's Hist. of the Government of Mass. Vol. II., p. 207).

Children:

1 ABBY J., b. Sept. 26, 1854: d. Dec. 25, 1900.
2 ARTHUR C., b. Sept. 21, 1858; d. Aug. 28, 1866.
3 NELLIE M., b. Feb. 25, 1864; d. May 28, 1882.
4 MINNIE J., b. Nov. 20, 1867.
5 BESSIE LOUISA, b. May 10, 1869.
6 LILLIAN W., b. Feb. 21, 1871; d. July 28, 1871.
7 EDWARD IRVING, b. March 4, 1873; d. May 22, 1873.
8 EDWIN B., b. Sept. 14, 1874.

---

65  94 (VI.) JAMES PRATT, of Weymouth (son of V. Matthew), b. July 17, 1754; d. Jan. 3, 1832; m. Aug. 1, 1776, Elizabeth Rice, dau. of David and Silence (Walker); b. Dec. 17, 1755; d. June 4, 1788. M. (2), Feb. 13, 1791, Mary Holbrook, dau. of ——, she d. Aug. 27, 1820, aged 67.

Children of Elizabeth:

1 ELIZABETH, b. Nov. 1, 1776; m. Apr. 6, 1794, Wm. P. Everson.
2 REBECCA, b. Oct. 20, 1778.
3 JAMES, b. June 20, 1783; d. Nov. 22, 1834.

Children of Mary:

102  96 4 JACOB, } b. Jan. 21, 1792. { m. Abigail L. Dyer.
103  96 5 JOHN, } m. May 26, 1823, Betsey Joy; d. Apr. 9, 1825.
6 MARY, b. July 14, 1795; m. Nov. 12, 1815, B. Burrell.

66   97 (VI.) JOSHUA PRATT, of Weymouth (son of V. Matthew), b.
Sept. 23, 1756; d. Sept. 25, 1828; m. Aug. 2, 1777, Lydia
Pratt, dau. of Joseph and Sarah; she d. Dec. 28, 1835, aged
78; b. Feb. 18, 1758.

Children:

    1   NANNY, b. Jan. 1, 1778; d. Aug. 22, 1861; m. Abner Pratt,
Feb. 7, 1799.
104   98   2   JOSHUA, b. Sept. 16, 1780.
107   99   3   JOSEPH, b. May 10, 1784.
101   100   4   ENOCH, b. June 27, 1787; m. Jan. 5, 1807, Sally Thompson.
    5   THOMAS, b. May 14, 1700; m. Ann Porter, Nov. 27, 1851-2.
    6   LYDIA RANDALL, b. Nov. 20, 1796; d. Jan. 4, 1867; m.
James Bicknell, 1822.
    7   JACOB, b. June 1790; d. young.

---

100   101 (VII.) ENOCH PRATT, of Weymouth (son of VI. Joshua),
b. June 27, 1787; m. Jan. 5, 1807, Sally Thompson.

Children:

    1   ENOCH, b. May 21, 1808.
    2   SALLY, b. Aug. 17, 1811.
    3   SUSAN, b. Nov. 4, 1813.
    4   ROSWELL HAWKES, b. —— 1826; m. Apr. 12, 1871, Betsey
Dyer Pratt; b. 1829, dau. of Jacob and Abigail L. (Dyer).

---

95   102 (VII.) JACOB PRATT, of Weymouth (son of VI. James), b.
Jan. 21, 1792; m. Oct. 30, 1825, Abigail L. Dyer; d. Oct.
28, 1875, aged 72.

Children:

    1   BETSEY DYER, b. Jan. 31, 1829.
    2   ABIGAIL A., b. Oct. 22, 1834; d. Aug. 19, 1836.
    3   CALVIN PHILIP, b. Apr. 20, 1838.
    4   JACOB FRANCIS, b. Feb. 20, 1840.

---

96   103 (VII.) JOHN PRATT, of Weymouth (son of VI. James), b. Jan.
21, 1792; d. Apr. 9, 1825; m. May 26, 1822, Betsey Joy.

Child:

BETSEY JOY, b. —— 1823.

98 104 (VII.) JOSHUA PRATT, of Weymouth (son of VI. Joshua),
b. Sept. 16, 1780; m. Sept. 29, 1803, Mary French, dau. of
Asa and Hannah (Wade), b. Dec. 1, 1784.

Children:
1 MARY, b. Jan. 23, 1804.
111 105 2 JOSHUA, b. Dec. 9, 1806; m. Feb. 28, 1827, Mercy V. Burrell.
119 106 3 QUINCY, b. May 20, 1809; m. May 27, 1835, Sally Pratt.
4 MARY, b. July 20, 1811; m. Aug. 11, 1830, Laban Dunbar.
5 EMELINE F., b. Jan. 5, 1814; m. (P.) Nov. 20, 1830, Warren
Dunbar.
6 HANNAH, b. March 22, 1817; d. 1817.
7 HANNAH W., b. Jan. 23, 1819; m. May 3, 1835, Hervey
Haydon.
8 BELINDA P., b. Feb. 28, 1821.
9 ELIZABETH, b. Feb. 6, 1827; d. Sept. 4, 1830.

---

99 107 (VII.) JOSEPH PRATT, of Weymouth (son of VI. Joshua),
b. May 10, 1784; d. Apr. 30, 1844; m. Oct. 24, 1802, Nancy
Dyer, b. Sept. 11, 1785; d. Jan. 16, 1857, dau. of Solomon
and Mary.

Children:
1 NANCY DYER, b. Feb. 13, 1803; m. Apr. 8, 1819, Wm. Rice.
2 BETSEY PLUMER, b. Jan. 7, 1805; m. Asa Dyer.
3 JOSEPH, b. Sept. 19, 1806 (never married).
120 108 4 JOHN DYER, b. Apr. 20, 1809; m. Catharine Porry.
5 DAVID, b. Dec. 8, 1811; d. Dec. 10, 1811.
6 MARGARET NEWELL, b. Apr. 5, 1812; m. Wm. Rice.
7 JANE, b. Aug. 31, 1813; m. March 18, 1831, Asa Kingman.
123 109 8 SOLOMON DYER, b. Dec. 3, 1816; m. Hannah Binney.
9 MARY DOWNING, b. Jan. 19, 1819; m. Enos Lincoln.
10 LUCY DYER, b. June 1, 1822; m. Jas. Haydon.
128 110 11 AUGUSTUS, b. Sept. 30, 1823.
12 SOPHRONIA S., b. Apr. 5, 1826; m. Nathan Hayward.
13 JOSIE,
14 JOSHUA P., } b. Jan. 10, 1828; all d. Jan. 14, 1828.
15 SALOME,
16 NANCY, b. Dec. 18, 1834; d. Jan. 10, 1836.

---

105 111 (VIII.) JOSHUA PRATT, of Weymouth (son of VII. Joshua),
b. Dec. 9, 1806; d.——; m. Mercy V. Burrell, Feb. 28, 1827.

Children:

  1 CYLENDA H., b. Sept. 16, 1828; m. J. Q. Denton.
  2 ELIZABETH B., b. July 16, 1830; m. Saml. Whitmarsh.
114 112 3 ASA BURRELL, b. Oct. 4, 1832; m. Sarah J. Bailey.
130 113 4 QUINCY, b. Dec. 14, 1834; m. Mary Pratt, dau. of Linsey
    and Elizabeth H.
  5 HELEN FRANCES, b. May 2, 1837; m. Henry Hicky.

---

112 114 (IX.) ASA B. PRATT, of Weymouth (son of VIII. Joshua),
  b. Oct. 4, 1832; m. (1) (P.) Nov. 24, 1853, Lillias B. Richmond, b. 1836; m. (2) Sarah J. Bailey, Oct. 9, 1867, dau.
  of Capt. Henry and Sarah (Gardner).

  Children of Lillias:

117 115 1 GUSTAVUS M., b. Feb. 23, 1857.
118 116 2 WILLIE A., b. Aug. 11, 1859.

  Child of Sarah J.:

  3 SUSIE EVELINE, b. Sep. 5, 1871.

---

115 117 (X.) GUSTAVUS M. PRATT, of Weymouth (son of IX. Asa B.),
  b. Feb. 23, 1857, m. May 29, 1879, Ansella P. Joy, dau. of
  Nathl. F.

  Children:

  1 EMMA MILTON, b. Dec. 27, 1879.
  2 HENRY CLIFFORD, b. Jan. 25, 1882.
  3 CHRISTIANNA J., b. Apr. 11, 1885; d. Apr. 24, 1885.

---

116 118 (X.) WILLIE A. PRATT, of Weymouth (son of IX. Asa B.),
  b. Aug. 11, 1859; m. Emma M. Tirrell, Nov. 6, 1881, dau.
  of Almer D., Jr., and Annie (Colston).

  Child:

  1 ANNIE HOLBROOK, b. May 13, 1882.

---

106 119 (VIII.) QUINCY PRATT, of Weymouth (son of VII. Joshua),
  b. May 20, 1809; d. May 31, 1872; m. May 27, 1835, Sally
  Pratt, dau. of Enoch.

Children :

1 LEONARD FRANCIS, b. March 7, 1836 ; d. March 5, 1865.
2 JULIA IRVING, b. Feb. 29, 1848 ; d. Jan. 27, 1850.
3 EDWARD, b. Jan. 17, 1851.

---

106  120 (VIII.) JOHN DYER PRATT, of Weymouth (son of VII. Joseph), b. Apr. 26, 1809 ; m. Catharine M. Perry.

Children :

1 ABBY ANN, b. Apr. 27, 1838 ; m. W. L. Salisbury.
2 SARAH MATILDA, b. Nov. 21, 1840 ; d. young.
3 SARAH MATILDA, b. Apr. 29, 1845 ; m. E. Blossom.
122  121  4 EBENEZER PERRY, b. March 12, 1847.
5 JOSEPHINE, b. June 12, 1849 ; m. Everett Bates.
6 LUCY ELLA, b. May 12, 1852 ; d. Apr. 29, 1853.

---

121  122 (IX.) EBENEZER P. PRATT, of Weymouth (son of VIII. John D.), b. March 12, 1847 ; m. Fanny Rebecca Cook, dau. of Wm. B. and Rebecca F., Oct. 7, 1903.

Child :

1 WALLACE HAYWARD, b. Nov. 21, 1875.

---

100  123 (VIII.) SOLOMON D. PRATT, of Weymouth (son of VII. Joseph), b. Dec. 3, 1816 ; d. Dec. 17, 1846 ; m. Oct. 20, 1838, Hannah Binney, of Hingham, and resided there.

Children :

1 JANE KINGMAN, b. June 16, 1845 ; d. Apr. 15, 1848.
126  124  2 JOSEPH, b. June 16, 1845 ; m. Eliza A. Pierce.
3 JANE K., b. Dec. 16, 1850 ; d. May 25, 1851.
127  125  4 HENRY AUGUSTUS, b. —— ; m. Ellen M. Edwards.
5 LUCINDA, b. —— ; m. J. R. Totman.

---

124  126 (IX.) JOSEPH PRATT, of Hingham (son of VIII. Solomon D.), b. Jan. 16, 1845 ; m. Nov. 23, 1870, Eliza Ann Pierce of Maine, dau. of James and Lucinda.

Children :

1 GARRY ADAMS, b. July 20, 1874.
2 EMMA ETHEL, b. June 1, 1877.

125  127 (IX.) HENRY A. PRATT, of Hingham (son of VIII. Solomon
     D.), b. ——; m. July 23, 1863, Ellen M. Edwards, of
     Quincy, dau. of John C. and Maria. Resided at Weymouth.

     Children :

     1  FREDDIE H. C., b. Feb. 11, 1866.
     2  MINOT FRANCES, b. Aug. 8, 1868.
     3  WILLIE F., b. Dec. 26, 1870.
     4  FLORENCE B. F., July 4, 1872.
     5  JANEY FRANCES, b. Jan. 19, 1875.
     6  ELLA WALLACE, b. Oct. 7, 1877.


110  128 (VIII.) AUGUSTUS PRATT, of Weymouth (son of VII.
     Joseph), b. Sept. 30, 1823; d. Oct. 3, 1885; m. (1) Nancy
     Binney, of Hingham, Jan. 9, 1845; she d. Dec. 16, 1848;
     m. (2) Ann Caroline Gardner, (P.) Dec. 25, 1850; also d.
     July 4, 1854; m. (3) Emeline S. Gardner, Dec. 6, 1855,
     dau. of Isaac and Sibyl; she d. Apr. 18, 1859; m. (4) Lucy
     T. Bicknell, Nov. 29, 1860, dau. of Thos. and Betsey.

     Children :

131  129  1  HENRY, b. July 11, 1846 (child of Nancy).
          2  NELLIE AUGUSTA (child of Lucy), b. July 4, 1862; m. Frank
             A. Veazie, Jan. 12, 1881.


113  130 (IX.) QUINCY PRATT, of Braintree (son of VIII. Joshua of
     Weymouth), b. Dec. 14, 1834; m. Aug. 2, 1855, Mary
     Elizabeth Pratt, dau. of Linsey and Elizabeth H.; she b.
     1837.

     Children :

     1  HERBERT NEVADA, b. Apr. 25, 1856.
     2  OSCAR QUINCY, b. Feb. 17, 1858.
     3  GENIFRED E., b. July 25, 1860.
     4  FANNY BELL, b. Jan. 15, 1867.
     5  BERTHA MAY, b. Aug. 3, 1869.


129  131 (IX.) HENRY PRATT, of Weymouth (son of VIII. Augustus),
     b. July 11, 1846; m. Nov. 25, 1868, Nora Everett Black-
     well, of Wareham, dau. of Franklin and Sarah.

     Children :

     1  NANCY BELL, b. Sept. 24, 1869.
     2  GRACE LINCOLN, b. May 22, 1875.

53 132 (III.) WILLIAM PRATT, of Weymouth (son of II. Matthew), b. May 5, 1673; d. Sept. 18, 1714; m. Hannah, who m. Dec. 23, 1719, Thomas Randall, of Easton. In 1727, the children of William, then minors, appoint their father-in-law, Thos. Randall, of Easton, their guardian, and live with him there. (Boston Probate Records, Vol. 27, pp. 32, 33; also Vol. 25, p. 333. Bristol Records, Vol. 43, p. 115, refers to them again).

Children:

    1 SARAH, b. Feb. 25, 1702; m. —— Spooner.

130 133 2 WILLIAM, b. Oct. 18, 1703.

175 134 3 JOSHUA, b. March 23, 1705; he moved to Bridgewater.

    4 JAMES, b. March 29, 1713; d. Nov. 31, 1713.

    5 JAMES, b. May 11, 1714; d. July 21, 1754, in Taunton, unmarried.

184 135 6 MATTHEW, b. ——.

    7 ANN, b. ——; m. Robt. Randall.

    8 BETTY, b. ——; m. Joshua Lovell.

    9 MARY, b. ——; m. James Nash. (?)

    10 HANNAH, b. ——; d. Aug. 29, 1739; m. Nathl. Ford.

---

133 136 (IV.) WILLIAM PRATT, of Abington (son of III. William), b. Oct. 18, 1703; d. Nov. 4, 1765; m. Oct. 25, 1733, Jane Torrey, dau. of Philip and Mary, b. Nov. 1, 1710; d. May 22, 1761. He lived in Abington and removed to Easton.

Children:

140 137 1 JONATHAN, b. July 25, 1734.

    2 JANE, b. May 24, 1736; m. (P.) Jan. 17, 1767, Joseph Bicknell.

160 138 3 WILLIAM, b. June 19, 1738; d. March 26, 1814.

    4 SARAH, b. June 4, 1741; d. Nov. 4, 1811.

    5 MARY, b. —— 1743; d. Nov. 6, 1805.

    6 ELIZABETH, b. Nov. 21, 1746; m. Gregory Belcher, June 29, 1775; she d. Oct. 10, 1808.

    7 HULDAH, b. May 9, 1749; m. John Carver, Feb. 1, 1795.

    8 MATILDA, b. Sept. 21, 1752; m. March 30, 1796, Isaac Allen or David Clark, Dec. 14, 1775.

172 139 9 PHILIP, b. Aug. 30, 1755; lived in Abington.

---

137 140 (V.) JONATHAN PRATT, of Easton (son of IV. William and Jane), b. July 25, 1734; d. March 28, 1808; m. June 24, 1762, Damaris Phillips; she d. Sept. 11; 1793. He m. (2)

Oct. 27, 179ti, Susannah Garbett, b. 1733; d. July 18, 1820.

Children:

|     |     |    |                                                                                   |
|-----|-----|----|-----------------------------------------------------------------------------------|
|     |     | 1  | JONATHAN, b. March 25, 1763; d. July 24, 1791.                                    |
| 145 | 141 | 2  | CALEB, b. July 26, 1764.                                                          |
|     |     | 3  | DAMARIS, b. Apr. 21, 1766; d. Sept. 11, 1793; m. Sept. 20, 1787, Ephraim Drake.   |
| 157 | 142 | 4  | JOSHUA, b. Feb. 2, 1768; d. Feb. 1, 1850.                                         |
|     |     | 5  | JANE, b. Jan. 34, 1770; d. Oct. 25, 1780.                                          |
|     |     | 6  | SAMUEL, b. Jan. 23, 1772.                                                          |
| 159 | 143 | 7  | JAMES, b. Feb. 20, 1774.                                                           |
|     |     | 8  | WILLIAM, b. March 9, 1776; m. Apr. 9, 1797, Amity Brett; no children.             |
| 164 | 144 | 9  | PHILIP, b. May 28, 1778.                                                           |
|     |     | 10 | MARY, b. July 18, 1780.                                                            |

---

141 145 (VI.) CALEB PRATT, of Easton (son of V. Jonathan), b. July 26, 1764; d. Jan. 31, 1840; m. Apr. 30, 1789, Olive Packard, b. 1764; d. Nov. 23, 1833.

Children:

|     |     |   |                                                                      |
|-----|-----|---|----------------------------------------------------------------------|
|     |     | 1 | JANE, b. Jan. 23, 1790; d. March 29, 1796.                           |
| 148 | 146 | 2 | JONATHAN, b. May 3, 1792; d. Oct. 23, 1802.                          |
|     |     | 3 | VINCENT, b. July 4, 1794; d. Apr. 14, 1796.                          |
|     |     | 4 | VINCENT, b. Nov. 13, 1796; d. Nov. 17, 1819.                         |
|     |     | 5 | MARTIN, b. May 4, 1799; d. Oct. 21, 1823, or Aug. 30, 1822.          |
| 151 | 147 | 6 | NAHUM, b. June 17, 1801; d. July 15, 1850.                           |

---

146 148 (VII.) JONATHAN PRATT, of Easton (son of VI. Caleb), b. May 3, 1792; d. Oct. 23, 1802; m. Dec. 4, 1817, Sophia Hayward, b. 1795-6; d. Dec. 26, 1851; dau. of Joseph and Lydia (Barrows). He is styled a Captain. He m. (2) Elizabeth Wood, of Middleboro.

Children:

|     |     |   |                                                                  |
|-----|-----|---|------------------------------------------------------------------|
| 153 | 149 | 1 | JONATHAN AVERY, b. Nov. 22, 1818; d. Feb. 1, 1886.               |
|     |     | 2 | HIRAM AUGUSTUS, b. March 4, 1821; d. Aug. 13, 1824.              |
|     |     | 3 | OLIVE JANE, b. March 6, 1823; d. Sept. 2, 1824.                  |
| 156 | 150 | 4 | HIRAM AUGUSTUS, b. Aug. 12, 1826.                                |
|     |     | 5 | MARTIN VINCENT, b. Nov. 10, 1828; m. Eveline E. Holmes.          |
|     |     | 6 | SHEPARD L., b. Oct. 9, 1830; m. Nov. 27, 1851, Huldah            |

Tinkham, b. Dec. 18, 1829; d. June 19, 1877; m. (2) Carrie E. Williams, Nov. 12, 1879.

7 DANIEL H., b. June 4, 1833; d. June 1881; m. Nov. 23 1862, Sarah E. Peckham.

----

147 151 (VII.) NAHUM PRATT, of Easton (son of VI. Caleb), b. June 17, 1801; d. July 15, 1850; m. Nov. 6, 1823, Eliza Perry; she d. Dec. 25, 1834. He m. (2) Dec. 31, 1835, Jerusha Hopkins, b. Sept. 30, 1813; d. March 6, 1864, dau. of Elisha Hopkins, of Rupert, Vt.

Children of Jerusha :

1 NAHUM, b. Sept. 3, 1837; d. Oct. 22, 1860; m. Oct. 14, 1858, Helen M. Townley, b. 1834, dau. of Elisha.

2 CALEB S., b. Aug. 4, 1840; d. Dec. 16, 1854.

171 152 3 GEORGE (Taunton Probate), m. Amy A. Dunbar, Jan. 15 1859.

4 ELISHA S. (Taunton Probate).

----

149 153 (VIII.) JONATHAN AVERY PRATT, of Easton (son of VII. Jonathan), b. Nov. 22, 1818; d. Feb. 1, 1886; m. Elizabeth, S. White, b. Aug. 5, 1818; d. July 24, 1867, dau. of Arunah and Milly (Drake) White, of Taunton. He m. (2) June 15, 1875, Lucy O. (Leach) Viles, b. 1822, dau. of Giles and Lucy H.

Children :

1 SOPHIA ELIZABETH, b. Apr. 15, 1843; m. Dec. 22, 1863, Deacon Lewis Morse of Sharon.

2 CLIFFORD AVERY, b. Jan. 28, 1845; m. Florence Hempstead, of Spring Prairie, Wis.

3 MARIA JANE, b. Apr. 13, 1850; d. Dec. 19, 1856.

4 LUTHERA E., b. —— 1853; m. May 14, 1874, Joseph E. Heath, of Fryeburg, Me.

155 154 5 FRANKLIN C., b. July 2, 1855; m. Sept. 12, 1877, Anna L. Heath.

6 OLIVE JANE, b. March 24, 1847; d. Sept. 24, 1849.

7 MARTIN ELMER, b. March 9, 1853. Lives in Idaho.

154 155 (IX.) FRANKLIN C. PRATT, of Easton (son of VIII. Jonathan A.), b. July 2, 1855; m. Sept. 12, 1877, Anna L. Heath.

Child:

BERTHA MAY, b. March 13, 1882.

150 156 (VIII.) HIRAM AUGUSTUS PRATT, of Easton (son of VII.
Jonathan), b. Aug. 12, 1826; m. June 3, 1853, or Jan. 3,
1854, Mary D. Williams, b. May 7, 1830, d. May 21, 1860,
dau. of Lewis Williams. He m. (?) Jan. 1, 1862, Louisa
C. Dean, dau. of Charles.

Children of Mary:

1 EUGENE W., b. Sept. 3, 1857.
2 MARY LOUISA, b. Feb. 27, 1860; d. July 16, 1860.

Children of Louisa:

3 CHARLES A., b. Oct. 23, 1862. ·
4 LOUISA F., b. Jan. 28, 1866.
5 HENRY W., b. May 20, 1871.

142 157 (VI.) JOSHUA PRATT, of Easton (son of V. Jonathan and
Damaris), b. Feb. 2, 1768; d. Feb. 1, 1850; m. Mar. 25,
1790, Sylvia Smith, of Mansfield, b. 1771; d. June 20,
1842.

Children:

1 BETSEY, b. July 18, 1791; d. Apr. 19, 1796.
2 DAMARIS, b. Dec. 29, 1793.
3 DANIEL, b. March 13, 1797.
4 BETSEY, b. Feb. 13, 1800.
5 LOWELL, b. June 15, 1802.
163 158 6 AZUBA, b. Apr. 7, 1806.

143 159 (VI.) JAMES PRATT, of Easton, (son of V. Jonathan), b.
Feb. 20, 1774; m. Sally Willbor. (?)

Children:

1 MELVIN WILLBOR, b. Nov. 22, 1803; d. March 19, 1806.
2 SALLY GILLMORE, b. Jan. 23, 1807.
3 FANNY WILLBOR, b. Sept. 27, 1809.

138 160 (V.) WILLIAM PRATT, of Easton (son of IV. William and
Jane), b. June 19, 1738; d. March 24, 1814; m. Jan. 1, 1766,
Hannah Williams, b. 1731; d. Feb. 15, 1776. He m. (2)
Dec. 12, 1776, Matilda Howard, b. 1738; d. Aug. 22, 1794.
He is styled "2d." Was a Deacon.

Children:

162 161 1 WILLIAM, b. Aug. 26, 1767.
    2 JAMES, b. Dec. 5, 1769; d. Dec. 25, 1769.

161 162 (VI.) WILLIAM PRATT, of Easton, (son of V. William and
Hannah), b. Aug. 26, 1767; d ——; m. Apr. 24, 1803, Mo-
linda Randall.

Child:
ANGELINE, b. Nov. 26, 1803.

158 163 (VII.) AZUNA, or ARUNA PRATT, of Easton (son of VI.
Joshua and Sylvia), b. Apr. 7, 1806; m. Milly ——.

Child:
ELIZABETH S., b. ——, 1819; d. July 24, 1867; m. ——.

144 164 (VI.) PHILIP PRATT, of Easton (son of V. Jonathan), b.
May 28, 1778; d. March 1, 1855; m. (1) Sept. 26, 1798,
Ruth Whiting, of Hanover; she b. Jan. 23, 1779; d. Feb.
22, 1806. He m. (2) Naomi Stiles; she b. June 17, 1789;
d. Oct. 24, 1813. He m. (3) Naomi G. Leonard; she b.
April 28, 1794, and d. suddenly.

Children of Ruth:
165a 164a 1 ELIAS WHITING, b. Feb. 11, 1799; d. Aug. 13, 1880.
166 165 2 GALEN, b. April 28, 1801.

Children of Naomi Stiles:
    3 JOSHUA R., b. Nov. 13, 1808; d. ——.
    4 PHILIP R., b. Aug. 5, 1811; lives (1887) Geneva, O.

Children of Naomi Leonard:
    5 MARY ANN, b. March 5, 1819; d. July 24, 1849.
    6 SUSAN LEONARD, b. Oct. 9, 1823; d. July 19, 1824.
    7 NAOMI JANE, b. May 22, 1825; d. March 27, 1839.

8  MARIA HILTON, b. July 17, 1827; d. Oct. 17, 1829.
9  MARIA HILTON, b. Apr. 21, 1831; d. Feb. 12, 1850.
10  JOSEPH WILLIAM, b. Apr. 20, 1833.
11  SUSAN FRANCES, b. Jan. 8, 1837; d. March 15, 1861; m. Wood.

---

164a 165a (VII.) ELIAS W. PRATT, of So. Scituate, Mass. (son of VI. Philip), b. Feb. 11, 1799; d. Aug. 13, 1880; m. (1) Ruth Briggs, Oct. 23, 1822, who d. Oct. 24, 1835. He m. (2) Rachel Copeland, Nov. 14, 1837; she. d. Oct. 26, 1848. He m. (3) Huldah Church, Sept. 9, 1849; she d. May, 1883.

Elias W. Pratt was born in Hingham, Mass. His mother died when he was very young. He went to live with his uncle, Justus Whiting, of Hanover, Mass. At the age of seventeen he was apprenticed to Col. John Barstow, of Hanover, Mass., to learn the ship-carpenter's trade, with whom he lived until he was twenty-one years of age. He afterwards carried on ship-building in Scituate, Mass. (now called South Scituate). Soon after his marriage with Ruth Briggs he purchased the homestead of William Briggs, of Scituate, on which he resided until his death, in August, 1880. In early life he was commissioned Captain of the Hanover Artillery Company, and afterwards was commissioned Major in the State service. He also held several town offices in South Scituate, and at one time was Selectman and Assessor.

Children of Ruth:

164h 164b 1  ELIZABETH BRIGGS, b. Nov. 28, 1824.
164i 164c 2  ABIGAIL WILDER, b. Aug. 2, 1826; d. Dec. 12, 1864.
164j 164d 3  ELIAS EDWARDS, b. April 26, 1829.
164k 164e 4  EMELINE AUGUSTA, b. Jan. 9, 1831.
      5  CHARLES BRIGGS, b. April 12, 1833; d. Nov. 6, 1840.
164l 164f 6  WILLIAM BRIGGS, b. Dec. 3, 1835; d. May 23, 1864.

Children of Rachel:

      7  RUTH CUSHING, b. Apr. 1, 1839; d. Dec. 16, 1878.
164m 164g 8  CHARLES COPELAND, b. Jan. 24, 1842.

---

164b 164h (VIII.) ELIZABETH B. PRATT, (dau. of VII. Elias W.), b. Nov. 28, 1824: m. Dec. 24, 1848, George W. Stetson.

Children :

1   LOUISA ELIZABETH, b. Sept. 12, 1849 ; d. May 27, 1857.
2   EMMA AUGUST, b. Jan. 12, 1852 ; d. Feb. 3, 1856.
3   CLARA ELDRIDGE, b. March 16, 1854 ; d. May 31, 1857.
4   ORILLA JUSTINA, b. Nov. 17, 1856 ; d. Dec. 13, 1863.
5   CHARLES BRIGGS, b. Aug. 12, 1861.
6   WARREN ABBOTT, b. Oct. 27, 1864 ; d. Aug. 14, 1867.

---

164c 164f  (VIII.) ABIGAIL W. PRATT, (dau. of VII. Elias W.), b. Aug.
2, 1826 ; m. May, 1852, Minot Gardner ; she d. Dec. 12,
1884.  He d. ——.

Children :

1   Willie, b. ——.
2   JUSTUS WHITING, b. March 1, 1852 ; m. Annie Hathaway,
of Taunton, June 6, 1874 ; she d. Jan. 1, 1877.  He m.
(2) Jennie Lucas, of Plymouth, Dec. 12, 1878.

    Children :

    1   *Ernest W.*, b. Sept., 1876.
    2   *Ethel*, b. Sept., 1879.

---

164d 164j  (VIII.) ELIAS E. PRATT, of Norwood, Mass. (son of VII.
Elias W.), b. April 26, 1829 ; m. May 4, 1851, Melinda A.
Hatch, who d. June 8, 1887.

Elias E. Pratt was born in Scituate (now South Scituate), Mass., and lived with his father until about seventeen years of age.  He then went to Marshfield to learn
the house-carpenter's trade of Benjamin Hatch, with
whom he served until he was twenty-one years of age,
when he returned to South Scituate and began business
for himself in this and neighboring towns.  In 1862 he
enlisted in Company F., 43d Regiment Mass. Volunteers,
and served his time in North Carolina.  At the expiration
of his enlistment he returned to his native town.  In the
following year was engaged in the Car Dep't of the Boston, Hartford and Erie R. R. (now New York & New
England), and was soon promoted to the position of
Master Car-Builder.  He occupied that position continu-
ously, with the exception of about eighteen months, until
April, 1887, when he resigned.  In June, 1887, he accepted
the position of inspector of Building for the New York,
New Haven and Hartford R. R.  In 1882, in company
with his son, Elias E., Jr., he purchased the stock and
good-will in the oil-cloth business owned and carried on

by the late Fisher Talbot, of Norwood, Mass., and has continued the business to the present time.

Children:

1  ANNA MARIA, b. July 18, 1852; m. May 1, 1873, George G. Upham.

   Child:

   *William Gilbert*, b. Oct. 6, 1880.

2  ELDON BRADFORD, b. Jan. 5, 1855; d. Oct. 7, 1881. Like his father, followed the railroad business, being station agent at Franklin, Mass., at the time of his death.

3  ELIAS EDWARD, b. Apr. 22, 1857.

4  MELINDA AGNES, b. June 5, 1860; m. Francis Eugene Everett, Dec. 25, 1878.

5  WILLIE ABBOT, b. Oct. 25, 1866; d. Apr. 24, 1869.

---

164e 164k (VIII.) EMELINE A. PRATT, (dau. of VII. Elias W.), b. Jan. 9, 1831; m. (1) Seth E. Bartlett, Nov. 10, 1850; m. (2) Loami B. Sylvester, of Hanover.

   Child of Seth:

1  HENRY FOSTER, b. May 30, 1851; m. Annie Eatough, of Taunton, Apr. 5, 1876.

   Children:

   1  *John Eldridge*, b. Jan. 31, 1879.
   2  *Sadie E.*, b. July 25, 1881.

   Child of Loami:

2  SARAH E., b. May 27, 1859; m. William Stearns, of Wayland, June 18, 1884.

---

164f 164l (VIII.) WILLIAM B. PRATT (son of VII. Elias W.), b. Dec. 3, 1835, in South Scituate; d. May 23, 1884; m. Sarah Vinal, Aug. 31, 1862.

He lived with his father until eighteen years of age, when he learned the carpenter's trade; afterwards purchased a box and planing mill, manufacturing boxes and trunks until the works were destroyed by fire. He held various town offices, such as Selectman, Assessor and Overseer of the Poor. Later in life he was engaged in the railroad business until his death.

Child b. and d. Sept. 5, 1865.

*164g 164m* (VIII.) CHARLES C. PRATT (son of VII. Elias W.), b. Jan. 24, 1842, in South Scituate; m. Hannah B. Hart, Dec. 5, 1867. He has been a successful farmer on the old home place.

---

165 166 (VII.) GALEN PRATT, of North Bridgewater, farmer (son of VI. Philip and Ruth, of Easton), b. Apr. 23, 1801; m. (1) Nancy, dau. of Benjamin Amos, Feb. 16, 1826; she d. May 2, 1842. He m. (2) Mary Rice, dau. of Charles Brackett, of West Bridgewater, Aug. 15, 1843.

He moved with his parents to Easton when a child; thence to Abington, 1806; thence to North Bridgewater in 1821, one month before the town was set off. He learned the shoe trade about 1821, and continued in it thirty-five years. Failing health compelled him to try farming, which he did on Cary Hill, afterwards moving to South Main street, Campello, where he now (1887) resides, and notwithstanding his age, is quite active. He was for many years a deacon in the South Congregational Church. Four generations reside at his home. In June, 1888, he was working in the hay-field.

Children of Nancy:

1 MARY, b. Dec. 7, 1826. School teacher.
2 DAMARIS AMES, b. June 2, 1829; d. May 30, 1830.
170 168    3 GALEN EMERY, b. Apr. 24, 1831.
169 167    4 BENJAMIN A., b. June 27, 1833.
5 HENRY LYMAN, b. June 23, 1835; d. March 11, 1848.
6 RUTH, b. May 3, 1839; d. Aug. 7, 1860.

Children of Mary:

7 MARILLA FRANCES, b. Apr. 11, 1849; d. June 6, 1854.
8 MINORA BRACKETT, b. June 1, 1845; d. Feb. 26, 1848.

---

167 169 (VIII.) BENJAMIN A. PRATT, of North Bridgewater (son of VII. Galen), b. June 27, 1833; m. Apr. 29, 1858, Diana Reed, dau. of Abia Reed, of Abington.

Children:

1 ERNEST, b. Feb. 17, 1860.
2 HANNAH, b. Dec. 6, 1862; m. Sept. 5, 1882, Fred. C. Kittrell, of Middleboro.
3 WALTER, b. Aug. 22, 1865; m. Jan. 4, 1887, Addie V. Loring.

4 FRANKLIN, b. Dec. 16, 1867.
5 ROBERT, b. Apr. 22, 1870; d. Aug. 10, 1872.
6 EMILY, b. Oct. 27, 1872.
7 LOIS ELVA, b. Mar. 3, 1877.

---

168 170 (VIII.) GALEN EMERY PRATT, of Brockton (son of VII.
Galen), b. Apr. 24, 1831; m. Nov. 11, 1856, Abigail Ellen,
dau. of John Little, of Hanover. He served in the war
of the Rebellion, and has also held town offices.

Children :

1 HENRY ELMER, b. Apr. 22, 1859; m. Ida F. Baker, of
Weymouth, Apr. 17, 1882.
2 GEORGE ELWIN, b. Oct. 18, 1862; not married.
They both live in Iowa.

---

152 171 (VIII.) GEORGE PRATT, of West Bridgewater (son of VII.
Nahum), b. ——; d. Aug. 9, 1867; m. Jan. 15, 1859, Amy
A. Dunbar.

Children :

HARRIET A., b. Sept. 15, 1858.
Child, b. July 26, 1860.

---

139 172 (V.) PHILIP PRATT, of Abington (son of IV. William), b.
Aug. 30, 1755; d. Dec. 16, 1830; m. Apr. 13, 1786, Rebec-
kah Shaw, b. Mar. 20, 1761; d. Apr. 16, 1842. (Will dated
Dec. 11, 1830.)

Children :

1 REBECKAH S., b. Oct. 2, 1786.
2 SUSANNA, b. June 10, 1788; d. Oct. 31, 1824.
3 HULDAH, b. Feb. 5, 1790.
4 JANE, b. May 22, 1792.
5 MARY, b. Oct. 15, 1794; d. July 3, 1818.
153 173 6 DANIEL, b. Dec. 7, 1796.
7 SARAH, b. Mar. 11, 1799; d. July 2, 1819.
180 174 8 PHILIP, b. Sept. 1, 1801.
9 WILLIAM, b. Jan. 21, 1804; d. Sept. 25, 1868. Will dated
July, 1868; probably never married, as he mentions no
children.

134 175 (IV.) JOSHUA PRATT, of Abington and East Bridgewater (son of III. William), b. Mar. 23, 1705, in Weymouth; d. Oct. 27, 1773. Epitaph:

"The sweet remembrance of the past
 Shall flourish when they sleep in dust."

He m. Jan. 22, 1728, Experience Washware. She d. 1773. He owned a mill with Matthew Pratt at Abington.

Children:

1 MATTHEW, b. July 3, 1720; d. July 19, 1747.
2 SARAH, b. June 20, 1734; d. Nov. 27, 1782.
3 EXPERIENCE, b. June 1, 1741; m. Apr. 29, 1762, Nathan Lowden.
177 176 4 JOSHUA, b. Jan. 21, 1743.
5 MARY, b. Aug. 13, 1737; m. Nathl. Ramsdell, 1753.
6 SUSANNA, b. May 10, 1745; d. Oct. 15, 1747.
7 HANNAH, b. ——; m. Saml. Allen, 1758.

---

176 177 (V.) JOSHUA PRATT, of Bridgewater (son of IV. Joshua), b. Jan. 21, 1743; d. ——, 1813; m. Oct. 30, 1783, Mary Pratt, b. 1756; d. Mar. 31, 1828; dau. of David Pratt. (Recorded as a "gentleman.")

Children:

179 178 1 WILLIAM, b. Sept. 26, 1784; d. Sep. 16, 1861; m. Celia.
2 NABBY, b. Oct. 6, 1785; d. Nov. 29, 1871; m. Elezer Whitman, Jr., 1812.
3 POLLY, or MARY, b. May 18, 1787; d. Nov. 24, 1861. Not married.
4 SARAH, b. June 21, 1789; m. Spencer Crane, 1809, afterwards Noah Pool.
5 DEXTER, b. Mar. 14, 1791; d. Apr. 5, 1866; m. June, 1830, Polly or Susan Pincin. Will dated May 14, 1861. No children named.

---

178 179 (VI.) WILLIAM PRATT, of E. Bridgewater (son of V. Joshua), b. Sept. 26, 1784; d. Sept. 16, 1861; m. Dec. 30, 1816, Celia Whitman, b. 1790; d. Aug. 4, 1853. Farmer.

No children.

4 180 (VI.) PHILIP PRATT, of Abington (son of V. Philip), b. Sept.
1, 1801; d. about 1849 (will dated May 24, 1849); m. Nov.
27, 1825, Lydia Brown, of East Bridgewater, b. 1809; d.
May 1, 1850. He owned mills in Abington.

Children:

2 181 1 PHILIP WATSON, b. Sept. 20, 1836.
2 SARAH JANE, b. Nov. 30, 1829; m. Nov. 3, 1849, Samuel
Eaton.
3 ELIZABETH BROWN, b. Aug. 20, 1832.
4 LYDIA MARIA, b. May 31, 1845.

———

11 182 (VII.) PHILIP W. PRATT, of Abington (son of VI. Philip),
b. Sept. 20, 1836; m. Jan. 1, 1863, Louisa F. Hunt.

Children:

1 SARAH ELIZABETH, b. Apr. 9, 1863.
2 DANIEL SHAW, b. Mar. 3, 1865..
3 SUSAN MARIA, b. Mar. 12, 1867; d. Apr. 4, 1878.
4 BENJAMIN A., b. Mar. 25, 1870.
5 MARCIA ANN, b. Jan. 2, 1873; d. Feb. 4, 1876.
6 ETHEL FRANCIS, } b. June 7, 1875, { d. Sept. 27, 1875.
7 GRACE LOUISA, { d. Sept. 28, 1875.

———

73 183 (VI.) DANIEL PRATT, of Abington (son of V. Philip), b. Dec.
7, 1796; d. Dec. 14, 1873; m. (P.) July 18, 1830, Marcia
Gage, of Woonsocket, R. I. He is recorded a farmer.

———

35 184 (IV.) MATTHEW PRATT, of Braintree (son of III. William
and Hannah), b. ——; d. ——; m. (P) Oct. 5, 1735, Abigail
Peck, of Barrington (Suffolk Deeds, 59, 29: bought estate
of Edmund and Josiah Quincy, May 19, 1739, in Braintree);
will (74, 47) dated Apr. 21, 1774. She d. 1775.

Children:

1 NATHANIEL, b. July 9, 1738.
36 185 2 MATTHEW, b. ——
3 EBENEZER, b. ——; m. Sarah Whitcomb (P), Mar. 15, 1776.
4 HANNAH, b. ——; m. — Hunt.
5 JUDITH, b. ——; m. Silas Clark (P), Oct. 26, 1765.

185   186 (V.) MATTHEW PRATT, (Jr.), of Braintree (son of IV. Matthew), m. (P.) Aug. 16, 1765, Lydia Hunt, of Weymouth.

Child:

188   187    MATTHEW, b. Jan. 19, 1766.

---

187   188 (VI.) MATTHEW PRATT, of Braintree, Vermont (son of V. Matthew), b. Jan. 19, 1766, in Braintree, Mass.; m. (1) March 21, 1784, Mary Niles, b. July 7, 1765, and d. Feb. 24, 1803. He m. (2) Oct. 9, 1803, Elizabeth Brown, b. in Oakham, Mass., Sept. 16, 1768; d. Nov. 19, 1817; m. (3) Apr. 9, 1818, Mrs. Polly Burrage. He d. June 26, 1819. He moved to Vermont 1812.

Children:

      1  POLLY, b. Nov. 10, 1784; m. ——
      2  RUTH, b. May 12, 1786; m. ——
193   189   3  SAMUEL, b. Febr. 1, 1788; d. Apr. 28, 1857.
      4  JOSHUA, b. Jan. 21, 1790; m. Dec. 1, 1814, Rebecca Hunt.
      5  SALLY, b. Jan. 22, 1793; m. March 24, 1812, Johial Ford; d. March 11, 1842.
      6  PHEBE, b. May 13, 1795; m.
198   190   7  ISAAC, b. Sep. 29, 1797; d. Aug. 19, 1871.
203   191   8  ENOCH, b. Oct. 13, 1799; d. Sept. 21, 1881.
      9  RELIEF, b. Feb. 8, 1802; d. Apr. 1, 1803.
      10  ELIZABETH, b. Sept. 19, 1804; m. June 10, 1828, Almon Morris; lives in Northfield, Minn.
206   192  11  MATTHEW, b. Dec. 5, 1806.
      12  JAMES BROWN, b. Apr. 19, 1809; m. Minerva Bradley.

---

189   193 (VII.) SAMUEL PRATT, of Braintree, Vermont (son of VI. Matthew and Mary), b. Feb. 1, 1788; d. Apr. 28, 1857; m. March 26, 1809, Lydia Claflin, of Hancock; she d. Feb. 24, 1848; aged 58.

Children:

      1  Infant, b. Aug. 6, 1809; d. next day.
      2  SAMUEL, b. Aug. 7, 1810; d. Feb. 26, 1811.
      3  SALLY, b. Jan. 15, 1812; m. Benj. F. Killman.
      4  LYDIA, b. Dec. 10, 1813; d. May 3, 1825.
      5  ANNA, b. Apr. 2, 1815; m. May 31, 1837, Willard Edson.
      6  HARRIET NEWELL, b. Feb. 16, 1818; d. Aug. 26, 1879; m.

Azro A. B. Coburn, who was killed by a grizzly bear, in California, Dec. 3, 1852.

196 194 7 GEORGE, b. Feb. 20, 1820.

8 NORMAN, b. June 16, 1822; d. May 3, 1848.

9
10 } Twins, b. Sept. 24, 1824; lived one day.

11 MATILDA, b. ——; d. Oct. 1827, aged 4 months and 9 days.

197 195 12 JAMES JACKSON, b. Dec. 15, 1829.

13 JOSEPH WARREN, b. Nov. 9, 1831; m. Lydia O. Nichols, of Roxbury. Resides at Calais.

---

194 196 (VIII.) GEORGE PRATT, of Braintree, Vermont (son of VII. Samuel), b. Feb. 20, 1820; m. Jan. 12, 1843, Zeruah S. Flint.

Children:

1 SARAH MATILDA, b. Oct. 6, 1844; m. Jan. 12, 1863, George Tarbell.

2 GEORGE LESTER, b. Sept. 22, 1847; d. Jan. 19, 1864.

---

195 197 (VIII.) JAMES J. PRATT, of Braintree, Vt. (son of VII. Samuel), b. Dec. 15, 1829; m. (1) June 22, 1853, Lucy A. Carpenter, of Randolph; she d. Jan. 10, 1856. He m. (2) July 16, 1857, Screpta B. Harrick, of Randolph.

Children:

1 VIOLA MARCELLA, b. June 22, 1854; m. March 28, 1876, Henry Cleveland.

2 MARY LUCY, b. July 10, 1862; d. Sept. 8, 1862.

3 CHARLES HERRICK, b. Nov. 2, 1863.

---

190 198 (VII.) ISAAC PRATT, of Braintree, Vt. (son of VII. Matthew), b. Sept. 29, 1797; d. Aug. 19, 1871; m. (1) Nov. 15, 1818, Jerusha Stedman; m. (2) Aug. 9, 1829, Ruby Whiting.

Children:

201 199 1 JOHN, b. Feb. 19, 1820.

202 200 2 JEFFERSON, b. July 28, 1822.

3 JUDSON, b. Apr. 26, 1830; d. March 25, 1835.

4 MARY NILES, b. March 31, 1832; d. March 27, 1835.

5 MARTHA BILLINGS, b. March 27, 1833; d. Apr. 5, 1835.

6 ELLEN LAVINA, b. Oct. 10, 1835; m. Dec. 23, 1868, Norman Goodale.

7 CARLOS BASS, b. Sept. 29, 1838; m. Jan. 1, 1867, Lucina S. Fitts, lives at West Randolph.

8 MARY OLIVIA, b. Nov. 5, 1841; m. May 30, 1866, Otis Riford.

9 BARNEY ISAAC, b. July 28, 1844; m. Nov. 30, 1869, Clemie R. Bass; lives at West Randolph.

---

199 201 (VIII.) JOHN PRATT, of Braintree, Vt. (son of VII. Isaac), b. Feb. 19, 1820; m. May 16, 1852, Mary Maxham, of Middlesex.

Children:

1 JOHN DANA, b. May 20, 1854; d. Nov. 8, 1866.
2 DELIA MARY, } b. ——; d. Aug. 2, 1861.
3 DAVID, }
4 ADDIE MARIA, b. Jan. 25, 1856.

---

200 202 (VIII.) JEFFERSON PRATT, of Braintree, Vt. (son of VII. Isaac), b. July 28, 1822; m. Nov. 25, 1852, Maria S. Maxham, of Middlesex.

Children:

1 EMMA CLARINDA, b. June 9, 1856.
2 ROLLA WILLIAM, b. June 3, 1865; d. Oct. 24, 1877.
3 ARTHUR DANA, b. Aug. 25, 1868.

---

191 203 (VII.) ENOCH PRATT, of Braintree, Vt. (son of VI. Matthew), b. Oct. 13, 1799; d. Sept. 21, 1881; m. (1) Abiah Track, (2) Sept. 10, 1873, Deborah (Parker) McAllister.

Children:

1 HIRAM, b. June 22, 1819; d. 1822.
2 MARIA M., b. Nov. 20, 1822; m. Nov. 2, 1848, Saml. L. Young, of Weymouth, Mass., and resided there (1883).
3 HIRAM J., b. Apr. 10, 1825; m. 1845, Elmira P. Riford, and settled in Warren.
4 Daughter, b. Apr. 16, 1827; lived about two weeks.
5 JACKSON JAMES, b. March 9, 1829; m. (1) Emma Gleason, of Warren, (2) a lady of Warren, where he resides.

      6 LUCRETIA THAYER COOLIDGE, b. May 15, 1831; m. Elisha Goodspeed, of Warren.

      7 EVALINE M., b. July 17, 1833; m. Augustus Haywood, of Bridgewater, Mass. They reside in Brooklyn.

      8 MARTHA MINORA, b. Sept. 4, 1835; m. Charles A. Badger, of West Randolph. They moved to Ft. Scott, Kan.

)5 204   9 ALMON MORRIS, b. May 23, 1839; m. Apr. 20, 1863, Orett Thurston.

     10 BETSEY LANORA ROXANA, b. March 16, 1842; m. (1) Apr. 26, 1863, Sylvester Thurston; m. (2) Nov. 6, 1875, Melvin Watson.

---

)4 205 (VIII.) ALMON MORRIS PRATT, of Braintree, Vt. (son of VII. Enoch), b. May 23, 1839; m. Apr. 20, 1863, Orett Thurston.

    Children:

    1 LILLA F., b. July 31, 1864; d. Aug. 5, 1867.

    2 HARRY ALMON, b. Feb. 2, 1877.

    3 INA MAY, b. March 23, 1879.

---

)2 206 (VII.) MATTHEW PRATT, of Braintree, Vt. (son of VI. Matthew), b. Dec. 5, 1806; m. (1) Oct. 21, 1832, Orra Claflin, of West Brookfield, who d. March 6, 1841, aged 32; m. (2) Dec. 12, 1841, Hannah Ford.

    Children:

    1 JASON MATTHEW, b. July 30, 1839; m. Feb. 11, 1860, Katie Keef, of Chicago, Ill. They reside in Gilmanton, Wis.

    2 HANNAH, b. Jan. 20, 1845. She was adopted by John Waite; lives in Gilmanton, Wis.

---

)4 207 (III.) SAMUEL PRATT, of Weymouth (son of II. Matthew), b. Apr. 3, 1676; m. Hannah ——: d. Oct. 16, 1715.

    Children:

3 208   1 SAMUEL, b. July 2, 1705.

0 209   2 DANIEL, b. Feb. 11, 1707; m. Mary Pratt.

      HANNAH, b. Sept. 29, 1710; m. Benj. Vining, Nov. 30, 1732.

    4 JOHN, b. July 13, 1713; d. Feb. 8, 1743.

209 210 (IV.) DANIEL PRATT, of Weymouth (son of III. Samuel), b.
Feb. 11, 1707; d. Nov. 6, 1799; m. Nov. 1, 1739, Mary
Pratt, dau. of III. Ephraim.

Children:

(See IV. Mary, dau. of III. Ephraim.)

    1 DANIEL, b. July 29, 1740; d. Sept. 1, 1740.
    2 HANNAH, b. Feb. 9, 1742; d. Feb. 15, 1742.
    3 MARY, b. Sept. 12, 1743; d. Feb. 4, 1768.
    4 MERIAM, b. Oct. 22, 1745.
215 211 5 ICHABOD, b. Apr. 8, 1748; d. May 4, 1822.
220 212 6 SAMUEL, b. Jan. 26, 1751; d. May 22, 1830.

208 213 (IV.) SAMUEL PRATT, of Weymouth (son of III. Samuel),
b. July 2, 1705; m. (P.) July 27, 1740, Lydia White.

Children:

239 214 1 JESSE, b. Mar. 30, 1743.
    2 LYDIA, b. May 22, 1744; d. May 30, 1744.
    3 PETER, b. May 17, 1745; d. Mar. 29, 1747.
    4 Child, b. ———; d. Jan. 17, 1756.

211 215 (V.) ICHABOD PRATT, of Weymouth (son of IV. Daniel and
Mary Pratt), b. Apr. 8, 1748; d. May 4, 1822; m. (P) June
5, 1773, Betty French, dau. of David and Mary (Carver),
b. Dec. 11, 1748; d. July 26, 1827.

Children:

    1 BETTY, b. Dec. 31, 1775; m. Feb. 22, 1798, Jno. Hawes.
    2 NANCY, b. May 1, 1780; m. Jan. 1, 1804, Thomas Arnold.
    3 THOMAS, b. July 16, 1786.
    4 ABNER, b. Jan. 15, 1789.
217 216 5 MARTIN, b. May 17, 1791; d. May 20, 1822.
    6 MARY, b. Mar. 15, 1796.

216 217 (VI.) MARTIN PRATT, of Weymouth (son of V. Ichabod), b.
May 17, 1791; d. May 20, 1822; m. Elizabeth French. She
m. (?) Joseph Perkins, Sept. 21, 1825, and removed to
Abington.

Children :

219   218   1   MARTIN KIDDER, b. Nov. 27, 1815.
         2   ALMIRA FRENCH, b. June 25, 1818.
         3   JOEL LANE, b. Mar. 27, 1822 ; d. Oct. 20, 1863, unmarried.

---

218   219   (VII.) MARTIN K. PRATT, of Weymouth (son of VI. Martin),
         b. Nov. 27. 1815 ; m. Jan. 29, 1844, Avis Thayer (Carpenter), dau. of Billings and Avis (Hayden), b. Nov. 29, 1815 ;
         d. Feb. 4, 1876.

Children :

         1   AVIS CAROLINE, b. Dec. 11, 1844 ; d. Nov. 2, 1864.
         2   ELIZABETH BILLINGS, b. July 30, 1848 ; d. Feb. 1, 1850.
         3   LIZZIE CARPENTER, b. June 18, 1850 ; m. Sept. 26, 1882,
            Edw. H. Frary.
         4   LOUISA MAY, b. Dec. 1, 1852.

---

212   220   (V.) SAMUEL PRATT, of Weymouth (son of IV. Daniel), b.
         Jan. 21, 1751 ; d. May 22, 1830 ; m. Dec. 3, 1770, Molly
         Porter, dau. of Ezra and Ruth (Richards), b. Jan. 25, 1753 ;
         d. Dec. 18, 1839.

Children :

         1   DANIEL, b. Sept. 20, 1771 ; d. ——, 1794.
         2   EZRA, b. Dec. 8, 1772 ; d. ——, 1773.
         3   HANNAH, b. Aug. 26, 1774 ; d. ——
         4   EZRA, b. Oct. 8, 1776 ; d. Feb. 10, 1813.
         5   MARY, b. Sept. 29, 1777 ; d. ——, 1777.
         6   MARY, b. Sept. 29, 1778 ; d. Oct. 16, 1825 ; m. Apr. 18, 1798,
            John Rogers.
         7   GIDEON, b. Apr. 20, 1780 ; d. Dec. 5, 1843.
224   221   8   DAVID, b. Mar. 6, 1782 ; d. Jan. 8, 1863.
         9   CALEB, b. May 13, 1784 ; d. Oct. 23, 1859 ; m. —— Wilson,
            of Boston.
        10   HANNAH, b. May 6, 1785 ; d. Apr. 6, 1823 ; m. June 29,
            1801, John Nash, Jr.
226   222   11   ASA, b. Apr. 19, 1787 ; d. Aug. 18, 1837.
        12   MIRIAM, b. Apr. 18, 1789 ; d. July 29, 1814.
        13   LEVINA, b. Dec. 28, 1790 ; d. Sept. 23, 1811.
        14   SAMUEL, b. June 22, 1792 ; d. July 25, 1820.

15  DANIEL, b. May 10, 1795; d. Feb. 7, 1819, at St. Pierre, Martinique.

16  LEVINA, } b. May 26, 1797; { d. Oct. 30, 1839; m. Nov. 28,
230  223  17  LEVI,     1822, Eveline Tirrell.

---

221  224 (VI.) DAVID PRATT, of Weymouth (son of V. Samuel), b. Mar. 6, 1782; d. Jan. 8, 1868; m. (P.) Feb. 15, 1805; m. Sept. 25, 1805, Polly or Mary Shaw, of Abington, b. Oct. 20, 1784; d. July 7, 1865; dau. of Abraham Shaw.

Children:

232  225  1  DAVID, b. Jan. 16, 1806; m. Mar. 28, 1827, Mercy G. French.

      2  ELVIRA B., b. Aug. 28, 1810; m. Apr. 14, 1844, John Hunt: d. May, 1879.

      3  MARY ANN, b. Oct. 15, 1819; d. Mar. 10, 1856.

      4  PRISCILLA SHAW, b. Jan. 22, 1822; m. Apr. 14, —, Jairus B. Lincoln.

---

222  226 (VI.) ASA PRATT, of Weymouth (son of V. Samuel), b. Apr. 19, 1787; d. Aug. 18, 1837; m. (1) Feb. 10, 1811, Sarah Bates, dau. of Robert and Susanna (Bicknell), b. Feb. 17, 1788; d. Aug. 22, 1811. He m. (2) May 11, 1814, Rebecca Badlam.

Children by Rebecca:

      1  MIRIAM, b. July 14, 1815; m. Rev. Willard Jones, July 4, 1839.

229  227  2  EDWIN, b. May 4, 1817; m. Lucy Ann Pratt.

      3  DEBORAH A., b. Nov. 2, 1821; m. Samuel Webb.

231  228  4  GEORGE HENRY, b. Oct. 11, 1825; m. Eliza Leach Pratt.

---

227  229 (VII.) EDWIN PRATT, of Weymouth (son of VI. Asa), b. May 4, 1817; m. Nov. 20, 1842, Lucy Ann Pratt, b. Apr. 10, 1823. He is a large lumber-dealer, and prominent in the Congregational Church.

Children :

1 WILLARD JONES, b. Sept. 13, 1844; d. Jan. 13, 1865.
230b 229a 2 JULIUS, b. Oct. 20, 1848.
3 HARRIET BEECHER, b. Jan. 11, 1854; m. Rev. Louis B.
Voorhees, Nov. 7, 1877.
4 ARTHUR EDWIN, b. Sept. 27, 1865.

---

229a 230b (VIII.) JULIUS PRATT, of Boston (son of VII. Edwin), b.
Oct. 20, 1848; m. Oct. 11, 1876, Mary Alice, dau. of Eben
Denton, b. Mar. 3, 1852. He is a wholesale dealer in
boots and shoes, of the firm of Pratt, Warren & Co., 110
Pearl Street, Boston.

Children :

1 ARCHIBALD DENTON, b. Mar. 4, 1882.
2 HAROLD STUDLEY, } b. Dec. 29, 1884.
3 HELEN JEWELL,

---

223 230 (VI.) LEVI PRATT, of Weymouth (son of V. Samuel), b. May
26, 1797; d. Oct. 30, 1839, at Boston; m. Nov. 28, 1822,
Eveline Tirrell; d. Jan., 1833.

Children :

1 BENJAMIN TIRRELL, b. July 27, 1823; d. Dec. 1, 1825.
2 WILLIAM E., b. Oct. 19, 1824; d. ——.
3 DEXTER, b. Apr. 22, 1826; lives in Boston.
4 ELIZABETH A., b. Mar. 18, 1829; d. ——.
5 PRINCE E., b. Feb. 18, 1830; d. Sept. 29, 1844.

---

228 231 (VII.) GEORGE H. PRATT, of Weymouth (son of VI. Asa
and Sarah Bates), b. Oct. 11, 1825; m. Eliza Loach
Pratt, dau. of Cornelius and Rebecca L.

Children :

1 REBECCA ELIZA, b. Oct. 30, 1859; d. Nov. 7, 1861.
2 REBECCA ELIZA, b. Jan. 17, 1862; d. Nov. 29, 1864.
3 ELIZABETH H., b. July 2, 1864; d. Apr. 30, 1865.
4 MIRIAM PERKINS, b. Apr. 10, 1870.

235 232 (VII.) DAVID PRATT, of Weymouth (son of VI. David and
Polly), b. Jan. 16, 1806; d. Dec. 17, 1875; m. Mar. 28,
1827, Mercy Gannett French, dau. of Stephen and Susan
(Jones), b. ——, 1807; d. Jan. 23, 1874.

Children :

    1 CHRISTIANNA JONES, b. Jan. 13, 1828; m. Dec. 6, 1846,
      Nathan P. Joy.
    2 ANSELLA, b. June 9, 1830; d. May 20, 1856; m. Mar. 22,
      1843, John P. Burrell.
236 233 3 HENRY CLIFFORD, b. Sept. 19, 1832.
237 234 4 DANIEL JUDSON, b. Aug. 4, 1835.
238 235 5 ORRIN THOMAS, b. Aug. 12, 1838.
    6 MIRIAM JONES, b. July 31, 1842; d. July 25, 1863; m.
      Apr. 1, 1863, John R. Bean.
    7 MARY SUSANNA, b. Jan. 16, 1849.

---

233 236 (VIII.) HENRY C. PRATT, of Weymouth (son of VII. David),
b. Sept. 19, 1832; d. July 20, 1878; m. July 20, 1857, Abby
Pittman, dau. of John and Abigail.

---

234 237 (VIII.) DANIEL JUDSON PRATT, of Weymouth (son of VII.
David), b. Aug. 4, 1835; m. June 25, 1863, Georgianna
Crafts, of Boston.

Children :

    1 MERION LOUISA, b. Apr. 1, 1864; d. Aug. 15, 1864.
    2 GUSTAVUS JUDSON, b. Apr. 14, 1865.
    3 ETHEL MERCY, b. Nov. 12, 1869.
    4 ANNIE FLORENCE, b. Feb. 20, 1873.
    5 HERMAN SAWYER, b. Feb. 16, 1885.

---

235 238 (VIII.) ORRIN T. PRATT, of Weymouth (son of VII. David), b. Aug. 12, 1838; m. Jan. 18, 1860, Eunice Clapp, of
Scituate, dau. of James S. and Elizabeth.

Children :

    1 ISABELLA ANSELLA, b. Jan. 1860; d. Jan. 27, 1880; m.
      Aug. 3, 1879, John F. Porter.
    2 EDWIN THOMAS, b. June 8, 1862.

214 239 (V.) JESSE PRATT, of Braintree, Mass. (son of IV. Samuel
and Lydia), b. Mar. 30, 1743; m. Feb. 15, 1766, Joanna
Adams. They moved (1811) to Braintree, Vt., with their
son Samuel, and both lived to be almost 100 years old.

Children:

    1  JERUSHA, b. Oct. 11, 1767; d. Sept. 25, 1769.

241 240   2  SAMUEL, b. Aug. 15, 1770; m. Persis Haydon, Dec. 5,
1795.

---

240 241 (VI.) SAMUEL PRATT, of Braintree, *Vermont* (son of V.
Jesse), b. in Braintree, *Mass.*, Aug. 15, 1770; d. 1830; m.
Dec. 5, 1795, Persis Haydon, of Braintree, Mass. She d.
at River Falls, Wis., 1867.

He moved to Braintree, Vt., 1812, soon after the settlement of the town (the original founders being from the
neighborhood of his home), with his family, consisting of
a wife and eight children; two were afterwards born in
Vermont.

The historian of Braintree, Vt., writes of him as follows: "Was connected by blood through the Adamses of
Revolutionary fame." Their religious principles were
firm and immovable, "which they transmitted to their
posterity, who, down to the present generation, have
preserved and perpetuated them intact and inviolate.
* * * * He believed with David that 'children are a herit-
age,' and had his 'quiver full of them.'" His mother
lived the last thirty years of her life at River Falls, Wis.,
with her daughter Lydia. "Of her it is enough to say
that she died as she had lived — a Christian." Of the
children, only one (Zebah) remained in Vermont, the re-
mainder removed west.

Children:

245 242   1  ZEBAH HAYDEN, b. Dec. 18, 1798; m. Mehitable Faxon,
of Hartford, and settled in Jericho, Vt.

    2  JOHN TILLSTON, b. Nov. 23, 1800; m. Sarah Smith of
Hartford; resided in Waterbury and Eden till 1854,
when he removed to River Falls, Wis., and d. there in
1879.

    3  SAMUEL, JR., b. Mar. 6, 1802; m. Sept. 18, 1821, Anna
White; lived in Waterbury, Vt., and Weymouth, Mass.,
whence he removed to River Falls, Wis., 1854, and d.
there 1879.

4 JERUSHA WEBB, b. Feb. 24, 1803, in Braintree; m. Apr.
6, 1830, Jeremiah Flint; removed to Wisconsin, 1854.
She d. 1872.

5 ASAPH, b. Mar. 28, 1806; m. Hermione Clark. They resided at Dover, Ill., and removed to River Falls, 1851,
but returned to Dover about 1874, where they now reside.

6 PHEBE HAYDEN, b. Aug. 18, 1808; m. Dec. 1, 1825, Ariel
Kellogg, of Brookfield; resided at Waterbury several
years, then went to Dover, Ill., where she d. in 1880.

7 LYDIA, b. Dec. 18, 1810; m. June 3, 1835, Joseph F. Nichols; removed, 1846, to Dover, and thence, 1854, to Wis.

244 243 8 GEORGE WASHINGTON, b. Apr. 3, 1812.

9 SARAH, b. Aug. 3, 1814; d. young.

10 JOANNA, b. Mar. 18, 1816; d. young.

---

243 244 (VII) GEORGE WASHINGTON PRATT, of River Falls, Wis.
(son of VI. Samuel); b. Apr. 3, 1812, in Braintree, Vt.;
m. 1857, Sophia A. White, of River Falls, Wis.

At the time of his father's death was only eighteen.
After studying a few years in Burlington and Montpelier,
Vt., he engaged in the music trade at New Orleans and
Memphis, and afterwards at St. Louis. In 1852 he moved
to River Falls, and was among the earliest settlers of
that place. There he became at once a leader in society
and took a prominent part in all that pertained to the
best interests of that town.

He was founder, and for many years president of River Falls Academy, an incorporated school of the first
order; was Chairman of Supervisors; Superintendent of
Public Instruction, and held other responsible offices.

He was, besides, one of the original founders of the
Congregational Church there, and a delegate to the
National Council at Boston Mass., in 1865. In the State
Normal School enterprise he was also a prime mover.

---

242 245 (VII) ZEBAH H. PRATT, of Jericho, Vt. (son of VI. Samuel),
b. Dec. 18, 1796; d. March 20, 1862; m. March 1, 1819,
Mehitable Faxon, dau. of Francis and Dorcas (Wild) b.
in Washington, N. H., May 4, 1791; d. Aug. 10, 1869.
He was a shoemaker.

Children :

1 JOHN T., b. Nov. 25, 1819; m. Sept. 22, 1844, Angelia Loomis of Fairfax, Vt., b. March 25, 1825, dau. of Ebenezer W. and Mehitable (Goodridge); she d. Aug. 7, 1864. He m. (2) Aug. 2, 1865, Hannah Smith, b. March 14, 1835, dau. of Richard O. and Lydia (Boyd). He is a painter and resides at Jericho, Vt.

2 CAROLINE A., b. May 5, 1821; m. Dec. 8, 1842, Zadoc W. Rockwood of Jericho, Vt., b. Oct., 1826.

3 CHARLES H., b. Jan. 15, 1823; m. May 12, 1855, Margaret Shelpman, dau. of Spicer and Elizabeth (Howard), b. Feb. 14, 1830; She d. Feb. 28 1863; He m. (2) Apr. 16, 1863, Margaret Booton, b. Apr. 6, 1834, dau. of Rev. John and Martha (Polley). He was for ten years in the service of the U. S., in the regular army. He was present at the principal battles of the Mexican War; he also served one year in Co. C., 91st Ohio Vols. Was for many years a school teacher. Is now a clergyman, residence, Bear Creek, Scitolo County, Ohio.

4 EDWIN E., b. June 13, 1824; m. April 20, 1847, Hannah Hapgood, b. July 10, 1826, dau. of Elmore and Rhenama (Smith). They reside at Saxonville, Wis. He is a farmer.

5 LUCETTA, b. Nov. 15, 1825 (unmarried).

6 LUCINDA A., b. Nov. 15, 1825; m. June 30, 1851, Benjamin F. Perry, of Lowell, Mass.

7 FRANCIS FAXON, b. Dec. 5, 1827; m. Nov. 1, 1853, Cynthia Blodgett of Jericho, Vt., b. July 15, 1831, dau. of Silvenas and Rachel (Woodward). He is a house and sign painter, and resides at Deloit, Wis.

8 DORCAS J., b. Nov. 20, 1829; m. May 23, 1861, William W. Martin, of Huntington, Vt.

9 GEORGE H., b. Nov. 23, 1831; d. Sept. 11, 1832.

10 MARTHA L., b. Feb. 26, 1833; m. May 6, 1868, Silas Ransom of Jericho, Vt., b. Apr. 8, 1822.

11 HELEN M., b. Nov. 15, 1836; m. Nov. 5, 1851, Spofford Wright of Williston, Vt. Residence, Jericho, Vt.

---

273  246 (II.) SAMUEL PRATT, of Weymouth (son of I. Matthew), b. ——; d. 1678; m. July 19, 1660, Hannah Rogers. She d. Oct. 16, 1715.

Samuel was, like his brothers, a town officer and large land-owner, being mentioned frequently in the records as such.

In his will he refers to "my brother Joseph Pratt." Estate valued at £275. 12s.

His son Samuel moved to Taunton, and was ancestor of most of the Pratts of Taunton, Norton, Mansfield and vicinity.

Children:

|   |   |   |   |
|---|---|---|---|
|   |   | 1 | JUDITH, b. July 25, 1661. |
| 395 | 246a | 2 | JOHN, b. Aug. 17, 1663; d. Feb. 8, 1744. |
|   |   | 3 | HANNAH, b. Dec. 21, 1665. |
|   |   | 4 | MARY, b. Mar. 3, 1668; m. Wm. Dyer. |
| 278 | 246b | 5 | SAMUEL, b. Nov. 15, 1670. |
|   |   | 6 | EXPERIENCE, b. Jan. 8, 1672. |
| 309 | 246c | 7 | EBENEZER, b. ——; mentioned as "nephew of Lieut. John." |

---

48  247  (IV.) JOHN PRATT, of No. Bridgewater (son of III. Matthew), b. ——; d. ——; m. ——.

He settled in North Bridgewater, 1737.

Children:

|   |   |   |   |
|---|---|---|---|
| 250 | 248 | 1 | BARNABAS. |
|   |   | 2 | JOHN. |
| 251 | 249 | 3 | THOMAS. |
|   |   | 4 | CONSIDER. |
|   |   | 5 | JESSE, m. Nov. 20, 1762, Lydia, Ramsdull, and moved to Medway, 1767, with family. |
|   |   | 6 | MARGERY, m. Thomas Tribou, July 11, 1745. |
|   |   | 7 | PRISCILLA, m. —— Smith. |

---

248  250  (V.) BARNABAS PRATT, of Bridgewater (son of IV. John), b. ——; d. 1788; m. Oct. 17, 1750, Isabella Downey, dau. of Walter. She went to Hebron, Maine, with son-in-law Davis, and lived to be 102 years of age.

Barnabas, Jr., appointed administrator, Apr. 6, 1791.

Children:

|   |   |   |
|---|---|---|
| 1 | THADDEUS, | went to { m. Rachel Churchill, July 23, 1777. |
| 2 | BARNABAS, | Maine. { m. Ruhama French, Aug. 23, 1787. |
|   | Had son Axell. |   |
| 3 | CATHARINE, m. Jeremiah Thayer, Jan. 17, 1781. |   |
| 4 | MARY, m. Asa Battles. |   |
| 5 | ISABEL, m. Levi Brannock, Apr. 15, 1789. |   |
| 6 | SUSANNA, m. Simeon Davis, Feb. 27, 1788. |   |

249  251 (V). THOMAS PRATT, of Bridgewater (son of IV. John),
b. ——; d. Apr. 4, 1777; m. Mary or Mercy Jones.

Children :

1  MICAH, b. Oct. 20, 1756.
2  CONSIDER, b. July 26, 1759; d. Oct. 4, 1775.
253  252  3  THOMAS, b. Aug. 30, 1761.
4  MARGERY, b. Feb. 5, 1764; m. John Bolton, Dec. 4, 1787.
5  LOT JONES, b. Jan. 1, 1766; d. Jan. 15, 1766.
6  LOT, b. Apr. 14, 1767; m. Polly Aldrich, Oct. 22, 1787.  He
removed to Vermont.
7  MERCY, b. Oct. 6, 1769; m. —— Spear.
8  PATIENCE, b. Nov. 5, 1771; m. John Crane, Apr. 29, 1793.
9  NOAH, b. Apr. 16, 1774; m. Desire Cole, Sept. 17, 1777.

(Lot and Noah went to Vermont.)

---

252  253 (VI.) THOMAS PRATT, of Bridgewater (son of V. Thomas),
b. Aug. 30, 1761; m. Feb. 27, 1788, Susanna, dau. of Seth
Thayer.

Children :

256  254  1  ASA, b. Oct. 31, 1793; m. Lydia Humphrey, Feb. 26, 1815.
258  255  2  ANNA, b. Dec. 24, 1806; d. Oct. 26, 1862.
3  EDWARD.
4  SILVIA.
5  AZUBA, m. Simeon Dunbar, Oct. 13, 1813.
6  REBECCA.
7  HENRIETTA.
8  SUSANNA.
9  EMILY.
10  POLLY.
11  ABIGAIL.

---

254  256 (VII.) ASA PRATT, of Andover, Me. (son VI. Thomas), b.
Oct. 31, 1793; d. Apr. 27, 1877; m. Lydia, dau. of James
Humphrey, Feb. 23, 1815.  She was b. Feb. 28, 1796; d.
Apr. 25, 1874.

Children :

1  SUSAN H., b. Feb. 27, 1816; d. Feb. 25, 1851; m. May 16,
1850, Mr. Low.
2  HARRIET A., b. Jan. 19, 1818; d. Dec. 18, 1818.

    3  HARRIET A., b. Nov. 1, 1819; m. May 16, 1840.

    4  RUEL, b. Feb. 5, 1822; d. Mar. 9, 1822.

    5  MARY, b. Apr. 4, 1823; d. Oct. 17, 1883; m. B. W. Tingley, June 22, 1854.

    6  ANGELINE, b. May 6, 1825; d. Aug. 17, 1873; m. May 20, 1846.

259  257  7  ABBA, b. Dec. 19, 1827.

    8  LAVINA, b. Mar. 29, 1831; d. Apr. 3, 1852.

---

255  258  (VII.) ARBA PRATT, of E. Stoughton (son of VI. Thomas), b. Dec. 24, 1806; m. Caroline Phillips of Duxbury.

Children:

    1  MARY A., b. Jan. 28, 1832; m. Samuel B. Harris, of Stoughton.

    2  ABIGAIL, b. Aug., 1834; d. 1834.

    3  EDWARD, b. July 27, 1836; d. May 17, 1860.

    4  LUTHER, b. Nov., 1845; d. Sept., 1847.

    5  CHARLES, b. July, 1847; d. Sept., 1847.

---

257  259  (VIII.) ARBA PRATT, of Andover, Maine (son of VII. Asa), b. Dec. 19, 1827; d. June 18, 1896; m. Nov. 11, 1855, Sarah Howey, b. Apr. 20, 1837; she d. June 21, 1874.

Children:

    1  EVA HARRIET, b. Oct. 7, 1856; m. Nov. 13, 1890, ——, in Brooklyn, N. Y.

    2  LYDIA LAVINA, b. June 17, 1858; m. Mar. 5, 1878, O. H. Carley.

    3  WILLARD ARETAS, b. Mar. 11, 1860; m. Sept. 14, 1884, ——, in Brooklyn, N. Y.

    4  EDWARD J., b. Apr. 21, 1862.

    5  HENRY LOVEJOY, b. May 5, 1866.

    6  SUSIE HERSEY, b. June 7, 1868.

    7  Irving, b. Aug. 15, 1879; d. Sept. 6, 1882.

---

49  200  (IV.) MICAH PRATT, of Taunton (son of III. Matthew, of Abington), b. ——, 1692; d. Dec. 31, 1758; m. Marcey ——, b. 1692; d. Apr. 26, 1762.

He was a Doctor, and is so recorded in the Taunton Records. Land was granted to him April 16, 1828, near that of Samuel, John, Peter, and Paul Pratt.

Micah was born in Weymouth, and when his Father moved from there to Abington, or a little later, he moved to Taunton, where he joined his cousin Samuel. He names his first daughter Mary after his mother, his second after his wife Marcey; Abigail and Elizabeth were family names.

He seems to have been a man of considerable prominence.

Children (given in his will, dated Apr. 7, 1763):

262 261 1 MICAH, b. ———. 1721 ("only son"); d. Oct. 5, 1765.
        2 MARY, b. ———; m. Abner Harris.
        3 MARCEY, b. ———; m. Edward Doan.
        4 ABIGAIL, b. ———; m. Job Deine.
        5 ELIZABETH, b. ———; m. Elmer ———.

261 262 (V.) MICAH PRATT, of Taunton (son of IV. Micah), b. 1721; d. Oct. 5, 1765; m. Sarah ———; b. 1723; d. Jan. 26, 1805. (Her name may have been Dier or Dyer, as a son is so named.) He was a Doctor, and like his father, had a large practice, and considerable property. His will is dated Sept. 26, 1765. His son Micah made a will Jan. 14, 1777, but does not mention any children, and it is safe to assume that he died without issue.

Children (as named in will):

        1 MICAH, b. ———; d. about 1777; m. Sept. 14, 1774, Marcey Burt.
        2 JOHN, b. ———.
265 263 3 DYER or DIER, b. 1754; d. March 3, 1841.
276 264 4 DAN, b. Oct. 7, 1761.
        5 SARAH, b. ———.
        6 MERCY or MARCEY, b. ———, 1745; d. Nov. 16, 1747.
        7 DESIRE, b. ———.
        8 ABI, b. ——— 1765; d. Oct. 24, 1773.

263 265 (VI.) DIER PRATT, of Taunton (son of V. Micah), b. 1754; d. March 3, 1841; m. Zilpha Macomber, Oct. 30, 1781; b. 1762; d. Sept. 29, 1830.

Children:

        1 MICAH, b. Aug. 6, 1782.
        2 ZILPHA, b. Aug. 21, 1784; m. Oct. 28, 1810, Benj. Morrill.
260 266 3 DIER J., b. Feb. 24, 1786; d. June 7, 1801.
        4 ABI, b. Feb. 11, 1788; m. Sept. 26, 1813, Joshua Turner.

275 267 5 JOB, b. March 19, 1790; m. Lucy ——,
      6 RUTH, b. Apr. 2, 1792.
      7 MARY or MERCY, b. March 18, 1794.
274 268 8 JAMES (M.), b. Apr. 25, 1796; d. Apr. 9, 1883.

---

266 269 (VII.) DIER J. PRATT, of Taunton (son of VI. Dier), b. Feb. 24, 1786; d. June 7, 1861; m. Ruth H. (Presbury?) His will dated Jan. 2, 1861.

Children:

272 270 1 MICAH N., b. Aug. 5, 1810; d. Jan. 12, 1865.
      2 CHARLES W., b. May 19, 1816; d. Oct. 16, 1838.
      3 MARTHA THOMAS, b. May 18, 1821; m. Wm. Pierce, Sept. 5, 1839.
      4 FOXWELL NELSON, b. Oct. 18, 1826.
      5 FRANCES LOUISA, b. Oct. 18, 1826; m. Jan. 17, 1865, Nelson Steele.
273 271 6 DIER L., b. ——,

---

270 272 (VIII.) MICAH N. PRATT, of Taunton and Vermont (son of VII. Dier L.), b. Aug. 5, 1810; d. Jan. 12, 1865; m. Maria C. or Merisa, she b. June 15, 1809; d. Oct. 15, 1869, dau. of John ——, of Ludboro, Vt. Some of his children are recorded as born in Vermont.

Children:

      1 LOYD W., b. May 6, 1842; d. May 3, 1863, at Fredericksburg, Va.
      2 JAMES H., b. Nov. 2, 1847.
      3 HIRAM, b. Oct. 28, 1850; d. July 7, 1851.
      4 MERISA E., b. ——, 1854; m. Apr. 13, 1870, Geo. H. Guillo.

---

271 273 (VIII.) DIER L. PRATT, of Taunton (son of VII. Dier J.), b. ——; d. ——; m. July 19, 1835, Elizabeth R. Hewitt.

Children:

      1 RHODA E., b. ——, 1836; m. March 25, 1855, Dyer S. Paull.
      2 MARTHA A., b. Sept. 13, 1844.
      3 Male Child, b. May 13, 1846.
      4 ANNA, b. Feb. 26, 1848.

208  274 (VII.) JAMES M. PRATT, of Taunton (son of VI. Dier), b.
Apr. 25, 1796; d. Apr. 9, 1883; m. Rebecca Presbury.

Children :

1  REBECCA, b. ——, 1831; m. Feb. 5, 1861, Geo. W. Wilson.
2  HARRIET, b. - , 1838; m. March 17, 1868, Wm. N.
Smith.
3  MARY B., b. ——, 1839; m. July 24, 1859, Abel W. Parker.
4  ADELINE, b. ——, 1840; m. Aug. 25, 1861, Ira M. Reed.

_____

267  275 (VII.) JOB PRATT, of Taunton (son of VI. Dier), b. March 19,
1790; m. Lucy ——,

Child :

JONATHAN W., b. —— 1823; m. June 24, 1845, Clarinda N.
Clapp, b. 1824, dau. of James O. and Orilla ——.

_____

264  276 (VI.) DAN or DANIEL PRATT, of Taunton (son of V. Micah),
b. Oct. 7, 1761; d. ——; m. Sept. 14, 1783, Deborah Jones,
b. March 22, 1766.

Children :

1  JOHN, b. July 14, 1785.
2  CYRUS, b. Apr. 20, 1787.
3  SALLA, b. May 19, 1790.
4  DANIEL, b. June 6, 1793.
5  BENJAMIN, b. March 15, 1796.
6  Infant son, b. Apr. 5, 1799; d. Apr. 14, 1799.

_____

246b 278 (III.) SAMUEL PRATT, of Taunton (son of II. Samuel and
Hannah), b. Nov. 15, 1670; d. Aug. 11, 1728; m. Patience
——, b. 1675; d. Jan. 8, 1735.

He was born in Weymouth, and removed to Taunton
shortly after the birth of Judith, 1695, as she is the only
child recorded at Weymouth. His name appears in the
Index of the Town Records of Taunton for Divisions of
Land between 1695 and 1700, but as some of these books
were destroyed by fire, his first location can not be ascer-
tained ; but later grants in the vicinity of Norton, in which
his dwelling-house is mentioned, undoubtedly prove that
he settled there.

July 26, 1714, Samuel Pratt had "set off" to him as follows: "Five acres at the northerly end of his land that Lyeth in Norton which is called Rumford." Also, Nov. 3, 1714, "Three quarters of an acre of land at the northerly side of my Rumford Lots on the northerly side of the road that leadeth from the grist mill to Norton Meeting House." As Norton was a part of Taunton, he is referred to as of the latter place in the records.

He was a man of considerable prominence, owning a large estate, as he was granted land in nearly every division up to 1714. His will is on record in Taunton, in which he names his children, and leaves property to the value of about £300.

His will is dated July 31, 1728, in which some of his children are mentioned as under twenty-one years of age.

Children:

|  |  | 1 | JUDITH, b. Nov. 23, 1695; m. Samuel Caswell. |
| 285 | 279 | 2 | SAMUEL, JR. |
| 292 | 280 | 3 | JOSIAH. |
| 311 | 281 | 4 | JONATHAN. |
| 315 | 282 | 5 | BENJAMIN, b. 1705; d. June 20, 1785. |
| 355 | 283 | 6 | PETER, b. 1711; d. Feb. 16, 1760. |
| 366 | 284 | 7 | PAUL. |
|  |  | 8 | HANNAH. |
|  |  | 9 | PATIENCE, m. Moses Knapp, Jan. 2, 1734. |

---

279   285 (IV.) SAMUEL PRATT, of Taunton (son of III. Samuel), b. ——; d. ——; m. (1) ——; m. (2) June 27, 1744, Abigail Atwood of Berkley; m. (3) Lydia ——.

He had land set off to him March 6, 1737, near Peter Pratt. Will dated July 4, 1758, in which he mentions his children. He left a large estate.

Children:

| 291 | 286 | 1 | NEHEMIAH. |
| 288 | 287 | 2 | SAMUEL. |
|  |  | 3 | LYDIA, m. Linkon. |
|  |  | 4 | MERCY, m. Samuel Wild. |
|  |  | 5 | PRUDENCE, m. Ebenezer Pitts, Jr. |
|  |  | 6 | PHEBE, m. Baird Arnold. |
|  |  | 7 | PATIENCE, m. John Smith. |

/ 288 (V.) SAMUEL PRATT, of Taunton (son of IV. Samuel), b. 1756; d. May 12, 1829; m. Phebe Hodges, b. Dec. 29, 1753. His will, dated March 20, 1824, mentions only four of his children, the others probably dead.

Child:

) 289 1 NEHEMIAH, b. July 15, 1781; d. before 1822.

———

) 290 (VI.) NEHEMIAH PRATT, of Taunton (son of V. Samuel), b. July 15, 1781; d. before 1822; m. Abigail Lincoln, Dec. 9, 1800; she d. March 19, 1829, aged 47.

Child:

HIRAM, b. about 1808; Samuel Pratt appointed guardian 1822.

———

8 291 (V.) NEHEMIAH PRATT, of Taunton (son of IV. Samuel), b. ——; d. ——; m. June 6, 1751, Mary Drake.

Child:

1 NEHEMIAH, b. ——; d. Aug. 24, 1770.
2 JAMES HODGES, b. June 12, 1784; d. Oct. 5, 1788.
3 POLLY, b. Jan. 14, 1786.
4 SAMUEL, b. Sept. 29, 1787; d. July 31, 1829.
5 BARNEY, b. Mar. 6, 1790.
6 PHEBE, b. July 22, 1798.

———

0 292 (IV.) JOSIAH PRATT, of Norton (son of III. Samuel), b. ——; m. (1) Nov. 22, 1716, Sarah Jones; she d. March 2, 1723. He m. (2) Tabethy Smith, of Norton, May 20, 1825; she d. Jan. 10, 1772. His will is dated 1745.

Children by Sarah:

0 293 1 JOSIAH, b. Feb. 14, 1719.
2 NEOME, b. March 18, 1721.
3 294 3 NEHEMIAH, b. Feb. 9, 1723.
4 JUDAH, b. July 30, 1727.
8 295 5 ZEPHENIAH, b. July 5, 1729.
2 296 6 SAMUEL, b. July 23, 1731.
7 SARAH, b. Feb. 22, 1736.
8 MERCY, b. Feb. 13, 1738.

9 CHARITY, b. Nov. 18, 1742; m. John Davenport, Feb. 29, 1764.

307 297 10 JOHN, b. June 19, 1744; d. Oct. 24, 1824.

Samuel settled in Westminster, Vt., before 1736.

---

295 298 (V.) ZEPHENIAH PRATT, of Norton (son of IV. Josiah), b.——; m. Abigail Rogers. He d. before 1752. His property was divided among his children and wife, 1753 (Taunton Probate).

Children:

1 ZEPHENIAH, "eldest son," d. 1772. (Norton Records give m. of Z. to Abigail Shephard, April 2, 1747, probably this one.)
2 SARAH, m. Stephen Briggs.
3 ABIEL.
4 ABIGAIL.

---

293 299 (V.) JOSIAH PRATT, of Stoughton (son of IV. Josiah of Norton), b. Feb. 14, 1719; m. Abigail ——. (Josiah's father gives him land in Stoughton in his will.)

Children:

1 JOSIAH, b. May 26, 1745.
301 300 2 ISAAC, b. Nov. 24, 1746.
3 JOSEPH, b. April 1, 1749; m. Ann Tucker, of Norton, Jan. 13, 1784. (?)

---

300 301 (VI.) ISAAC PRATT, of Stoughton (son of V. Josiah), b. Nov. 24, 1746; m. Mary ——.

Children:

1 JOSIAH, b. Sept. 14, 1769.
2 ISAAC, b. June 18, 1771.
3 ELIZABETH, b. Sept. 12, 1773.

---

296 302 (V.) SAMUEL PRATT, of Norton (son of IV. Josiah), b. July 23, 1731; m. Experience White, of Norton, Jan. 15, 1756. She d. Aug. 15, 1779.

Children :

1 SAMUEL, b. May 2, 1753 ; m. Apr. 13, 1780, Abigail Col-
  well.
2 MERCY, b. Nov. 2, 1756.
3 LOUXO, b. May 6, 1761.
4 *ABRAHAM, b. May 17, 1763 ; d. June 10, 1763.
5 EXPERIENCE, b. May 11, 1764.

---

294  303  (V.) NEHEMIAH PRATT, of Norton (son of IV. Josiah),
          b. ——; m. June 28, 1748, Abigail Newland, of Norton.

          Children :

          1 NEHEMIAH, b. Apr. 11, 1749 ; m. Nov. 15, 1709, Judith
            Pratt.
303  304  2 DAVID, b. March 8, 1751.
          3 NAOMI, b. Feb. 20, 1753.
          4 ABIGAIL, b. May 4, 1755.
          5 ANNE, b. Aug. 18, 1757 ; d. Nov. 20, 1832.
          6 MARY, b. Nov. 28, 1759.
          7 DANIEL, b. June 15, 1765.

---

304  305  (VI.) DAVID PRATT, of Mansfield (son of V. Nehemiah), b.
          March 8, 1751 ; m. Lois Forbes, of Easton, Nov. 10,
          1774.

          Children :

          1 OTIS, b. June 18, 1775.
306  306  2 AMASA, b. Aug. 24, 1777 ; m. July 7, 1796, Eunice Wil-
            liams.
          3 SALLY, b. Jan. 2, 1781.
          4 DAVID, b. June 13, 1783.
          5 LOIS, b. May 5, 1785.
          6 ANNA, b. April 18, 1790.

---

297  307  (V.) JOHN PRATT, of Mansfield (son of IV. Josiah), b. June
          19, 1744 ; d. Oct. 24, 1824 ; m. Nancy——.

          Children :

          1 JOHN, b. July 21, 1780.
          2 HERBERT, b. Feb. 20, 1790.
          3 ALLEN, b. Apr. 20, 1792.
          4 NANCY, b. Feb. 4, 1794.

5 MILLA, b. July 12, 1796.
6 ALBERT, b. June 5, 1798.
7 AURELIUS, b. Mar. 24, 1800.
8 LOUISA, b. Feb. 23, 1802.
9 MARIA, b. Sept. 22, 1804.

---

306 308 (VII.) AMASA PRATT, of Mansfield (son of VI. David), b. Aug. 24, 1777; d.——; m. July 7, 1798, Eunice Williams.

Children:

310 309   1 AMASA, b.——; d. Sept. 5, 1879.
         2 CHARLES F. b.——; d. Aug 15, 1884.

---

309 310 (VIII.) AMASA PRATT, of Mansfield (son of VII. Amasa), b.——; d. Sept. 5, 1879; m. Feb. 12, 1829, Sally Woods.

Children:

  1 MARY A., b. June 26, 1845; d. Sept. 24, 1865.
  2 HENRY, B., b.——; d. Aug. 31, 1865.

---

281 311 (IV.) JONATHAN PRATT, of Mansfield (son of III. Samuel), b.——; d.——; m. Abigail Mory, of Norton, July 25, 1728; she d. Sept. 11, 1745. Brother Benjamin mentioned in Records; also John. He m. (2) Rachel Bramen, March 12, 1745.

Children:

322 312   1 JONATHAN, b. Oct. 17, 1729.
         2 ABIGAIL, b. Sept. 23, 1732; d. young.
         3 ABIGAIL, b. Feb. 18, 1734; m. Shepardson.
         4 BATHSHEBA, b. March 7, 1737; m. Abiel Clapp; she d. before 1771.
         5 { EBENEZER, b. April 20, 1739; d. 1739.
         6 { ANNA, b. April 20, 1739; d. 1739.
         7 NATHAN, b. Nov. 24, 1741; d. Nov. 14, 1743.
         8 NATHAN, b. Nov. 14, 1743; d. Sept. 14, 1745.
         9 RACHEL, b. Nov. 14, 1746; d. May, 1750.
320 313  10 SPENCER, b. June 25, 1749.
        11 RACHEL, b. Aug. 1751; d. Jan. 1754.
321 314  12 DANIEL, b. July 14, 1755.

32 315 (IV.) BENJAMIN PRATT, of Mansfield (son of III. Samuel),
b. ——, 1705; d. June 29, 1785; m. Mary Turner, Jan.
22, 1729. He was styled a Captain.

Children:

1 WALTHA, or WEALTHY, m. May 8, 1774, Job Brintnell.
2 MARY, m. Hoges.
3 KATHARINE, m. Williams.
4 SARAH, m. Billings.
17 316 5 SOLOMON, d. Nov. 6, 1776.
6 JEBEL, m. Dean.

---

16 317 (V.) SOLOMON PRATT, of Mansfield (son of IV. Benj.), d.
Nov. 6, 1776; m. May 13, 1767, Hannah White, or Hues.
She m. (2) Timothy Billings, Jan. 9, 1785, and d. Feb.
2, 1790.

Children:

1 BENJAMIN, b. Nov. 26, 1767.
23 318 2 SOLOMON, b. Feb. 26, 1771.
28 319 3 JONATHAN, b. May 13, 1773.
4 HANNAH, b. May 26, 1775.

---

13 320 (V.) SPENCER PRATT, of Mansfield (son of IV. Jonathan),
b. June 25, 1749; m. Lucy.

Children:

1 LUCY, b. Dec. 6, 1771.
2 SPENCER, b. Nov. 5, 1773.
3 APTOLLAR, b. June 26, 1776.
4 JONATHAN, b. Feb. 2, 1779.
5 RACHEL, b. Oct. 4, 1781; d. Feb. 19, 1817.
6 LEWIS SWEETING, b. Oct. 3, 1784.
7 BETSEY CHARLOTTE, } b. May 11, 1788.
8 GREENLEAF JENNISON, }

---

14 321 (V.) DANIEL PRATT, of Mansfield (son of IV. Jonathan),
b. July 14, 1755; m. Sept. 7, 1780, Chloe Hawes of
Mansfield.

Children:

1 ELIJAH HAWES, b. July 29, 1782.
2 CHLOE, b. Sept. 1, 1784.

3 ROXY, b. April 9, 1787.
4 POLLY, b. July 30, 1790.
5 SCYLAR, b. Nov. 22, 1793.
6 GEORGE, b. Oct. 6, 1796.

---

312 322 (V.) JONATHAN PRATT, of Mansfield (son of IV. Jonathan), b. Oct. 17, 1729; d. Oct. 13, 1771; m. 1758, Hepzibah Billings, of Stoughton. He was (1757) styled a "Dr." on the "Alarm List" of soldiers in the North Precinct.

No Children.

---

318 323 (VI.) SOLOMON PRATT, of Mansfield (son of V. Solomon), b. Feb. 26, 1771; m. May 19, 1803, Polly Bates of Mansfield. He was a Justice of the Peace, 1823.

Children :

326 324 1 HARRISON BILLINGS, b. March 3, 1804.
327 325 2 HORATIO, b. June 5, 1805; d. May 24, 1872.
3 GEORGE ERASTUS, b. July 4, 1809.
4 MARY BATES, b. May 6, 1814; m. March 7, 1837, Rev. J. H. Sargent.
5 CHARLES, b. June 2, 1818; m. Caroline A. Pratt, of LeRoy, N. Y., April 25, 1855.

---

324 326 (VII.) HARRISON B. PRATT, of Mansfield (son of VI. Solomon), b. March 3, 1804; m. Dec. 25, 1828, Stella Bates, of Mansfield. He was styled a Captain; was Town Clerk in 1826.

Children :

1 HARRISON WARREN, b. April 26, 1831.
2 HENRY LORING, b. March 29, 1833; d. Jan. 17, 1878.
3 DELIA AUGUSTA, b. June 10, 1835; d. Oct. 11, 1835.
4 FRANCIS EDWARD, b. May 20, 1837; d. June, 1838.
5 ELIZABETH AUGUSTA, b. Jan. 19, 1840; m. Nov. 15, 1871, Avery O. Dunham, of Mansfield.

27 (VII.) HORATIO PRATT, of Mansfield (son of VI. Solomon), b. June 5, 1805; d. May 24, 1872; m. July 6, 1837, Elizabeth Williams. He was a lawyer.

Children:

1 MARY ELIZABETH, b. Feb. 4, 1846; d. July 23, 1847.
2 JOHN W. W., b. Dec. 16, 1847.
3 CHARLES CAMDEN, b. Feb. 22, 1849.

———

28 (VI.) JONATHAN PRATT, of Mansfield (son of V. Solomon), b. May 13, 1773; d. at Pelham, April 16, 1846; m. March 19, 1794, Abigail Phillips, dau. of John and Priscilla; she b. May 5, 1776; d. Oct. 16, 1861.

Children:

29    1 SOLOMON, b. Nov. 8, 1797, at Mansfield.
30    2 BENJAMIN, b. Feb. 1, 1800, at Attleboro; d. May 8, 1852, at Hatfield.
31    3 JOHN, b. Sept. 3, 1802, at Mendon; d. Sept. 8, 1850, at Springfield.
32    4 LUKE, b. April 6, 1805, at Mendon; d. Jan. 3, 1865, at Springfield.
33    5 BETSEY BISHOP, b. Aug. 29, 1807, at Mendon; d. Feb. 8, 1880, at Pelham.
      6 POLLY, b. Feb. 11, 1810, at Mendon; d. Sept. 19, 1830.
34    7 WILLIAM FOSTER, b. Sept. 14, 1812, at Mendon; d. Sept. 9, 1882, at E. Bridgewater.
35    8 OLNEY PAINE, b. Oct. 5, 1815, at Mendon.
      9 HANNAH, b. Nov. 20, 1818, at Mendon; d. Aug. 7, 1820.
     10 ASENETH, b. Sept. 25, 1821, at Mendon; d. Sept. 18, 1824.

———

36 (VII.) SOLOMON PRATT, of Mendon (son of VI. Jonathan), b. Nov. 8, 1797; m. Lydia Aldrich.

Children:

1 SUSAN.
2 ASENETH.
3 ABIGAIL.
4 HANNAH.
5 AURELIUS.
6 EZRA.

330 337 (VII.) BENJAMIN PRATT, (son of VI. Jonathan) b. at Attleboro, Feb. 1, 1800; d. at Hatfield, May 8, 1852; m. Aug. 5, 1828, Amy, dau. of Elisha and Narissa Chase, of Sterling, Mass. She was b. Feb. 27, 1807; d. Oct. 4, 1874.

Children:

    1  JOHN, b. July 1, 1830, at Mendon; d. July 28, 1854, at Hatfield.

    2  ELISHA, b. June 19, 1833, at Mendon; d. Sept. 6, 1854, at Hatfield.

    3  EDWIN CHASE, b. Sept. 9, 1837, at Pelham; d. May 17, 1838.

    4  AMY ANN, b. Sept. 22, 1839, at Pelham; m. Nov. 20, 1875, Geo. F. Davidson.

    5  BETSEY MARIA, b. July 11, 1841, at Pelham; m. April 2, 1868, Charles Otis Vixon.

339 338  6  BENJAMIN LUKE, b. Jan. 8, 1849, at Hatfield.

---

338 339 (VIII.) BENJAMIN LUKE PRATT, of Sterling, Mass., (son of VII. Jonathan), b. Jan. 8, 1849; m. May 16, 1802, Ella O., dau. of Eben P. and Eliza    lood.

Child:

AMY ELIZA, b. Feb. 26, 1876.

---

331 340 (VII.) JOHN PRATT (son of VI. Jonathan), b. Sept. 3, 1802, at Mendon; d. Sept. 8, 1850, at Springfield; m. Jan. 5, 1826, Adeline Aldrich; she b. Oct. 1, 1805; d. Oct. 16, 1848.

Children:

343 341  1  JOHN FRANKLIN, b. Feb. 12, 1827; d. Sept. 4, 1860, at Ludlow.

344 342  2  GEORGE MORTIMER, b. Feb. 7, 1829, at Ludlow.

---

341 343 (VIII.) JOHN FRANKLIN PRATT (son of VII. John), b. Feb. 12, 1827, at Ludlow, Mass.; d. there Sept. 4, 1860; m. April 30, 1860.

Child:

FRANKIE, M., b. Feb. 8, 1861; m. March 27, 1879, Geo. A. Allen, of Bellefonte, Pa.

342  344 (VIII.) GEORGE MORTIMER PRATT, of Ludlow, Mass. (son of VII. John), b. Feb. 7, 1829; m. Jan. 20, 1850, Elizabeth, dau. of James and Elizabeth Tidgewell; she b. Nov. 14, 1831, at Sheffield, Eng.

Children:

   1  JOHN WILLIAM, b. Nov. 25, 1850, at Middletown, Conn.
   2  GEORGE FRANK, b. Dec. 22, 1854, at Middletown, Conn.
   3  CHARLES FOSTER, b. Jan. 31, 1858, at Middletown, Conn.

---

332  345 (VII.) LUKE PRATT, of Springfield, Mass. (son of VI. Jonathan), b. April 6, 1805, at Mendon; d. Jan. 3, 1835, at Springfield; m. Sept. 15, 1829, Eliza, dau. of Russell and Betsey Pratt Sage, of Saybrook; she b. June 6, 1805, in Saybrook; d. May 5, 1879.

Children:

   1  SOPHIA AMELIA, b. June 27, 1830; d. Nov. 29, 1849.
   2  SARAH FRANCES, b. May 13, 1832; m. Feb. 15, 1853, Fred'k S. Strong, of Coventry, Ct.; son Charles Pratt Strong, b. Dec. 11, 1855, a physician in Boston.
347  346  3  BENJAMIN OLNEY, b. June 24, 1834.
   4  HARRIET ELIZA, b. Oct. 13, 1837; m. Nov. 8, 1860, Jas. M. Bly, of Chicopee Falls.
   5  CHARLES FOSTER, b. Dec. 28, 1839; d. Oct. 28, 1849.
   6  LURANNA PHILLIPS, b. Nov. 6, 1842; m. Nov. 22, 1866, Lewis Warner.

---

346  347 (VIII.) BENJAMIN OLNEY PRATT, of Springfield, Mass. (son of VII. Luke), b. June 24, 1834; m. May 31, 1857, Lucy C. Carrol.

Child:

ANNIE E., b. Oct. 23, 1863; d. Aug. 27, 1865.

---

333  348 (VII.) BETSEY B. PRATT, of Pelham, Mass. (dau. of VI. Jonathan), b. Aug. 29, 1807; d. Feb. 8, 1880; m. Aug. 26, 1827, Thomas, son of George and Waity Buffum.

Children:

   1  ANGELINE A., b. June 23, 1828; m. March 2, 1847, Jos. G. Ward.

2 DAVID, b. Oct. 1, 1829 ; d. May 2, 1853 ; m. May 11, 1852, Emeline E. Taylor.

3 GEORGE H., b. Jan. 20, 1831 ; d. July 21, 1859.

4 ELIZA ANN, b. Feb. 8, 1833 ; m. Oct. 13, 1857, Granville H. Leonard.

5 WILLIAM F., b. Jan. 4, 1835 ; d. March 30, 1837.

6 JOHN PRATT, b. Jan. 4, 1836 ; m. Jan. 1, 1861, Helen M. Johnson ; (2) Mary Kirk.

7 JOSEPH C., b. July 11, 1839 ; d. Oct. 21, 1840.

8 MYRON, b. Sept. 20, 1841 ; d. April 7, 1868 ; m. Julia A. Jenks.

9 MARY J., b. June 22, 1844 ; d. July 22, 1848.

10 THOMAS, b. Aug. 20, 1846 ; m. Sept. 1, 1869, Mary E. Graves.

11 WILLIAM OSCAR, b. July 18, 1849 ; d. Dec. 25, 1885 ; m. April 10, 1872, Mary E. Powers.

---

334 349 (VII.) WILLIAM FOSTER PRATT, of East Bridgewater (son of VI. Jonathan), b. Sept. 14, 1812, at Mendon, Mass. ; d. Sept. 9, 1882, at East Bridgewater ; m. Oct. 18, 1835, Huldah Howard, dau. of Timothy and Huldah Harlow ; she b. April 7, 1812.

Children :

1 ALMIRA WILLIAMS, b. Jan. 20, 1837 ; m. Oct. 1, 1856, Francis Washburn.

2 MARY ABIGAIL, b. June 26, 1840 ; m. Jan. 19, 1859, Oliver Holmes Wade.

3 HULDAH ESTHER, b. Sept. 11, 1842 ; m. Dec. 7, 1860, Constant S. Peterson ; m. (2) John Burrill, Dec. 24, 1873.

4 LUCY ANN, b. Feb. 22, 1845 ; d. June 24, 1848.

5 WILLIAM FOSTER, b. March 23, 1847 ; d. June 24, 1857.

6 GEORGE FRANKLIN, b. April 16, 1852 ; d. Aug. 14, 1858.

351 350 7 PRESCOTT HENRY, b. April 4, 1858.

---

350 351 (VIII.) PRESCOTT HENRY PRATT, of East Bridgewater (son of VII. William F.), b. April 4, 1858 ; m. June 9, 1881, Agnes Clifton, dau. of Henry and Sally Gurney ; she b. June 10, 1861. (To him is due the credit of furnishing most of the matter relating to the descendants

of Solomon Pratt of Mansfield, in which line he belongs.)

Child:

LOUISE FOSTER, b. July 6, 1883.

———

335  352 (VII.) OLNEY PAINE PRATT, of Mendon (son of VI. Jonathan), b. Oct. 5, 1815; m. July 14, 1839, Harriet N. Sage.

Children:

    1  JULIA.

354  353    2  OLNEY.

———

353  354 (VIII.) OLNEY PRATT (son of VII. Olney P.), b. Jan. 25, 1852; m. Dec. 24, 1872, Ida P. Westcott; she b. Oct. 12, 1855.

Children:

    1  WILLIAM FOSTER, b. Oct. 29, 1873.

    2  OLNEY P., b. Feb. 17, 1876.

———

283  355 (IV.) PETER PRATT, of Taunton (son of III. Samuel), b. 1711; d. Febr. 16, 1760, aged 49; m. Jan. 1, 1732, Mary Lincoln.

        He had land set off to him, 1737, 1743, 45, 46, 53, 58, "near the Dighton Line." (See Taunton Probate for children; will dated, Nov. 14, 1759.)

Children:

358  336    1  JOHN, "eldest."

    2  NATHANIEL.

    3  EBENEZER.

350  357    4  ABIJAH, d. 1800; m. Elizabeth Briggs, May 24, 1774.

    5  MOLLY.

    6  SUSANNA.

    7  BATHSHEBA.

    8  RACHEL.

    9  ELIZABETH, b. ——, 1753; d. Aug. 5, 1767.

———

356  358 (V.) JOHN PRATT, of Taunton (son of IV. Peter), b. ——; d. Oct. 1771; m. Hepsebah; d. June 23, 1770.

Children :

1 PETER.
2 DARIUS, or DERIAS.
3 MOLLY.
Nathl., Micah, and Ebenezer, guardians, 1771.

---

357 359 (V.) ABIJAH PRATT, of Taunton (son of IV. Peter),
b. ——; d. 1800; m. May 24, 1774, Elizabeth Briggs.
(Will approved, June 2, 1800.)

Children :

361 360 1 ABIJAH, JR., m. Betsey Walker, Apr. 15, 1802.
2 SILAS, b. ——, 1745; d. Oct. 20, 1768.
3 SPENCER.
4 CHARLES.
5 NATHANIEL.
6 ELIZABETH, m. Elisha Thayer.
7 ASENATH, m. May 6, 1804, Wm. Codding.
8 OLIVE.
9 REME.

---

360 361 (VI.) ABIJAH PRATT, of Taunton (son of V. Abijah),
b. ——; d. ——; m. April 15, 1802, Betsey Walker.

Child :

303 302 EBENEZER W., b. Nov. 9, 1802; d. Sept. 6, 1885.

---

302 303 (VII.) EBENEZER W. PRATT, of Taunton (son of VI. Abijah), b. Nov. 9, 1802; d. Sept. 6, 1885; m. Abigail L.

Child :

305 304 GILBERT W., b. ——, 1833.

---

304 305 (VIII.) GILBERT W. PRATT, of Taunton (son of VII. Ebenezer W.), b. ——, 1833; m. May 20, 1855, Sarah A. Lincoln, b. 1833.

Children :

1 CORA E., b. April 17, 1862.
2 CHARLES GILBERT, b. Jan. 9, 1865.

166 (IV.) PAUL PRATT, of Taunton (son of III. Samuel), b. 1713; d. March 19, 1798; m. Nov. 18, 1733, Mehetable White; she d. aged 34. He m. (2) Abigail, d. June 5, 1782. He m. (3) Hannah Lincoln, Feb. 13, 1783; she b. 1732; d. Oct. 26, 1821, aged 90.

The Division (dated Dec. 31, 1798), of Paul's property is on record at Taunton, in which the wife Hannah is mentioned, also the children. His estate was valued at $3,371.51, a considerable sum for the time.

He was granted land, near the Dighton Line, 1737, 1745, 1748, and 1771, and was a prosperous farmer.

Children:

1  JEMIMA, b. ———; m. Shore.
2  SARAH, b. ———; m. French.
167  3  PAUL, b. June 9, 1735; d. April 24, 1769.
168  4  RUFUS, b. ———, 1749; d. May 9, 1770.
169  5  LEMUEL.

170 (V.) PAUL PRATT, of Taunton (son of IV. Paul), b. June 9, 1735; d. April 24, 1769 (record states, "as he was holding a plow, very suddenly);" m. Marcia Hoskins, Dec. 4, 1755; she afterwards m. Capt. James Andrews, a captain of Artillery in the French war. Paul Pratt was a farmer and shoemaker.

Children:

171  1  PAUL, b. Oct. 25, 1756; m. Caroline, dau. of Simeon Crossman.
2  BENJAMIN, b. May 28, 1758; lost at sea, 1778.
172  3  PRUDENCE, b. May 25, 1760; m. Timothy Smith, June 30, 1779.
173  4  MEHETABLE, b. Sept. 11, 1762; m. David Mason, of Cheshire, Mass.; she d. 1851.
174  5  WEALTHY, b. July 14, 1765; m. Oded Eddy.
175  6  JONATHAN, b. April 13, 1768.
176  7  MARCY, b. Jan. 13, 1770; m. Nathl. Crossman.

177 (VI.) PAUL PRATT, of Taunton (son of V. Paul), b. Oct. 25, 1756; d. Sept. 25, 1839; m. ———, Caroline, dau. of Simeon Crossman, of Taunton. He moved to Cheshire, Mass., and afterwards to Herkimer County, N. Y. He was a farmer.

Children :

1 WEALTHY, b. ——; m. Shubat Westcott.
379 378 2 BENJAMIN, b. March 17, 1786; d. Sept. 17, 1809.
.3 ROXY, b. June 22, 1799; m. Lawrence Root.
4 MARCIA, b. Dec. 0, 1800; m. Lyman Biddlecome; she
d. Sept., 1886.
5 RILEY, } b. Dec. 22, 1802; never married.
6 MAHALA, }
7 BARTON, b. Sept. 23, 1806; left one son and daughters.

---

378 370 (VII.) BENJAMIN PRATT (son of VI. Paul), b. in Taunton,
Mass., March 17, 1786; d. Sept. 17, 1809; m. Sept. 17,
1800, Lucy Biddlecome, b. Nov. 30, 1791; d. April 10,
1835. He m. (2) Botsey Cornell, b. June 7, 1773; d. Sept.
12, 1840.

Children :

1 DANIEL, b. June 26, 1810; m. Fannie Herrick, and had
several sons.
2 CAROLINE, b. Sept. 21, 1814; m. Lewis Gilbert, March,
1848.
3 BENJAMIN, b. April 28, 1817; m., and had a large family.
4 LYMAN, b. Nov. 27, 1820, had two wives (the first d. Jan.
8, 1877, by whom he had several children (one named
Otis). They settled in Huntington, Ohio (W. Va.?)

---

372 380 (VI.) PRUDENCE PRATT (dau. of V. Paul), b. May 25, 1760;
d. March, 1822; she m. June 30, 1779, Timothy Smith.

Children :

1 TIMOTHY, m. widow Leviah Barnes.
2 PRATT, m. (1) widow Judith Christian, (2) widow Eleanor
Dutcher.
3 PRUDENCE, m. Zenas Dewey.
4 RUFUS, m. Lucinda De Groat.
5 MARTIN, m. Botsey De Groat.
6 GILBERT, m. widow Roswell Wood.
They all moved to Deerfield, N. Y.

---

373 381 (VI.) MEHITABLE PRATT (dau. of V. Paul), b. Sept. 11,
1762; d. 1851; m. David Mason, of Cheshire, Mass.
They settled at Marion, Wayne Co., N. Y. They had
twelve children.

THE PRATT FAMILY.

Children:

| | | | |
|---|---|---|---|
| 1 | Jewel. | 7 | Mehitable. |
| 2 | Benjamin. | 8 | Jerusha. |
| 3 | David. | 9 | Achsah. |
| 4 | John. | 10 | Mary. |
| 5 | Henry. | 11 | Arvilla. |
| 6 | Melinda. | 12 | Electa. |

---

12 (VI.) WEALTHY PRATT (dau. of V. Paul), b. July 14, 1765; d. Nov. 29, 1820; m. Dec. 12, 1781, Rev. Oded Eddy, of Taunton. They moved to Cheshire, Mass., 1782, and from there to Deerfield, N. Y., 1790.

She was a very large woman, weighing over 400 pounds. There was not a seat large enough for her in the church, and one was made especially for her use, by the side of the pulpit.

Children:

1 Jonathan, b. June 16, 1786.
2 Wealthy, b. May 31, 1788.
3 Oded, b. Sept. 12, 1790; m. Lucy Ann Northroup, Feb., 1810.
4 Anna, b. Oct. 1802; m. Ammi Roat, 1822 or 1823.

---

13 (VI.) JONATHAN PRATT (son of V. Paul), b. Apr. 12, 1768; m. 1789, Rachel Dean, b. Apr. 12, 1768; d. 1842.

They moved from Taunton to Cheshire, Mass., and from there to Deerfield, N. Y.

Children:

14 1 Jonathan, b. Jan. 28, 1790; d. 1829.
2 Harriet, b. July 22, 1796; m. Orrin Biddlecome, Sept., 1817. (Still living, 1867.)

---

15 (VII.) JONATHAN PRATT (son of VI. Jonathan), b. Jan. 28, 1790; d. 1829; m. Elizabeth Tisdale.

Children:

1 William, m. Eliza Moulton; had son Milton and two daughters.

2 JEROME, m. Ann Haddon; had son Jerome.

3 SILAS. His eyesight failing him, he committed suicide in a fit of despondency.

4 HARRIET, m. James Biddlecome.

5 MILTON, did not marry.

6 JEANETTE.

7 ELIZABETH.

---

376 386 (VI.) MARCY PRATT (dau of V. Paul), b. Jan. 13, 1770; d. Jan. 4, 1856; m. May 6, 1780, Nathaniel Crossman, son of Simeon Crossman, of Taunton, Mass.

They moved first to Cheshire, Mass., and afterwards to Deerfield, N. Y. He was a carpenter and farmer.

Children:

1 NATHANIEL, b. Feb. 22, 1790; m. Elizabeth Stewart, 1815; d. Mar. 3, 1848.

2 SIMEON.

3 MARCY, b. March 18, 1795; m. Scott M. Willmarth, April 4, 1815; she d. Feb. 10, 1868.

4 CAROLINE.

388 387 5 WARREN, b. Feb. 27, 1798; d. Oct. 1, 1880.

6 CURTIS, b. Jan. 12, 1800; m. (1) Nancy Biddlecome, Dec., 1823; (2) Anstrus Joslyn, Oct. 27, 1870.

7 BENJAMIN PRATT, b. Dec. 11, 1801. He was a noted physician and surgeon; d. Sept. 3, 1846.

8 PATTY (MARTHA), b. Dec. 20, 1803; m. James Samson, Oct., 1821; d. Aug. 6, 1881.

9 NANCY, b. Feb. 15, 1805; m. Henry Fowler, Feb., 1830.

10 LUTHER, b. Feb. 10, 1808; m. Amanda H. Burlingame, April 19, 1837; d. April 7, 1879.

11 SALLY (SARAH), b. Oct. 9, 1809; lives in Utica, N. Y.

---

387 388 (VII.) WARREN CROSSMAN (son of VI. Marcy Pratt), b. Feb. 27, 1798; d. Oct. 1, 1880; m. Dec. 1819, Susan D. Clapp. They moved to Rock, Wis. He was a carpenter and Farmer.

Children:

1 HELEN M., b. Aug. 27, 1820; m. John Hassett Chandler, Feb. 7, 1841. She was for many years a mission-

ary and teacher in Burmah and Siam, under the appointment of the Baptist Missionary Union. She went to Burmah in 1841, thence to Siam in 1843. On account of ill health returned to the United States, Oct. 3, 1880.

2  JANE A., b. July 15, 1822; m. Rev. Wm. H. Eddy, Sept. 10, 1840; had nine children.

3  JENNETTE A., b. May 20, 1824; m. Robert J. Evans, Dec. 31, 1845; d. Jan. 31, 1875.

4  LUCY M., b. June 17, 1826; m. Josiah M. Truesdell, Sept. 1, 1843; d. March 7, 1854; had six children.

5  ELDANA C., b. Aug. 1, 1828; m. (1) Electa M. Buck, Dec. 13, 1847; (2) Widow Sarah Morse, Dec. 4, 1883; had three children.

6  GEORGE W., b. Nov. 29, 1831; m. Philena C. Baldwin, Jan 21, 1854; had two sons.

7  BENJAMIN P., b. Oct. 13, 1846; m. (1) Alice P. Crisman, Nov. 24, 1876; (2) Lillie L. Forbes, May 30, 1883.

---

309  389  (V.)  LEMUEL PRATT, of Taunton (son of IV. Paul), b. ——; d. before 1815; m. Oct. 20, 1789, Elizabeth Baker.

Children :

    1  ELIZABETH, b. May 6, 1790; d. May 7, 1790.
301  390  2  LEMUEL, b. July 4, 1791.
    3  ITHIEL, b. Aug. 6, 1793; d. Oct. 21, 1793.
    4  LIXUM, b. Dec. 1, 1795.
    5  LEONARD, b. April 29, 1797.

---

390  391  (VI.)  LEMUEL PRATT, of Dighton (son of V. Lemuel), b. July 4, 1791; d. before 1869; m. ——, (Jonathan Pratt, administrator of estate).

Children :

    1  ALFRED.
    2  ELIZABETH A., m. Oliver P. Simmons.
    3  Daughter, m. Talbot.

The above two Lemuels and families are from Taunton Records; the last is not authentic, but probably correct.

368 322 (V.) RUFUS PRATT, of Taunton (son of IV. Paul), b. 1749;
d. May 9, 1770; m. ——.

    CHILD:

394 393 1 RUFUS, m. Hannah Hicks.

---

393 394 (VI.) RUFUS PRATT, of Taunton (son of V. Rufus), b. ——;
d. ——; m. Feb. 11, 1784, Hannah Hicks, of Rehoboth.

    Children:

    1 PAUL, b. Aug. 8, 1794.
    2 RUFUS, b. Oct. 22, 1798.
    3 PRUDENCE H., b. Feb. 1, 1800.
    4 HEZEKIAH H., b. Jan. 19, 1804.

---

245a 395 (III.) LIEUT. JOHN PRATT, of Weymouth (son of II.
Samuel), b. Aug. 17, 1663; d. Feb. 8, 1744; m. (1) Mary
——; (2) Elizabeth Swift, dau. of Thomas Swift, of Milton; she d. Dec. 25, 1736, aged 75. He m. (3) Mrs.
Sarah Gardner, Dec. 8, 1737.

    He is one of the heirs of his uncle John, being styled
a "Lieut." In the Town Records his name ("Lieut.
John") appears many times, and almost always as having been elected to fill some position of trust. He appears to have been a man of great energy and business
ability, being not only associated with the military and
town's business, but a prominent man in the Church.
His pew was near his brother Ebenezer's, on the "west
side of the great dore" of the Meeting House, for which
he paid £3.

    Children:

587 396 1 SAMUEL, b. Oct. 15, 1683.
594 397 2 NATHANIEL, b. Oct. 25, 1702.
656 398 3 THOMAS, b. Jan. 3, 1705.

---

245c 399 (III.) EBENEZER PRATT, of Weymouth (son of II. Samuel),
b. 1674; d. 1752; m. (1) Martha ——, who d. May, 1720;
m. (2) Waitstill Washburn, Dec. 25, 1720.

    Like his brother John, he was a prominent man of
Weymouth, holding many positions in the town affairs,

his name frequently appearing on the records. He was, 1714, identified with the establishment of the fishing trade between Weymouth and Cape Sable, being with others granted land called "Hunt's Hill" and "the Beach," in North Weymouth, on which to prosecute the business. He paid £4. 5s. 0d., for a pew in the Meeting House, on the "west side of the great dore."

Children:

| | | | |
|---|---|---|---|
| 402 | 400 | 1 | EBENEZER, b. Aug. 6, 1702. |
| | | 2 | ANN, b. April 24, 1704. |
| | | 3 | MARY, b. Aug. 23, 1706. |
| | | 4 | SARAH, b. Oct. 3, 1708. |
| 409 | 401 | 5 | SAMUEL, b. Dec. 19, 1712. |

---

400 402 (IV.) EBENEZER PRATT (son of III. Ebenezer), b. Aug. 6, 1702; d. Oct. 9, 1760; m. Tabatha Crane, 1726, Weymouth; she d. 1754.

Children:

| | | | |
|---|---|---|---|
| | | 1 | SILAS, b. Sept. 9, 1729; d. ——, 1776. Had a son Silas, who went to New York. |
| | | 2 | TABATHA, b. April 8, 1732; m. 1754, Lt. Ebenezer Porter. |
| 406 | 403 | 3 | EBENEZER, b. May 9, 1734. |
| 508 | 404 | 4 | ANNER, b. Jan. 14, 1736; d. April 6, 1776. |
| | | 5 | HANNAH, b. Aug. 7, 1738; m. 1754, Samuel Bate. |
| 534 | 405 | 6 | STEPHEN, b. March 27, 1740; d. Jan. 16, 1806. |
| | | 7 | REBECCA, b. July 14, 1741; m. Oct. 26, 1760, Stephen Pain, Jr. |
| | | 8 | SHEREBIAH, b. April 5, 1745. |
| | | 9 | RELIANCE, b. Nov. 16, 1749; m. 1766, Ebenezer Hovey. |
| | | 10 | MOLLY, m. 1777, Zach. Bicknoll, Jr. |

---

403 406 (V.) EBENEZER PRATT, of Weymouth, Blacksmith (son of IV. Ebenezer), b. May 9, 1734; d. Jan. 10, 1760; m. (1) Hannah Reed, April 14, 1757, dau. of John and Mary (Torrey), b. May 16, 1736; d. Jan. 10, 1760; m. (2), (P.) Nov. 28, 1761, Molly Kingman, dau. of Saml. and Mary (Lovell), b. Feb. 10, 1742.

Children:

| | | | |
|---|---|---|---|
| 406 | 407 | 1 | ROBERT, b. May 1, 1758; son of Hannah. |
| | | 2 | SOLOMON, b. July 15, 1763. |

3  EDWARD, b. Aug. 4, 1764.
4  EBENEZER, b. Dec. 6, 1766.
5  MOLLY, b. July 4, 1769.

---

407  408  (VI.) ROBERT PRATT (son of V. Ebenezer), b. May 1, 1758; m. 1779, Rebecca Burrell. He moved to Bridgewater, where his last two children were born.

Children:
1  HANNAH, b. Sept. 17, 1781.
2  ELIZABETH, b. June 3, 1783.
3  COTTON, b. March 24, 1785.
4  EBENEZER, b. May 27, 1789.

---

401  400  (IV.) SAMUEL PRATT, of Weymouth (son of III. Ebenezer), b. Dec. 19, 1712; d. Dec. 28, 1793; m. Feb. 17, 1737, Betty Bicknell, dau. of Benj. and Susanna (Humphrey), b. July 16, 1720. He m. (2) Mary ——.

Children:
1  BETTY, b. April 15, 1738; m. James Humphrey, Jr.
2  ASA, b. July 8, 1742.
3  DAVID,    } b. Feb. 12, 1745; { moved to Freeport, Me.
414  410  4  JONATHAN,
477  411  5  BENJAMIN, b. May 20, 1757; m. (P.) Jan. 18, 1783, Betty Dyer.
465  412  6  PETER, b. ——, 1750; (P.) m. Dec. 26, 1772, Amity Porter.
       7  CHLOE, b. ——, 1755; (P.) m. March 19, 1775, VI. Matthew Pratt.
476  413  8  SILVANUS, b. June 8, 1758; (P.) m. June 22, 1782, Hannah Bates.
       9  THOMAS, b. ——; m. Mary ——; had Polly, Aug. 6, 1770. Lived in Braintree.

---

410  414  (V.) JONATHAN PRATT, of Weymouth (son of IV. Samuel), b. Feb. 12, 1745; d. July 6, 1832; m. (P.) March 1, 1766, Sarah Dyer; d. Dec. 25, 1833, aged 86, a widow. He, or his son Jonathan removed to Braintree.

Children:
419  415  1  JOSIAH, b. Jan. 21, 1768; m. Deborah Tower.
       2  SUSA, b. Jan. 8, 1770; m. Thos. Cook. (?)

JONATHAN, b. April 18, 1772; m. Sarah Cook, 1793.
BETSEY, b. May 3, 1774; m. Wm. Everson.
SARAH, b. Aug. 20, 1776; m. ——.
MARY, b. March 15, 1779; m. Samuel Bent.
NATHANIEL, b. Nov. 8, 1780; m. Lydia Hunt.
WILLIAM, b. June 3, 1785.
HANNAH, b. March 15, 1788; m. Danl. Penhallow.
CLARISSA, b. Oct. 30, 1791; m. James Bates.

---

JOSIAH PRATT, of Windsor, Mass. (son of V. Jonathan), b. Jan. 21, 1768, in Weymouth; d. May 14, 1845, in Windsor. He m. (P.) Jan. 14, 1789, Deborah, dau. of Peter and Deborah (Stowell) Tower, b. in Hingham, Oct. 4, 1767.

Children:

DEBORAH, b. Aug. 3, 1792; m. Solomon Snow, of Windsor.
JOSIAH, b. Aug. 5, 1794.
GORHAM DOUGLASCE, b. May 21, 1797; m. Maria Boyd; both dead; no issue.
ALONZO, b. 1803; d. March 9, 1806.
TINNIE or TIRZA PHILENA, b. Oct. 9, 1805; d. Oct. 24, 1831, unmarried.
MARY ANN, b. May 4, 1809; m. Henry F. Pomeroy.
CAROLINE, b. May 30, 1812; m. Emory Bruce.

---

JOSIAH PRATT, of Wilson, N.Y. (son of VI. Josiah), b. Aug. 5, 1794; d. Oct. 30, 1864; m. Jan. 17, 1819, Ann Lutz, of Wilson; she d. Aug. 6, 1850, aged 53 yrs., 11 mos., 1 day. She was dau. of Michael and Ruth (Doop) Lutz.

Children:

RUTH, b. May 28, 1820; m. Dudley Frink; she d. July 19, 1863.
LUTHER, b. April 25, 1822; m. Diantha Ash; he d. in Mich.
JOSIAH N., b. Feb. 1, 1825; m. Abzina Parker; he d. in Mich.
PETER T., b. Nov. 26, 1828; m. twice and resides (1887) in Cal.
SARAH A., b. Sept. 7, 1830; m. Ralph Stockwell.
RUFUS W., b. Dec. 12, 1833; m. Hannah M. Barnes.

417 422 (VI.) NATHANIEL PRATT (son of V. Jonathan), b. Nov. 8,
1780; d. May 27, 1852; m. June 12, 1803, Lydia Hunt,
dau. of Asa and Silence (Orcutt), b. Jan. 11, 1786.

Children :

  1 LUCINDA, b. Nov. 24, 1805 ; m. June 11, 1826, Roswell
    Trufant.
  2 SUSAN HOBART, b. Oct. 22, 1808 ; d. ——.
  3 SUSAN HOBART, b. Dec. 21, 1811 ; m. John L. White,
    July 5, 1829.
  4 CYRUS KINGSBURY, b. Dec. 16, 1817 ; d. May 28, 1865,
    at Braintree.

------

418 423 (VI.) JONATHAN PRATT, of Quincy (son of V. Jonathan of
Weymouth), b. Apr. 18, 1772 ; d. March 20, 1846 ; m.
Aug. 11, 1793, Sarah Cook.

Children :

  1 SUSAN, b. Feb. 19, 1794 ; m. Philip Bates, of Weymouth.
  2 SALLY, b. 1796 ; m. Nov. 16, 1818, Hosea Hollis.
  3 JANE S., b. 1804 ; m. Dec. 6, 1832, William Stiles.
  4 CLARISSA, b. —— ; m. 1828, Alden French.
  5 HANNAH, b. Apr. 27, 1806 ; m. Antipas Harrington, b. 7 ?
428 424   6 NATHAN, b. Dec. 8, 1793.
432 425   7 LEMUEL, b. —— ; d. June 15, 1828.
435 426   8 ALBERT, } b. ——.
  9 ALMIRA, }
433 427  10 JONATHAN, b. Nov. 5, 1814.

------

424 428 (VII.) NATHAN PRATT, of Braintree (son of VI. Jonathan, of
Quincy), b. Dec. 8, 1793 ; m. (1) Dermila Clary ; d. June
12, 1828 ; m. (2) Sarah Clary, Nov. 29, 1832 ; d. March
21, 1841 ; m. 3, Sophia, (b. 1802), (P.) March 12, 1842 ; d.
at San Francisco, Nov. 11, 1881.

Children of Dermila :

  1 SARAH CLARY, b. March 20, 1820 ; m. Webber Harring-
    ton, b. ......
431 429   2 NATHAN O., b. Jan. 3, 1821 ; m. Bethia Pratt.
434 430   3 RODOLPHUS, b. March 3, 1823 ; m. Ada Phillips.
  4 FRANCIS, b. March 4, 1827 ; d. Jan., 1828.

Children of Sarah :

  5 HENRY LYMAN, b. March 1, 1841.
  6 JONATHAN, b. ——.

429  431 (VIII.) NATHAN C. PRATT, of Braintree, (son of VII. Nathan), b. Jan. 3, 1821; m. Dec. 2, 1841, Bethia Pratt, dau. of Lemuel and Bethia (Clary).

Children:

1  WILLIAM C., b. April 22, 1845.
2  GEORGE F., b. Nov. 9, 1847.
3  GEORGE F., b. July 31, 1852.

---

425  432 (VII.) LEMUEL PRATT, of Braintree (son of VI. Jonathan), b. ——; m. Dec. 25, 1820, Bethia Clary; d. July 17, 1823.

Children:

1  Infant, d. Oct. 29, 1822.
2  BETHIA, b. 1823; m. Nathan Pratt, 1841.

---

427  433 (VII.) JONATHAN PRATT, of Braintree (son of VI. Jonathan, of Quincy), b. Nov. 5, 1814; m. Aug. 15, 1838, Jane C. Follansbee, of Braintree, dau. of Joshua and Sarah (Jones).

Children:

1  MARIA ELIZABETH, b. May 15, 1847; d. June, 1847.
2  SARAH ADELAIDE, b. May 11, 1848; m. Nov. 21, 1880, William T. Winebeyer.

---

430  434 (VIII.) RODOLPHUS PRATT (son of VII. Nathan of Braintree), b. March 3, 1823, at Braintree; d. Jan. 6, 1865, at San Francisco; m. May 15, 1856, Adeline Philips, of Weymouth. She m. Sept. 2, 1866, Isaac W. Tirrell. He (Rodolphus) was a sea-captain.

Children:

1  SARAH ADELINE, b. May 25, 1857; d. Oct. 28, 1864.
2  WALTER HERBERT, b. Oct. 7, 1859; d. Nov. 16, 1864.
3  EMMA FLORENCE, b. June 9, 1862; m. June 15, 1882, Thomas Wilder, of Whitman, Mass.

426 435 (VII.) ALBERT PRATT, of Quincy (son of VI. Jonathan and Sarah), b. ——; m. (1) Susanna Nightingale; m. (2) Oct. 9, 1855, Celia C. Hayden.

Children of Susanna:

 1 SUSANNA R., b. ——; d. Dec. 27, 1854.
 2 LUCY ANN HARRIET, b. July 26, 1840.

437 436  3 CHARLES A., b. July, 1844.

---

436 437 (VIII.) CHARLES A. PRATT, of Quincy (son of VII. Albert), b. July, 1844; m. Oct. 28, 1865, Georgietta F. Blanchard, of Quincy.

Child:

GEORGE A., b. ——; d. July 26, 1870.

---

418 438 (VI.) WILLIAM PRATT, of Weymouth (son of V. Jonathan), b. June 3, 1785; d. May 16, 1853; m. Nov. 8, 1804, Martha Dunbar, dau. of Daniel and Phillipi (Damon), of Hingham, b. Feb. 28, 1788.

Children:

452 439  1 WILLIAM, b. Jan. 29, 1805; d. Sept. 20, 1847; m. (P.) Sept. 18, 1825, Nancy Baker.

 2 A son, b. July 15, 1806; d. July 17, 1806.

447 440  3 DAVID MATTHEW, b. July 13, 1807; m. Oct. 21, 1827, Eleanor G. Cushing.

454 441  4 HOSEA D., b. June 13, 1809; d. Aug. 6, 1874; m. (P.) Feb. 20, 1830, Phebe H. Baker.

459 442  5 WASHINGTON, b. Apr. 5, 1812; d. Jan. 11, 1883.

460 443  6 ALVIN, b. July 9, 1814; d. Nov. 19, 1863; m. Apr. 21, 1836, Mary T. Pierce.

 7 MARTHA S., b. Oct. 6, 1816; d. Dec. 31, 1833. (Unmarried.)

 8 MARY, b. Dec. 27, 1818; d. Sept. 21, 1847; m. Edwin Everson.

 9 DANIEL, b. Dec. 27, 1820; d. May 17, 1864. (Unmarried).

463 444  10 CHARLES, b. March 12, 1821.

451 445  11 SETH, b. Sept. 23, 1823; d. Feb. 4, 1854; m. Sarah Jane Dodge.

453 446  12 SARAH LOUISA, b. Feb. 16, 1828; m. Thos. F. Cleverly.

 13 JONATHAN, b. June 14, 1830; d. Feb. 5, 1859. (Unmarried).

A son and dau. b. and d. infants.

440  447 (VII.) DAVID M. PRATT, of Weymouth (son of VI. William),
b. July 13, 1807; m. (1) Oct. 21, 1827, Eleanor G. Cushing, b. 1805; d. Aug. 21, 1871. He m. (2) Caroline
Cushing (Sprague), Aug. 28, 1872 (sister of his first wife),
of Hingham. He is now (1887) in good health, and
although not actively employed, is remarkably preserved for one of his age. He was a boot and shoe
maker.

Child of Eleanor:

449  448      1  DAVID JACKSON, b. June 4, 1828; m. Jan. 1, 1852, Mary
Dodge.

────────

448  449 (VIII.) DAVID J. PRATT, of North Weymouth (son of David
M.), b. June 4, 1828; m. Jan. 1, 1852, Mary Abigail
Dodge, of Quincy, b. Nov. 24, 1835; dau. of Benjamin
and Sarah Ann Dodge. He was, like his father, a boot
and shoe maker.

Children:

1  MARY ELEANOR, b. Sept. 14, 1855; d. May 18, 1873. She
was a very promising and bright girl, her death oc-
curring a few days before she would have graduated
from school. She was also a pupil of the New England Conservatory of Music, where she displayed a
remarkable talent for music. Her death caused very
deep sorrow among her many friends.

458  450      2  WALTER DODGE, b. July 17, 1857; m. Carrie E. White,
dau. of Edward and Sarah.

────────

445  451 (VII.) SETH PRATT, of Quincy (son of VI. William and
Martha), b. at Weymouth, Sept. 23, 1823; d. Feb. 4,
1854; m. Dec. 26, 1852, Sarah Jane Dodge, of Quincy.

Child:

SETH ARTHUR, b. March 30, 1854, at Quincy; m. Carrie
Louisa Farren, Oct. 12, 1882; she b. 1854; no children.
He (Seth A.) is the American consul at Zanzibar, East
Africa.

────────

439  452 (VII.) WILLIAM PRATT, of Weymouth (son of VI. William),
b. Jan. 29, 1805; d. Sept. 20, 1847; m. (P.) Sept. 18,
1825, Nancy Baker; d. ──.

Children :

1 ABIGAIL, m. Bryant Newcomb Fernald, of Quincy.
2 WILLIAM, m. Florinda Mary Harding. They are both dead (1887), leaving no children.
3 NANCY, d. in infancy.
4 MARTHA, m. (1) Henry Holmes, of Quincy; m. (2) —— Seaton. They reside in Canada.
5 LUCINDA, m. Lorenzo Goodwin.
6 CHARLES HENRY, d. in infancy.
7 GEORGE W., m. Annie Bradley; she d.

NOTE.—They are all d. (1887), but Martha and George W., and the writer cannot find him.

———————

446 453 (VII.) SARAH L. PRATT (dau. of William and Martha), b. Feb. 16, 1828; m. Sept. 9, 1852, Thomas Francis Cleverly, of North Weymouth, b. June 21, 1828, son of Thomas and Elizabeth (Lincoln) Cleverly. He is much interested in genealogical and historical work, having given more attention than any other person in Weymouth to the history of North Weymouth ("Old Spain"), and especially the original grants of land and location of their boundaries. To him the author of this work is much indebted for valuable information.

Child :

MARY LOUISA, b. Nov. 10, 1853.

———————

441 454 (VII.) HOSEA D. PRATT (son of VI. William), b. June 13, 1809; d. Aug. 8, 1874; m. (P.) Feb. 20, 1830, Phebe H. Baker, of Duxbury.

Children :

1 ROXENA B., b. April 1, 1831; m. (1) Ebenezer Bacon; m. (2) Benj. F. Foss.
2 EDWIN AUGUSTUS, b. Dec. 16, 1835; m. Sept. 6, 1857, Ellen M. Willis, and had Edward Francis. They live at Oakdale, Iowa.
456 455 3 LEANDER, b. March 26, 1839.
4 ELLEN JANE, b. Jan. 2, 1845; d. March 6, 1872; m. March 13, 1860, Jos. Bates, Jr.
5 LAURA ANN, b. March 16, 1846; m. George Joy.

455  456 (VIII.) LEANDER PRATT (son of VII. Hosea D.), b. March
26, 1839; m. Oct. 8, 1859, Sarah Ann Willis, dau. of John
M. and Fanny.

Children:

1  EMMA I., b. July 21, 1860.
2  SARAH J., b. Feb. 8, 1862; m. Feb. 8, 1879, Luthor O.
Crocker.

462  457      3  ALVIN A., b. Nov. 4, 1863.

---

450  458 (IX.) WALTER D. PRATT, of North Weymouth (son of
VIII. David J.), b. July 17, 1857; m. Sept. 14, 1876, Carrie Etta White, dau. of Edward and Sarah.

He was in the employ of Churchill, Gilchrist, Smith &
Co., of Boston, after which he removed to Emerson, Ia.,
where he occupied several offices, including that of post
master. He now (1887) resides at Red Oak.

Children:

1  FRANCIS FORSAITH, b. Feb. 28, 1877, in No. Weymouth.
2  EDWARD DODGE, b. Feb. 16, 1886, in Emerson, Ia.; d.
Aug. 1886.

---

442  459 (VII.) WASHINGTON PRATT, of Weymouth (son of VI.
William), b. April 5, 1812; d. Jan. 11, 1883; m. Jan. 5,
1834, Narissa H. Baker, of Marshfield, dau. of Thomas
and Nancy, b. Feb. 16, 1816.

Children:

1  NARISSA, b. July 11, 1835; m. Wm. L. Hesscy.
2  LEONARD, b. April 30, 1840; d. July 1863, at Peters-
burg, Va.
3  ABBY ELIZA, b. Jan. 31, 1849; m. George Covell; d.
April 23, 1886.
4  FRANCES A., b. March 3, 1854; d. April 13, 1877.
5  CLARA BELL, b. June 17, 1856.

---

443  460 (VII.) ALVIN PRATT (son of VI. William), b. July 9, 1814;
d. Nov. 19, 1863; m. Mary T. Pierce, April 21, 1836;
she d. Aug. 9, 1881, aged 64 years, 10 mos.

Children:

454  461  1  BENJAMIN FRANKLIN, b. March 29, 1837.
         2  EDWARD AUGUSTUS, b. Dec. 2, 1843.
         3  GEORGE A., b. Nov. 13, 1845.
         4  HENRY W., b. May 12, 1847; d. Oct. 2, 1864.
         5  ALVIN F., b. Aug. 12, 1855; d. Sept. 9, 1855.

---

457  463  (IX.) ALVIN AUGUSTUS PRATT, of Braintree (son of VIII.
         Leander), b. Nov. 4, 1863; m. Dec. 9, 1885, Elizabeth
         Ann Souther, b. 1866, dau. of Martin and Eliza J.
         (Morse).

         Child:

         MABEL AMELIA, b. Nov. 5, 1886.

---

444  463  (VII.) CHARLES PRATT, of Weymouth (son of VI. William),
         b. March 10, 1821; d. ——; m. (P.) Feb. 21, 1847, Maria
         O. Totman, b. Oct. 27, 1822, of Hingham.

         Children:

         1  CHARLES MORRIS, b. April 23, 1849.
         2  ELIZABETH HARRISON, b. July 31, 1853; m. Geo. Mit-
            chell.
         3  WILLIAM AUSTIN (Rev.), b. May 9, 1855; m. Dora
            Roberts, of Ludlow, Vt. He is now (1887) pastor of
            the Universalist Church in Cedar Rapids, Iowa; no
            children.
         4  ELLA MARIA, b. March 14, 1857.

---

461  454  (VIII.) BENJAMIN F. PRATT, of Weymouth (son of VII.
         Alvin), b. March 29, 1837; d. ——; m. Lydia Robinson,
         of Hingham; she (1887) is dead.  He served in the war
         of the Rebellion, and was confined in the Confederate
         Prisons.

         Children:

         1  EDWARD AUGUSTUS, b. March 27, 1859; d. Sept. 10, 1860.
         2  ELLIS W., b. Nov. 4, 1860.
         3  ALVIN FRANKLIN, b. Oct. 2, 1866.

PETER PRATT, of Weymouth (son of IV. Samuel), b. 1750; d. Dec. 5, 1833; m. (P.) Dec. 26, 1772, Amy or Amity Porter, d. Sept. 1838.

Children:

SAMUEL, b. Dec. 8, 1774.
SAMUEL, b. Dec. 7, 1775.
REBECCA, b. May 12, 1777.
MOLLY, b. Sept. 22, 1779; d. Dec. 13, 1855; m. Jan. 25, 1800, Jona. Cleverly, d. March 18, 1820.

   Children:

| 1 | *Henry.* | 5 | *Mary J. D.* |
| 2 | *Thomas.* | 6 | *Caleb S.* |
| 3 | *John.* | 7 | *George W.* |
| 4 | *Asa P.* | | |

JENNY, b. Nov. 2, 1782; m. Dec. 1, 1803, Isaac Damons, and moved to Northampton.
ASA, b. 1786; d. 1821; m. Feb. 21, 1809, Betsey Leavett. (?)

---

SAMUEL PRATT (son of V. Peter), b. Dec. 7, 1775; d. ——; m. March 8, 1798, widow Nabby Cushing, dau. of Regemelech and Sarah (Farrar), b. Sept. 27, 1778; she m. (2) Nov. 9, 1817, Capt. Robert Bates.

Children:

PETER, b. Sept. 13, 1799; d. Aug. 27, 1830; m. April 19, 1825, Mary Bicknell.
HARRIET, b. April 22, 1803; m. May 17, 1826, Daniel W. Bates.
SAMUEL P., b. Sept. 16, 1806; m. (P.) Feb. 12, 1825, Clarissa Bates; m. (2) May 19 1839, Lydia S. Jordan.

---

SAMUEL P. PRATT, of Weymouth (son of VI. Samuel and Nabby), b. Sept. 16, 1806; m. (P.) Feb. 12, 1825, Clarissa Bates; m. (2) Lydia S. Jordan, May 19, 1839.

Children:

JOHN BATES, b. Jan. 11, 1826; m. (P.) in Weymouth, Nov. 1, 1846, Elizabeth Little.
SARAH, b. Jan. 25, 1837; m. ——, Perkins.
SAMUEL P. P., b. Feb. 5, 1832; d. Sept. 4, 1872.
HARRIET, b. Aug. 12, 1834.

471  472 (VIII.) SAMUEL P. P. PRATT, of Weymouth (son of VII.
Samuel P.), b. Feb. 5, 1832; d. Sept. 4, 1872; m. Nov.
22, 1854, Abbie Alden Bates, dau. of Albert and Abigail.

Children :

1  CLARISSA B., b. Jan. 27, 1857.
2  ABBY ELLA, b. March 15, 1861; d. Aug. 27, 1876.
3  CLARA BATES, b. Nov. 27, 1867.
4  ALBERT SAMUEL, b. July 21, 1869; d. April 8, 1871.

468  473 (VII.) PETER PRATT (3d), of Weymouth (son of VI. Samuel
of V. Peter), b. Sept. 13, 1790; d. Aug. 27, 1830; m. April
19, 1825, Mary Bicknell; she m. (2) John White.

Children :

475  474  1  LEONIDAS F.
2  CAROLINE, m. Nelson Thomas.

474  475 (VIII.) LEONIDAS F. PRATT, of Fall River, Mass. (son of
VII. Peter), b. Nov. 5, 1826, in Weymouth; m. Nov. 14,
1849, Bertha Bates, dau. of Joseph and Rebecca, of
Weymouth, b. March 9, 1828. He is (1868) in the print-
ing business in Fall River.

Children :

1  WALTER FRANCIS, b. June 5, 1850; d. July 18, 1851.
2  WILFRED SEABURY, b. Oct. 24, 1851; m. Emily F. Hun-
tress, and has one daughter.
3  MARY ELIZA, b. July 22, 1854; m. John Franklin.
4  JOSEPH WALTER, b. Aug. 24, 1856; m. ——; no children.

413  476 (V.) SILVANUS PRATT (son of IV. Samuel), b. June 8,
1758; d. Nov. 26, 1836; m. (P.) June 22, 1782, Hannah,
dau. of Urban and Hannah (Holbrook) Bates, b. Aug. 16,
1765; d. Sept., 1844.

Child :

1  HANNAH, b. 1784; m. Stephen Richards; d. Sept. 27,
1812.

Child :

Mary, b. Dec. 27, 1804; d. March 29, 1816.

177 (V.) BENJAMIN PRATT, of Weymouth (son of IV. Samuel and Betty, b. May 20, 1757; m. (P.) Jan. 18, 1783, Betsey Dyer, dau. of Joseph, Jr., and Hannah Bate, b. Aug. 6, 1757.

Children :

178   1  LUTHER, b. Oct. 27, 1783; d. Jan. 8, 1863.

      2  BETSEY, b. July 1, 1788; m. Ebenezer Humphrey, Dec. 5, 1809.

      3  ABIGAIL D., b. Sept. 6, 1794; m. Sept. 22, 1816, James Thomas.

---

179 (VI.) LUTHER PRATT (son of V. Benjamin), b. Oct. 27, 1783; d. Jan. 8, 1863; m. Dec. 27, 1804, Sophia Holbrook, dau. of Elisha and Sarah (Burrell), b. April 30, 1787.

Children :

      1  ANGELINE, b. March 27, 1809; m. Charles R. Thompson.

180   2  ELISHA, b. Feb. 26, 1811; m. Mary Torrey.

      3  SOPHIA, b. March 28, 1813; m. Nehemiah Lovell.

      4  ELIZA, b. June 27, 1815; m. William Lovell.

181   5  ABIEZER, b. May 27, 1817.

182   6  BENJAMIN, b. Oct. 23, 1819; d. Dec. 12, 1886.

183   7  JAMES, b. June 26, 1822.

---

184 (VII.) ELISHA PRATT, a merchant, of No. Weymouth (son of VI. Luther), b. Feb. 26, 1811; m. (P.) April 27, 1831, Mary, dau. of John and Mary (Field) Torrey.

Children :

185   1  ELISHA FRANCIS, b. Nov. 11, 1833.

      2  GEORGE HORACE, b. March 16, 1840; d. Aug. 31, 1840.

      3  GEORGE HORACE, b. Sept. 11, 1841; d. Nov. 16, 1842.

      4  WENDELL PHILLIPS, b. Aug. 31, 1843; d. Sept. 10, 1843.

186   5  MARY JANE, b. ——; m. Alden Whiting, Nov. 1, 1856.

187   6  LUTHER JAMES, b. May 23, 1846.

188   7  SARAH WHITE, b. Oct. 14, 1848; d. June 25, 1880; m. Lewis E. Bradford, Dec. 22, 1866.

---

190 (VIII.) ELISHA F. PRATT, of No. Weymouth (son of VII. Elisha), b. Nov. 11, 1833; m. May 10, 1857, Mary Freeman Josephs, of Quincy, Mass; she b. Feb. 22, 1836.

Children:
1  ARTHUR FRANCIS, b. Sept. 20, 1860; d. Oct. 13, 1869.
2  CHARLES WALTER, b. Sept. 19, 1865; d. Oct. 7, 1869.
3  WALTER FRANCIS, b. April 8, 1871.

---

481  490 (VII.) ABIEZER PRATT, of Weymouth (son of VI. Luther),
b. May 27, 1817; m. July 30, 1843, Hannah Nash Hawes,
dau. of James and Lucy; b. April 16, 1823; d. April 15,
1873.

Children:
1  ABIEZER FOSTER, b. Nov. 11, 1844; m. Sarah J. Cloverly,
Jan. 12, 1867; she b. Dec. 13, 1844.
2  FRANCIS JACKSON, b. Nov. 26, 1846.
3  FANNIE C., b. July 12, 1855.

---

482  491 (VII.) BENJAMIN PRATT, of Weymouth (son of VI. Luther),
b. Oct. 22, 1819; d. Dec. 12, 1886; m. Feb. 28, 1841, Eliza
Reed, of East Weymouth.  (Shoemaker.)

Children:
1  EMILY W., b. Dec. 29, 1841; d. May 4, 1842.
2  BENJAMIN EDWARD, b. Sept. 25, 1843; d. March 20,
1883, in Taunton, unmarried.
494  492  3  STEPHEN AUSTIN R., b. March 31, 1848.
495  493  4  CHARLES HENRY, b. July 20, 1854.
5  MARY ANN REED, b. June 13, 1859; m. Nov. 2, 1877,
G. H. Hunt.
Children:
1  George P., b. May 1, 1878.
2  Edward P., b. Feb. 22, 1884.

---

493  494 (VIII.) STEPHEN A. R. PRATT, of Weymouth (son of VII.
Benjamin), b. March 31, 1848; m. Aug. 28, 1872, Ann R.
Orcutt, dau. of Samuel J. and Ann Stetson.
Child:
STEPHEN AUSTIN, b. April 1, 1873.

493  495 (VIII.) CHARLES H. PRATT, of Weymouth (son of VII.
          Benjamin), b. July 20, 1854; m. Feb. 12, 1874, Maria F.
          Orcutt, dau. of Samuel and Ann Stetson.

          Children:
      1  CHARLES B., b. Sept. 12, 1874.
      2  FREDERICK F., b. Feb. 15, 1876; d. Aug. 23, 1876.

483  496 (VII.) JAMES PRATT, of Weymouth (son of VI. Luther), b.
          June 26, 1823; m. (P.) May 9, 1847, Charlotte E. Cor-
          tholl, of Hingham.

          Children:
      1  ERNEST M., b. June 15, 1856; d. Oct. 18, 1856.
499  497  2  LESTER MERTON, b. Dec. 7, 1858.
      3  WINTHROP E., b. Feb. 27, 1862.
500  498  4  JAMES W., b. 1863.

497  499 (VIII.) LESTER M. PRATT, of Weymouth (son of VII. James),
          b. Dec. 7, 1858; m. Feb. 3, 1880, Nellie A., dau. of Sam'l
          and Caroline Davis.

          Children:
      1  LILLIAN MERTON, b. May 27, 1880.
      2  BURLEIGH ELWOOD, b. April 5, 1882.

498  500 (VIII.) JAMES W. PRATT, of Weymouth (son of VII. James),
          b. 1863; m. Nov. 18, 1883, Emma F. Tarbox.

          Children:
      1  WARREN WINTHROP, b. April 20, 1884.
      2  LAWRENCE ENRICK, b. March 29, 1884.

489  501 (VIII.) MARY J. PRATT (dau. of VII. Elisha), b. ——; m.
          Nov. 1, 1856, Alden Whiting, of East Marshfield.

          Children:
      1  FLORA MAY, b. May 6, 1858; d. Jan. 10, 1860.
      2  HOWARD ALDEN, b. Oct. 19, 1860; d. Oct. 22, 1865.
      3  RUSSELL HOWARD, b. Jan. 19, 1868.
      4  CLARA MAY, b. Aug. 18, 1872.

457  502 (VIII.) LUTHER J. PRATT, of Weymouth (son of VII. Elisha),
b. May 23, 1846; m. Martha Wales Richmond, May 23,
1866, at Quincy, dau. of Wm. B. and Eveline; she b.
Sept. 17, 1850.

No children.

---

488  503 (VIII.) SARAH W. PRATT (dau. of VII. Elisha), b. Oct. 14,
1848; m. Dec. 22, 1866, Lewis E. Bradford.

Children:
1 NETTIE E., b. May 1, 1867.
2 ——, b. May 5, 1873; d. young.
3 ——, b. April 20, 1874; d. young.

---

397  504 (IV.) NATHANIEL PRATT, of Abington (son of III. John
and Elizabeth), b. Oct. 26, 1702; d. 1779; m. Dec. 7,
1724, Elizabeth Whitcomb of Scituate. He lived in
Abington. Will dated Feb. 7, 1779. He was a selectman
of Abington in 1752.

Children:
536  505  1 WHITCOMB, b. Oct. 7, 1725; m. Botty Gurney
2 ELIZABETH, b. Sept. 25, 1727; d. Jan. 10, 1749.
3 NOAH, b. Jan. 22, 1730; d. Sept. 2, 1730.
539  506  4 NOAH, b. Oct. 19, 1731; m. (P.) Mary Whitmarsh.
5 ELIZABETH, b. Jan. 16, 1734; m. Stetson.
543  507  6 NATHANIEL, b. ——.

---

404  508 (V.) ABNER PRATT, of Weymouth, a cordwainer (son of
IV. Ebenezer and Tabitha), b. Jan. 14, 1736; m. (1) (P.)
June 19, 1756, Mary Porter, dau. of Ebenezer and Mel-
kea, b. Dec. 15, 1739; d. 1758; m. (3) Dec. 19, 1758,
Margaret Humphrey, b. Feb. 8, 1739; d. Jan. 29, 1832;
dau. of James and Ann.

Children:
1 LABAN, b. May, 1758; d. 1758 (child of Mary.)
519  509  2 LABAN, b. 1759.
3 MARY, b. 1760.
4 ALVAN, b. Oct. 1, 1762.
5 LUCY, b. Aug. 26, 1764; m. April 22, 1784, Levi Bates.

        6  Esther, b. April 6, 1768; m. May 22, 1788, Jona. Darby, Jr.

        7  Sarah. b. Nov. 1, 1770; m. May 28, 1789, John Rice.

        8  Hannah b. March 12, 1773; m. (P.) (2) April 20, 1793, Seth Johnson.

511  510    9  Abner, b. Sept. 1, 1775; d. Oct. 9, 1845.

---

510  511  (VL.) ABNER PRATT, of Weymouth (son of V. Abner), b. Sept. 1, 1775; d. Oct. 9, 1845; m. Feb. 7, 1799, Nabby Pratt, dau. of Joshua and Lydia (Pratt), b. Jan. 1, 1778.

        Children :

        1  Mary, b. Dec. ——, 1800; d. 1801.

515  512    2  Abner b. Aug. 25, 1802.

        3  Jared, b. May 27, 1805; d. May 12, 1831; m. 1826, Sarah Lincoln.

          Child :

          *Caleb L.*, b. Aug. 5, 1827.

        4  Mary B., b. Sept. 19, 1807; d. Jan. 25, 1853.

        5  Nabby, b. Dec. 12, 1810; m. Wm. Loud.

        6  Lydia, b. Oct. 11, 1813; d. Sept. 19, 1864.

518  513    7  Palmer, b. Aug. 9, 1816.

534  514    8  Harvey, b. March 27, 1819; m. Aug. 27, 1800, Susan C. Current.

---

512  515  (VII.) ABNER PRATT, Jr., of Weymouth (son of VI. Abner and Nabby), b. Aug. 25, 1802; d. Aug. 1, 1870; m. March 25, 1832, Hannah Wilder, of Hingham, b. Oct. 5, 1806.

        Children :

        1  Sarah Lincoln, b. Nov. 30, 1832; m. Jacob Burrell.

517  516    2  Benjamin Franklin, b. Nov. 8, 1836.

---

516  517  (VIII.) BENJAMIN F. PRATT, of Hingham (son of VII. Abner and Hannah), b. Nov. 8, 1836; m. March 17, 1860, Mary M. Hyland, of Scituate, dau. of Isaiah and Deborah A. He (1888) resides in Hingham.

Children:
1 CLARA MAY, b. Nov. 6, 1861; m. E. B. Young, of Hingham.
2 MARY L., b. Nov. 22, 1862.
3 ISAIAH P., b. Sept. 23, 1866.
4 FRANK D., b. June 8, 1868.
5 WENDELL A., b. March 31, 1870.

———

513 518 (VII.) PALMER PRATT, of Weymouth (son of VI. Abner and Nabby), b. Aug. 9, 1816; m. M. Augusta Hamilton, Nov. 17, 1869, at Braintree.

Child:
FLORA A., b. Sept. 8, 1870; d. May 28, 1885.

———

509 519 (VI.) LABAN PRATT (son of V. Abner), b. ——, 1759; d. ——; m. April 14, 1785, Lucy Pratt, dau. of V. Matthew and Mary Pratt, b. Sept. 2, 1765; d. Oct. 13, 1837.

Children:
1 LUCY, b. Aug. 16, 1786; m. Samuel Loring of Hull.
529 530 2 LABAN, b. June 27, 1788; d. Aug. 6, 1838; m. (P.) Feb. 21, 1807, Nancy Thayer, of Randolph.
3 AZIEL, b. April 9, 1790; never married.
4 SOPHIA, b. June 26, 1791; m. (P.) Oct. 24, 1822, Daniel Dyer.
5 LEWIS, b. Jan. 12, 1796; m. (P.) Sept. 10, 1819, Elizabeth Wilder, of Hingham; m. (2) May 19, 1827, Mary Gould. No issue by either marriage.
523 521 6 JONATHAN D., b. May, 1798; d. June 22, 1808; m. (P.) Sept. 26, 1823, Mary W. Whiton, of Hingham.
526 522 7 NORTON, b. Dec. 22, 1800; m. Jan. 20, 1823, Priscilla Loud; (2) Emeline Merritt.
8 MARY L., b. May 21, 1804; m. May 20, 1831, Lemuel French, Jr.

———

521 523 (VII.) JONATHAN D. PRATT (son of VI. Laban), b. May 9, 1798; d. Jan. 22, 1808; m. (P.) Sept. 26, 1823, Mary W. Whiton of Hingham.

Children:

1 CHRISTOPHER, b. July 30, 1827; (never m.)
525 524 2 OSBORN, b. Dec. 4, 1829; m. Jan. 1, 1856, Georgiana Arnold.
3 CATHARINE, b. April 10, 1832; m. Ansel Burrell.
4 MARY DERBY, b. ——; m. Harry Burns.

---

524 525 (VIII.) OSBORN PRATT, of Braintree (son of VII. Jonathan D.), b. Dec. 4, 1829; m. Jan. 1, 1856, Georgiana Arnold, dau. of George W. and Sarah A. (Wales); she b. Nov. 14, 1832. He resides at Holbrook.

Child:

ARNOLD, b. Aug. 29, 1866.

---

522 526 (VII.) NORTON PRATT, of Braintree (son of VI. Laban), b. Dec. 22, 1800, in Weymouth; d. Oct. 27, 1879; m. (1) Priscilla Loud, Jan. 20, 1823; m. (2) Emeline Merritt, Dec. 11, 1844; b. July 4, 1806; d. Feb. 20, 1878.

Children of Priscilla:

1 LUCY ANN, b. April 16, 1823; m. Edwin Pratt, of Weymouth.
2 MARY NORTON, b. Feb. 9, 1825.
528 527 3 FRANCIS B., b. Jan. 15, 1827.
4 LABAN, b. Nov. 15, 1829; m. in Abington, March 4, 1856, Elizabeth Bradford Bartlett.
5 MARGARET H., b. June 29, 1832.
6 MARINA, b. Aug. 15, 1835; m. Daniel Potter.
7 BETSEY TIRRELL, b. Dec. 11, 1836; d. Feb. 1, 1843.
8 HARRIET P., b. Oct. 27, 1839.
9 MEHITABLE R., b. March 27, 1842; d. Aug. 7, 1842.

Child of Emeline:

10 EDWARD NORTON, b. Oct. 1851; m. June 16, 1880, Harriet D. Whittier.

---

527 528 (VIII.) FRANCIS B. PRATT, of Braintree (son of VII. Norton), b. Jan. 15, 1827; m. (1) Abigail A. Nash, May 1, 1850; d. May 19, 1850; m. (2) Lavina A. Nash, Nov. 27, 1856.

Children :
1 FRANCIS NORTON, b. June 19, 1858; d. Dec. 19, 1860.
2 ABBY PRISCILLA, b. Aug. 7, 1861.
3 A son, } b. May 14, 1866; d. May 14, 1866.
4 A daughter,
5 FANNIE BARTLETT, b. Oct. 27, 1869.

---

520  529 (VII.) LABAN PRATT, of Weymouth (son of VI. Laban), b. June 27, 1788; d. Aug. 6, 1826; m. Feb. 21, 1807, Nancy Thayer, of Randolph.

Children :
1 EVELINE, b. June 21, 1807; d. Oct. 25, 1825.
2 SOPHIA, b. Feb. 28, 1810; d. March 13, 1869; m. Oct. 24, 1825, Daniel Dyer.
531  530  3 ATHERTON, b. May 9, 1820; d. Oct. 1, 1863.
4 HIRAM, b. Sept. 18, 1825.

---

530  531 (VIII.) ATHERTON PRATT, of Weymouth (son of VII. Laban), b. May 9, 1820; d. Oct. 1, 1863; m. (P.) Aug. 7, 1842, Margaret Rice, dau. of William and Nancy Dyer; b. April 18, 1826.

Child :
533  532  GEORGE HIRAM, b. Sept. 19, 1843.

---

532  533 (IX.) GEORGE H. PRATT, of Weymouth (son of VIII. Atherton), b. Sept. 19, 1843; m. Sept. 13, 1860, at Quincy, Susan M. Elmes, dau. of Theodore and Sarah E.

Children :
1 MARY ELLEN, b. June 3, 1861.
2 LILLY ATHERTON, b. Dec. 20, 1864; d. Oct. 4, 1865.

---

514  534 (VII.) HARVEY PRATT, of Weymouth (son of VI. Abner and Nabby), b. March 27, 1819; m. Aug. 27, 1860, Susan Cushman Current, dau. of James and Susan, of Boston.

Child :
A son, b. Nov. 2, 1861.

505 535 (V.) WHITCOMB PRATT, of Abington (son of IV. Nathaniel and Elizabeth), b. Oct. 7, 1725; d. before 1782; m. Elizabeth (Betty) Gurney, Jan. 14, 1748.

Children:

545 536    1   Elizabeth, b. Nov. 7, 1745.
546 537    2   Thomas, b. Feb. 1, 1752.
547 538    3   Whitcomb, b. March 23, 1761.
         4   Daniel L., b. March 17, 1766.

---

506 539 (V.) NOAH PRATT, of Abington (of IV. Nathaniel and Elizabeth), b. Oct. 19, 1731; m. (1) Jan. 11, 1753, Mary Jones; she d. March 28, 1767, aged 41 years; m. (2) March 17, 1768, Mary Whitmarsh.

Children:

548 540    1   Robert, b. Dec. 18, 1753.
557 541    2   Noah, b. July 20, 1758.
580 542    3   Seth Jones, b. June 26, 1762.
         4   Molly Hearsey, b. Sept. 29, 1755.

---

507 543 (V.) NATHANIEL PRATT, of Abington (son of IV. Nathaniel and Elizabeth), b. ——; d. ——; m. (P.) Feb. 20, 1773, Grace Bien.

Child:

581 544    1   Nathaniel, b. March 28, 1775.

---

538 545 (VI.) ELIZABETH PRATT, of Abington (dau. of V. Whitcomb), b. Nov. 7, 1745; m. Dec. 30, 1766, Levi Stetson, of Abington.

Children:

   1   Elizabeth, b. July 25, 1767.
   2   Lucinda, b. Oct. 25, 1769.
   3   Whitcomb, b. Feb. 7, 1775.
   4   Levi, b. March 10, 1777.
   5   Nancy, b. Dec. 21, 1779.
   6   Olive, b. Jan. 30, 1785.
   7   Jedson, b. Jan. 7, 1789.

537  546  (VI.) THOMAS PRATT, of Abington (son of V. Whitcomb),
b. Feb. 1, 1752; d. March 8, 1820; m. (P.) June 5, 1773,
Susannah Tirrill; she d. Nov. 24, 1829, aged 73 years.

Children:

    1  ELIZABETH, b. Sept. 14, 1773; m. Sept. 11, 1794, Charles
      Brown, of Bridgewater.
    2  SARAH, b. Nov. 29, 1775.
    3  CHLOE ("Cloa"), b. Nov. 26, 1779.
    4  NATHANIEL, b. June 25, 1783.
    5  THOMAS, b. Dec. 12, 1790.

538  547  (VI.) WHITCOMB PRATT, of Abington (son of V. Whitcomb), b. March 23, 1761; m. Dec. 5, 1785, Ruth Lovel.

540  548  (VI.) ROBERT PRATT, of Abington (son of V. Noah), b.
Dec. 16, 1753; d. 1791; m. Jan. 27, 1779, Jane Bicknell
of Abington, b. 1758; d. Nov. 20, 1811.

Children:

    1  MEHITABLE, b. Jan. 26, 1781.
550  549  2  SETH, b. April 17, 1783.
    3  MOLLY, b. March 21, 1786.

549  550  (VII.) SETH PRATT, of Abington (son of VI. Robert), b.
April 17, 1783; d. Jan. 30, 1844; m. (P.) April 18, 1819,
Martha Pulling Reed.

Children:

553  551  1  HENRY JONES, b. Sept. 8, 1821.
554  552  2  ISAAC REED, b. Feb. 3, 1824; m. Sarah W. Ford, Jan.
      5, 1846.
    3  JANE BICKNELL, b. April 7, 1826; m. Bela Wilkes,
      Sept. 19, 1845.
    4  MARTHA ANN, b. Feb. 3, 1834.

551  553  (VIII.) HENRY JONES PRATT, of Abington (son of VII.
Seth), b. Sept. 8, 1821; m. (P.) Sept. 14, 1845; m. Sept.
3, 1846, Mary N. Brown.  He m. (2) Maria J. Hunter.

Children:

MARY N. B., b. Jan. 14, 1853, in Philadelphia.
CLIFFORD BROWN, b. July 27, 1846.
HENRIETTA BROWN, b. Oct. 21, 1848.
ALFRED REED, b. May 11, 1862.
HARVEY H.

---

)ISAAC REED PRATT, of Abington (son of VII.
Seth), b. Feb. 3, 1824; d. April 13, 1896; m. Jan. 5,
1846, Sarah W. Ford.

Children:

MARTHA EMELINE, b. Oct. 5, 1846.
SARAH F. b. March 17, 1854.
CHARLES WALDRON, b. March 24, 1861.
SETH ELDERT, b. Dec. 23, 1862.
LILLIAN GERTRUDE, b. Nov. 18, 1864.

---

CHARLES W. PRATT, of Abington (son of VIII.
Isaac R.), b. March 24, 1861; m. May 27, 1885, Jennie
F. Thomas of South Weymouth.

Child:

GORDON REED, b. Oct. 8, 1886.

---

NOAH PRATT, of Abington (son of V. Noah), b. July
20, 1758; d. 1825; m. Else Jenkins, Nov. 24, 1780; pub. as
" Alice," recorded "Olive," recorded in Births "Else,"
and in her Will "Else." She d. 1836, in Hanover, a
widow, and mentions all of her children then living, in
her Will (recorded at Plymouth). Some of the children's
births recorded in Abington, the rest mentioned in her
Will.

Children:

MOLLY, b. Jan. 13, 1781; d. Sept. 21, 1805, "aged 25."
CYRUS, b. Nov. 13, 1783; d. Jan. 10, 1846.
ROBERT, b. July 18, 1792; d. July 4, 1820, "aged 28."
JAMES, b. May 15, 1795.
PHINEHAS, b. May 25, 1796; d. Jan. 28, 1830, "aged 32."

573 561   6  NATHANIEL.
574 562   7  DAVID, b. 1786; d. March 6, 1863, in East Bridgewater.
576 563   8  NOAH, m. (1) Nancy Reed; m. (2) Lydia ——.

---

558 564 (VII.) CYRUS PRATT, of Abington (son of VI. Noah), b. Nov. 13, 1783; d. 1846; m. Dec. 7, 1800, Cyntha Orcutt.

    Children :

566 565   1  GEORGE WASHINGTON, b. March 27, 1809.
      2  MARY JENKINS, b. Nov. 15, 1813.
      3  MARILLA, b. Nov. 30, 1819; m. Oct. 4, 1862, Worthy C. Dunham.

---

565 566 (VIII.) GEORGE WASHINGTON PRATT, of Abington (son of VII. Cyrus), b. March 27, 1809; m. May 6, 1835, Harriet Meserve.

    Children :

      1  HARRIET EMILY, b. May 28, 1836; m. Jan. 27, 1856, Edmund A. Shaw.
      2  GEORGE A., b. April 10, 1838; d. June 19, 1842.
      3  CYNTHIA ANN, b. April 23, 1843.

---

559 567 (VII.) JAMES PRATT, of Abington (son of VI. Noah), b. May 15, 1795; d. 1860; m. (P.) May 10, 1817, Polly Shaw, of Abington. He m. (2) Sept. 27, 1857, Bathsheba Curtis.

    Children :

      1  MARY PORTER, b. Nov. 3, 1818; m. Harrison C. Leavitt, Oct. 24, 1850.
      2  MARY PORTER, b. May 1, 1822; d. young.
      3  BETSEY STETSON, b. Aug. 13, 1826; m. Ira Blanchard.
      4  JAMES MONROE, b. July 10, 1828; d. Sept. 10, 1828.
      5  MARTIN LUTHER, b. Oct. 1, 1831.
569 568   6  JAMES NEWTON, b. ——.

---

563 569 (VIII.) JAMES NEWTON PRATT, of Abington (son of VII. James), b. ——; m. April 26, 1851, Betsey Stetson.

Children:

        1  MARY CAROLINE, b. Nov. 21, 1854.

2  570   2  HENRY MARTIN, b. March 20, 1856; m. Jan. 17, 1877, Alice M. Hollis.

        3  A child, b. Aug. 25, 1864.

---

0  571 (VII.) PHINEHAS PRATT, of Abington (son of VI. Noah), b. May 25, 1796; d. Jan. 26, 1830; m. Dec. 6, 1821, Louisa Gurney, of Abington; b. 1797; d. Feb. 4, 1861.

    • Children:

3  572   1  LEANDER, b. 1825.

        2  LOUISA GURNEY, b. June 6, 1826; d. Jan., 1872.

---

1  573 (VII.) NATHANIEL PRATT (son of. VI. Noah), b. ——; d. ——; m. (P.) May 10, 1812, Orpha Bisby.

        Had 6 or 8 children; had no sons to come to maturity; no record.

---

2  574 (VII.) DAVID PRATT (son of VI. Noah), b. 1786; d. March 6, 1863; m. Feb. 6, 1812, Lydia Corthell, of Halifax. He died in East Bridgewater, Mass.

Children:

7  575   1  ADDISON, b. Dec. 24, 1812 ("not born in Abington").

        2  ADALINE, b. Sept. 25, 1822.

        3  ALMORA B., m. —— Felton.

---

3  576 (VII.) NOAH PRATT (son of VI. Noah), b. ——; d. ——; m. (P.) Nancy Reed, April 12, 1818.

---

5  577 (VIII.) ADDISON PRATT, of Rockland (son of VII. David), b. Dec. 24, 1812; m. March 29, 1843, Eliza Ann, dau. of Daniel Holbrook; she d. Jan. 12, 1890, aged 69 years.

Children:

        1  HORACE GREELEY, b. Sept. 22, 1844.

0  578   2  CHARLES W., b. Feb. 27, 1848.

578  579  (IX.) CHARLES W. PRATT, of East Bridgewater (son of
VIII. Addison), b. Feb. 27, 1848; m. April 22, 1884, Ella
A. Wade, b. 1857.

Child:
Lawrence Prevost, b. May 4, 1885.

---

568  580  (VI.) SETH JONES PRATT, of Abington (son of V. Noah),
b. June 28, 1762; d. ——; m. Jan. 21, 1784, Hannah
Hunt.

Child:
Jones, b. March 29, 1785.

---

544  581  (VI.) NATHANIEL PRATT, of Abington (son of V. Nathaniel and Grace), b. March 24, 1775; d. ——; m. Lydia
——

Children:
1  Lydia, b. July 28, 1797.
2  Nathaniel, b. Sept. 11, 1800.

---

570  582  (IX.) HENRY M. PRATT, of Rockland (son of VIII. James
N.), b. March 20, 1856; m. Jan. 17, 1877, Alice M., dau.
of Henry and Patience Hollis.  Shoe cutter.

Children:
1  James Lester, b. Oct. 31, 1878.
2  Alice Louise, b. Aug. 20, 1880.
3  Elsie Idella, b. Sept. 1, 1885.

---

572  583 (VIII.) LEANDER PRATT, of E. Abington (son of VII. Phinehas), b. May 1825; m. Jan. 23, 1861, Anna Fryer, of
Boston.  He is an artist.

Children:
1  A child, b. April 23, 1864.
2  George F., b. Nov. 17, 1808; d. Nov. 17, 1808.
3  George, b. Aug. 4, 1872.

405  584  (V.)  STEPHEN PRATT, of Weymouth (son of IV. Ebenezer),
              b. May 27, 1740; d. Jan. 16, 1806; m. (1) Betsey ——, d.
              July 20, 1788.  He m. (2) Mary Whitman, d. Aug. 20,
              1801.

          Children:

586  585      1  ABIAH, b. March 15, 1762; m. Betsey ——.
              2  JOSEPH, b. July 30, 1790.
              3  EBENEZER, b. about 1804; went to Hingham, 1818.

---

585  586  (VI.)  ABIAH PRATT, of Weymouth (son of V. Stephen), b.
              March 15, 1762; m. May 10, 1787, Patience Bicknell,
              b. 1763; d. April, 1842.

          Children:

              1  PATIENCE, b. June 17, 1787; d. Oct. 2, 1868; m. Abiah
                 W. Salisbury.
              2  ABIAH, b. March 25, 1790.
              3  JOTHAM, b. Oct. 1, 1793; d. July 12, 1875, or Sept. 1877,
                 at sea.
              4  CYNTHIA, b. 1801; d. March 26, 1875; m. Isaac Reed,
                 May 24, 1819.
              5  HANNAH, b. ——; m. Samuel Orcutt, July 30, 1818.
              6  ELIEZER, b. ——.
              7  SILAS, lived in a cave and died 1824.
              8  A child, d. 1805.

---

306  587  (IV.)  SAMUEL PRATT, of Weymouth, weaver (son of III.
              John and Elizabeth), b. Oct. 15, 1668; d. ——; m. Jan.
              10, 1719, Christian Tower, of Hingham; she d. 1765,
              aged 77. (?)

          Children:

              1  LYDIA, b. Dec. 21, 1719; m. May 24, 1743, Thomas
                 Whiton.
              2  SARAH, b. Oct. 27, 1721.
591  588      3  JOSEPH, b. Oct. 22, 1723; d. Nov. 5, 1788.
596  589      4  MICAH, b. Nov. 13, 1726.
606  590      5  BENJAMIN, b. Nov. 2, 1730; d. March 30, 1815.

---

588  591  (V.)  JOSEPH PRATT (son of IV. Samuel), b. Oct. 22, 1723;
              d. Nov. 5, 1788; m. July 24, 1745, Sarah Dyer, dau. of
              Joseph and Jane (Stephens), b. March 20, 1727; d. Jan.
              19, 1803.

Children:

    1  SARAH, b. Dec. 19, 1745; m. (P.) Aug. 15, 1767, Eliot Loud.

    2  SOLOMON, b. May 9, 1749; d. 1751.

594  592   3  SOLOMON, b. Nov. 30, 1752.

    4  JOSEPH, b. Jan. 18, 1757.

    593  5  LYDIA, b. Feb. 18, 1758; d. Dec. 28, 1835; m. Joshua Pratt, son of V. Matthew, (P.) Aug. 2, 1777.

    6  LEAH, b. Nov. 24, 1764; m. Oct. 16, 1783, Zael Hunt.

    7  ELIZABETH, b. ——; m. (P.) Dec. 14, 1782, Alpheus Bates.

---

592  594  (VI.) SOLOMON PRATT (son of V. Joseph), b. May 9, 1749; d. 1751; m. Aug. 3, 1775, Remember Bate. Removed to Abington.

Children:

    1  THOMAS, b. Feb. 16, 1776; m. Nov. 27, 1811, Mary Salisbury.

    2  JOSEPH.

    3  WHITCOMB.

603  595   4  OTIS.

---

580  596  (V.) MICAH PRATT (son of IV. Samuel), b. Nov. 13, 1726; d. ——; m. Nov. 3, 1748, Elizabeth Lincoln, d. April 10, 1801, aged 71. He removed to Abington.

Children:

000  597   1  MICAH, b. Aug. 15, 1749.

001  598   2  ELAM, b. Oct. 5, 1751.

    3  ELIZABETH, b. May 31, 1756.

002  599   4  JOSEPH, b. Oct. 23, 1758.

    5  ISAAC.

    6  DANIEL, b. Oct. 7, 1782.

---

597  600  (VI.) MICAH PRATT, of Abington (son of V. Micah), b. Aug. 15, 1749; d. ——; m. Jan. 2, 1773, Mary Parkman.

---

596  601  (VI.) ELAM PRATT, of Abington (son of V. Micah), b. Oct. 5, 1751; m. (P.) Lydia Hunt, Jan. 22, 1782.

599  602 (VI.) JOSEPH PRATT, of Abington (son of V. Micah), b. Oct.
             23, 1758; m. (1º.) March 19, 1790, Lois Pratt.

_____

595  603 (VII.) OTIS PRATT (son of VI. Solomon, of Abington), b.
             ——; m. Clarissa.

             Children :
605  604      1  BERNICE, b. ——; m. Sept. 30, 1852, L. Amelia Pool.
              2  MARY L., b. ——; m. Nov. 22, 1848, Leavitt Torrey.

_____

604  605 (VIII.) BERNICE PRATT (son of VII. Otis), b. ——; m. Sept.
             30, 1852, L. Amelia Pool, of Abington.

             Child :
             CLARENCE HAROLD, b. April 28, 1856, at Plainfield.

_____

500  606   (V.) BENJAMIN PRATT, of Weymouth (son of IV. Samuel),
             b. Nov. 2, 1730; d. March 30, 1815; m. Feb. 8, 1752,
             Love Lincoln, dau. of Elisha and Mellea, b. Dec. 19,
             1734; d. Sept. 13, 1809.

             Children :
              1  ELISHA, b. Dec. 27, 1753.
              2  LOVE, b. Aug. 27, 1755; d. Sept. 19, 1843.
              3  BENJAMIN, b. July 10, 1758; d. Sept. 20, 1818.
              4  LOIS, b. Dec. 10, 1759; m. April 8, 1779, John Blancher.
611  607      5  ROBERT, b. Dec. 10, 1762; d. Feb. 2, 1847.
              6  JAMES, b. April 16, 1765.
610  608      7  JOHN,
647a 609      8  WILLIAM P., } b. Feb. 17, 1767; } m. Oct. 16, 1790, Ruth
                 Wild, of Braintree.
              9  MELLEA, b. June 7, 1773.
             10  CONTENT, m. March 20, 1799, Bela Vining, of Weymouth.

_____

606  610 (VI.) JOHN PRATT, of Weymouth (son of V. Benjamin and
             Love), b. Feb. 17, 1767; m. Nov. 22, 1802, Hannah Bates.

             Children :
              1  REUBEN BATES, d. Aug. 27, 1875.
              2  JOHN, d. Feb. 17, 1826.

607 611 (VI.) ROBERT PRATT, of Weymouth (son of V. Benjamin
and Love), b. Dec. 10, 1762; d. Feb. 2, 1847; m. May 1,
1787, Polly Loud, dau. of John and Mercy (Vining), b.
July 18, 1766; d. Dec. 25, 1851.

Children:

622 612 1 BENJAMIN, b. April 2, 1788; m. Silence Thayer, of
Randolph, 1809.
616 613 2 JOHN LOUD, b. Aug. 7, 1789.
633 614 3 ROBERT L., b. Aug. 29, 1793.
4 POLLY,                          d. May 8, 1855.
643 615 5 ELEAZER, } b. Sept. 16, 1797;
6 LOIS,                           m. (1) Apr. 15, 1821, Azel
Cushing; m. (2) —— Dyer.

---

613 616 (VII.) JOHN LOUD PRATT, of Weymouth (son of VI. Robert),
b. Aug. 7, 1789; d. July 30, 1863; m. Sept. 18, 1814,
Hannah H. Bates, b. June 20, 1791; d. May 20, 1872.

He was a shoemaker; also served in the war of 1812;
she was a cousin of Joshua Bates, the founder of Bates
Library, Boston, also a prominent merchant and bank-
er of that city.

Children:

1 ELIZABETH BATES, b. June 26, 1815; m. March 31, 1836,
John Holbrook, of Weymouth.
642 617 2 NATHAN, b. Feb. 5, 1818.
3 JOHN LOUD, b. Aug. 27, 1820; d. Oct. 18, 1821.
621 618 4 JOHN LOUD, b. Sept. 23, 1822.
5 HANNAH H., b. Feb. 1, 1825; d. Sept. 18, 1830.
640 619 6 JOSIAH BATES, b. Oct. 25, 1828; d. May 22, 1866.
7 HANNAH HUMPHREY, b. Sept. 8, 1830; m. Augustus
Bailey.
641 620 8 GEORGE WEBSTER, b. Jan. 20, 1835; m. Mercy B. Jones.

---

618 621 (VIII.) JOHN L. PRATT, JR., of Weymouth (son of John L.),
b. Sept. 23, 1822; m. May 4, 1847, Sarah Jane Woodward,
of Lowell, Mass.; b. March 4, 1825; d. June 24, 1863.

Children:

1 BERTRAND WOODWARD, b. April 14, 1861; d. May 15,
1861.
2 JENNIE THERESA, b. Jan. 19, 1863.

12   622 (VII.) BENJAMIN PRATT, of Randolph (son of VI. Robert),
b. April 2, 1788; d. Jan. 21, 1871; m. 1809, Silence Thayer, b. July 1, 1790; d. Feb. 10, 1842.

Children:

16   623    1   ABRAM, b. May 29, 1810; d. Oct. 6, 1853.
15   624    2   JASON, b. Dec. 26, 1814.
           3   MARY ANN, b. March 31, 1818; m. E. Wales Thayer,
              (P.) Oct. 0, 1836.
           4   SUSAN, b. ——, 1821; never married; d. Feb. 12, 1848.

---

14   625 (VIII.) JASON PRATT, of Randolph, now Holbrook (son of
VII. Benjamin), b. Dec. 26, 1814; m. Sept. 19, 1837,
Susannah Thayer, b. Sept. 9, 1818; dau. of Robert M.
Thayer, of Braintree.

Children:

           1   LYDIA ANN, b. Nov. 16, 1839; m. George W. Batchelder,
              April 15, 1861.
           2   MARY JANE, b. Oct. 9, 1845; m. Josiah W. Chamberlin,
              July 5, 1864.

---

23   626 (VIII.) ABRAM PRATT, of Holbrook (son of VII. Benjamin),
b. May 29, 1810; d. Oct. 6, 1853; m. (1) (P.) Aug. 7, 1831,
Almira Pratt, of Braintree; she d. Aug. 22, 1843, aged
37. He m. (2) Hannah Holbrook.

Children:

30   627    1   ABRAM W., b. 1833.
31   628    2   RICHMOND T.,
32   629    3   CHARLES EDWIN,
           4   EMILY J., b. 1840; m. Jan. 12, 1866, George Patten.
           5   HANNAH A., 1845; m. J. E. Daniels, June 6, 1869.

---

27   630 (IX.) ABRAM W. PRATT, of Holbrook (son of VIII. Abram),
b. ——, 1833; m. Feb. 13, 1856, Mary H. Bryant, b. 1838.

Children;

           1   ALICE W., b. Nov. 19, 1858.
           2   EMILY J., b. April 22, 1861.
           3   NELLIE A., b. April 10, 1869.
           4   MINNIE M., b. Oct. 15, 1871.

5 Anna F.,
6 Abram Berton,
7 Arthur Richmond, b. July 3, 1874.

---

628 631 (IX.) RICHMOND T. PRATT, of Holbrook (son of VIII.
Abram), b. ——, 1833; m. R. Lizzie Porter, April 25,
1859, b. ——, 1840, dau. of Reuben and Rhoda Porter.

Children:
1 Martha L., b. Feb. 28, 1859; d. May 15, 1860.
2 Mary J., b. Jan. 5, 1863.
3 Laura R., b. April 4, 1868.

---

629 632 (IX.) CHARLES E. PRATT, of Holbrook (son of VIII.
Abram), b. ——; m. Harriet Clark, Sept. 3, 1857.

Children:
1 Sarah L., b. March 11, 1859; m. Nov 24, 1877, William
N. Pendegrass.
2 Hattie A., b. Sept. 20, 1864; d. July 28, 1867.
3 Lizzie.
4 Myra W., b. 1867; d. Aug. 18, 1868.

---

614 633 (VII.) ROBERT L. PRATT, of Holbrook (son of VI. Robert),
b. Aug. 29, 1793; m. (1) Silvia Thayer, Nov. 26, 1812,
dau. of Phinehas and Ann Q. Thayer, of Randolph; she
d. Oct. 31, 1860, aged 65. He m. (2) June 12, 1861, Mary,
dau. of James and Anna Loud, b. ——, 1803.

Child:
635 634 1 Henry

---

634 635 (VIII.) HENRY PRATT, of Holbrook (son of VII. Robert
L.), b. ——; m. (1) (P.) June 12, 1831, Harriet Mad-
den; m. (2) (P.) July 19, 1835, Sarah Drake; m.
(3) July 10, 1850, Susan Hardy; she d. Aug. 29, 1859,
aged 38; m. (4) Eliza Dorr, Jan. 11, 1860. (The records
state the last to be his fourth marriage.)

Children:
1 Henry W., b. 1837; d. Sept. 15, 1849.
638 636 2 John Loud.

3 EDWIN FRANCIS, b. 1840; m. Elmira M. Dyer, July 10, 1873.

19 637    4 ROBERT PHINEAS THAYER, b. 1842; m. May 17, 1874, Desire C. Dyer.

- - -

16 638 (VIII.) JOHN L. PRATT, of Randolph (son of VII. Henry), b. ——; m. July 31, 1851, Ann Q. Thayer.

Child:

1 JOHN W., b. Aug. 31, 1870.

---

17 639 (VIII.) ROBERT PHINEAS T. PRATT, of Braintree (son of VII. Henry), b. ——, 1842; m. May 17, 1874, Desire C. Dyer, b. in Weymouth 1854, dau. of Benjamin and Louisa (Cushing).

Child:

1 ERNEST LINWOOD, b. Aug. 5, 1878; d. Oct. 27, 1878.

---

9 640 (VIII.) JOSIAH H. PRATT, of Weymouth (son of VII. John L.), b. Oct. 25, 1829; d. May 22, 1866; m. 1850, Elvira C. Richardson, of Scituate; b. in Scituate, Mass., 1834; d. Aug. 20, 1884. He was a "nailer" by occupation.

Children:

1 WALTER HERBERT, b. Sept. 22, 1852; d. Aug. 27, 1853.
2 ARTHUR HERBERT, b. 1854; m. March 13, 1876, at Brockton, Alice Maud Richardson, dau. of James W. and Maria. Arthur H. is a cooper.
3 FRANK WALTER, b. Aug. 30, 1858; m. Feb. 22, 1885, Cora A. Burgoyne. He is a mason.
4 MERTON ELLSWORTH, b. June 28, 1864; d. Sept. 18, 1864.

---

0 641 (VIII.) GEORGE WEBSTER PRATT, of Weymouth (son of VII. John L.), b. Jan. 20, 1835; m. Mercy Baker Jones, of Scituate.

Children:

1 CORA E., b. March 15, 1857; m. W. F. Burrell.
2 ADELLA ATWOOD, b. Feb. 21, 1861; d. Dec. 17, 1883.

3 WEBSTER LINCOLN, b. Nov. 4, 1865.
4 RUSSELL BAKER, b. Oct. 23, 1872.
5 JESSIE JONES, b. Feb. 6, 1882.

---

617 642 (VIII.) NATHAN PRATT, of Weymouth (son of VII. John L.), b. Feb. 5, 1818; m. (1) Nov. 7, 1847, Sarah E. Hyde, of Norwich, Ct.; b. ——, 1818; d. Sept. 1, 1849, dau. of Jarius; m. (2) Jan. 5, 1852, Julia S. Carow of Norwich, Ct., b. Feb. 17, 1817; dau. of William M. Carew. He keeps a general grocery store at Weymouth.

Children:

1 NATHAN H., b. Aug. 31, 1848; unmarried (1887); a lawyer in Boston.
2 MARY H., b. April 10, 1827; m. Oct. 25, 1882, George H. Bass, of Rockland.

---

5 643 (VII.) ELEAZER PRATT, of Weymouth (son of VI. Robert), b. Sept. 16, 1797; m. (1) Lois Penniman, Aug. 31, 1820; m. (2) Hannah N. Howes, July 30, 1843; she d. April 15, 1873.

Children:

1 MARY L., b. Aug. 27, 1821.
2 DRUSILLA, b. June 29, 1823.
3 JAMES, b. Feb. 26, 1825; d. Jan. 5, 1887.
4 BRYANT C., b. March 21, 1827; m. Sept. 17, 1848, Lydia B. Hatch, b. Oct. 6, 1831.
5 CLARINDA E., b. Nov. 12, 1830.
645 644 6 BENJAMIN, b. Aug. 23, 1832.
7 ELIZA C., b. Aug. 23, 1834; m. Hiram D. Pock, April 23, 1853.
8 JEPTHA, b. 1840.
9 FANNIE C., b. July 12, 1855; d. Aug. 28, 1855.
10 ELEAZER PARKER, b. March 22, 1857.

---

644 645 (VIII.) BENJAMIN PRATT, of Weymouth (son of VII. Eleazer), b. ——, 1833; m. March 13, 1853, Hannah Williamson, dau. of Anthony, of Marshfield.

Children :

1  ISABELLA SPRAGUE, b. Dec 5, 1854; m. Carleton, of Weymouth.

647  646        2  MARY AGNES, b. Aug. 11, 1863.

---

646  647 (IX.) MARY A. PRATT (dau. of VIII. Benjamin), b. Aug. 11, 1863 ; m. June 23, 1880, William H. Pratt, son of Asa T. and Mercy (Clapp), of Braintree.

Children :

1  CORA BELLE,        } b. Nov. 1, 1880; { d. Nov. 17, 1880.
2  CARRIE BRADFORD,   }                 { d. Aug. 20, 1881.
3  ELEANOR SPRAGUE, b. Oct. 12, 1881.
4  OLIVE MERCY, b. Sept. 15, 1882.
5  ALTON RUSSELL, b. Sept. 28, 1883 ; d. April 13, 1884.
6  GEORGE WINSLOW, b. May 20, 1885.

---

609  647 a (VI.) WILLIAM PRATT, of Braintree (son of V. Benjamin and Love of Weymouth), b. Feb. 17, 1767 ; d. —— ; m. (P.) Oct. 16, 1790, in Weymouth ; m. in Braintree Feb. 13, 1791, Ruth Wild, dau. of Micah and Deborah (Hollis).

Children :

1  EUNICE H., b. 1808; m. Aug. 12, 1822, Joseph Much-more; m. (2) Jacob Blackburn; m. (3) Francis Woodward, d. Jan. 2, 1866.

650  648        2  LINSEY, b. Nov. 29, 1810.
655  649        3  STEPHEN, b. 1818 ; d. March 9, 1865.
              4  BARNABAS, b. 1800 ; d. July 17, 1882 ; m. Isabella M. Wilson, Sept. 15, 1845.

---

648  650 (VII.) LINSEY PRATT, of Braintree (son of VI. William), b. Nov. 29, 1810 ; m. Dec. 25, 1834, Eliza H. Dyer, dau. of Abraham and Lydia (Hobart).

Children :

653  651        1  WILLIAM L., b. Nov. 25, 1836 ; m. Sally Hollis.
              2  MARY E., b. July 5, 1838 ; m. Quincy Pratt.
654  652        3  HENRY O., b. June 22, 1840.
              4  RUTH, b. Dec. 12, 1844.
              5  LYDIA J., b. Dec. 29, 1847.

651 653 (VIII.) WILLIAM L. PRATT, of Braintree, resides (1887) in Weymouth (son of VII. Linsey), b. Nov. 25, 1836; m. (P.) May 30, 1857, Sally Hollis, dau. of Reuben and Sally (Thompson), of Weymouth.

Children :

1 NELLIE THOMPSON, b. Feb. 19, 1860.
2 MABEL, b. March 4, 1864; d. Sept. 27, 1864.
3 LILLIAN GLEASON, b. Jan. 16, 1866; d. Feb. 28, 1869.
4 WILLIE PRESTON, b. Dec. 22, 1867; d. June 4, 1877.

---

652 654 (VIII.) HENRY O. PRATT, of Braintree (son of VII. Linsey), b. June 22, 1840; m. (1) Sarah B. Faunce, May 23, 1866; m. (2) Maria L. Hunt, Nov. 21, 1870.

Children :

1 SARAH LOUISA, b. Dec. 17, 1871.
2 HENRY STEPHEN, b. April 9, 1873; d. July 26, 1873.
3 VIOLA M., b. Aug. 9, 1874; d. Sept. 5, 1874.
4 LILLIAN GERTRUDE, b. Dec. 14, 1877.

---

649 655 (VII.) STEPHEN PRATT, of Braintree (son of VI. William), b. ——; m. Dec. 13, 1846, Helen W. Packard, dau. of James and Dorothea, she d. May 4, 1862, aged 34.

Children :

1 FRANCIS W., b. Dec. 7, 1856.
2 WILLIAM T., } b. March 4, 1862; { d. July 12, 1862.
3 A son, } { d. March 4, 1862.
4 OCEANA R., b. 1851; d. Sept. 5, 1855.
5 WILLIAM JAMES, d. June 20, 1860.

---

306 656 (IV.) THOMAS PRATT, of Weymouth (son of III. John and Elizabeth), b. Jan. 3, 1705; d. March 25, 1760; m. (1) May 30, 1732, Mary Vinson, dau. of John and Sarah, b. July 12, 1708; d. Dec. 21, 1754; m. (2) (P.) May, 1757, Mrs. Abigail Gay, of Dedham, d. May 26, 1818, aged 90.

Children by Mary :

1 ABNER, b. April 7, 1733; d. June 24, 1733.
2 MARY, b. Oct. 15, 1737.

3  HANNAH, b. Nov. 4, 1741; m. July 15, 1759, Hezekiah
    White.

4  ELIZABETH, b. Dec. 27, 1742; m. March 12, 1761, Jona.
    Derby, Jr.

5  EUNICE,  } b. April 6, 1746; { m. Aug. 18, 1763, Isaac
6  LOIS,    }                  { Porter, son of John and
    Sarah (Nash). He d. June 15, 1800, aged 64. She d.
    Jan. 8, 1821, aged 74.

658  657    7  THOMAS, b. Sept. 30, 1748.

            8  SARAH.

            Child by Abigail:

            9  BENJAMIN, b. Aug. 27, 1758.

---

657  658  (V.) THOMAS PRATT, of Quincy (son of IV. Thomas, of
            Weymouth), b. Sept. 30, 1748; d. March 1, 1811; m. (1)
            Mary Green, Oct. 2, 1769; she d. Feb. 13, 1801, at
            Quincy; m. (2) Sarah (Hubbard) Thayer, of Quincy,
            June 7, 1801.

            Children:

            1  MARY or POLLY, b. Aug. 6, 1770; m. John R. Newcomb.

            2  COTTON, m. Sarah Newcomb, 1797.

662  659    3  JAMES, b. 1766; a minister in Philadelphia, Pa.

            4  JOANNA, m. Oct. 4, 1795, Benj. Faxon.

            5  ESTHER, m. Feb. 14, 1802, Benj. Faxon.

661  660    6  THOMAS O., b. Dec. 25, 1784; m. Jan. 12, 1809, Nancy
                Miller.

            7  BETSEY, m. Nov. 9, 1804, John Veazie.

            8  RELIEF, m. March 17, 1815, Thos. Reed.

---

660  661  (VI.) THOMAS PRATT, of Quincy (son of V. Thomas), b.
            Dec. 25, 1784; m. Jan. 12, 1809, Nancy Miller, dau. of
            Thomas and Thankful (Field), b. March 16, 1787. Tho-
            mas Miller was a soldier, impressed in Burgoyne's
            army, and afterwards settled in Quincy.

            Children:

            1  GEORGE THOMAS, b. Oct. 30, 1809; d. Nov. 20, 1816,
                drowned.

            2  EDWARD, b. May 30, 1812; d. Oct. 23, 1812.

            3  ELIZA A., b. April 20, 1815; m. K. B. Nickerson, Oct.
                29, 1835.

    4  GEORGE T., b. June 15, 1817; d. May 8, 1822.

    5  MARIA B., b. May 7, 1820; d. Aug. 1, 1838.

    6  CAROLINE L., b. Aug. 20, 1822; d. April 24, 1853; m. M. Merrott, Nov. 14, 1841.

    7  JOHN Q. A., b. May 17, 1825; m. Ellen M. Chase.

    8  FANNY JENKINS, b. March 29, 1828; m. Amos Buckman.

---

660  662 (VI.) **JAMES PRATT**, of Quincy (son of V. Thomas), b. 1776; d. Sept. 3, 1828, aged 52; m. Sarah Newcomb, of Braintree (b. Dec. 15, 1777), Sept. 17, 1797; she d. April 21, 1860. His son James was a clergyman and was stationed at Philadelphia.

Children:

    1  COTTON, b. March 12, 1799; m. Mary Newcomb, of Braintree, Dec. 7, 1820.

665  663 ·  2  HENRY GARDNER, b. July 6, 1806; m. 1829, Elizabeth G. Gould.

    3  JAMES, b. July 27, 1809; d. Jan. 17, 1874.

668  664  4  WILLIAM, b. March 31, 1812; d. Feb. 18, 1867; m. Harriet Gibson.

    5  An infant, d. young.

    6  "  "  "  "

---

663  665 (VII.) **HENRY GARDNER PRATT**, of Quincy (son of VI. James), b. July 6, 1806; m. 1829, Elizabeth G. Gould.

Children:

    1  ELIZABETH, b. June 3, 1844.

    2  CHARLES H., b. Jan. 1, 1854.

    3  GEORGE, d. March 7, 1837.

    4  CHARLES F., b. 1847; d. Nov. 8, 1848.

    5  CHARLES F., d. Sept. 23, 1851.

667  666  6  HENRY G., m. Feb. 17, 1853, Mary D. S. Pope.

    7  SARAH J., m. Feb. 7, 1856, Wm. H. Willson.

    8  WILLIAM H., m. May 8, 1860, Ellen F. Totman.

    9  GEORGE F., m. Jan. 20, 1864, Abbie A. Pope.

---

666  667 (VIII.) **HENRY G. PRATT** (son of VII. Henry G.), b. ——; m. Feb. 17, 1853, Mary D. S. Pope.

Children:

    1  CHARLES HENRY, b. Jan. 1, 1854; d. March 24, 1878.

2  Infant, b. Aug. 20, 1856.
3  FRANK G., b. 1859; m. April 25, 1883, Carrie E. Stoddard.
4  NELLIE ETTA, b. June 21, 1863; d. July 14, 1865.

———————

664  668 (VII.) WILLIAM PRATT, of Quincy (son of VI. James), b.
          March 31, 1812; d. Feb. 18, 1867; m. Harriet Gibson, d.
          April 28, 1866.

     Children:
     1  HARRIET NEWELL, b. June 13, 1835; d. April 22, 1844.
     2  ELIZABETH COOLEDGE, b. April 14, 1837; m. Feb. 3,
          1868, H. W. Gray.
     3  MARIA BEECHER, b. Nov. 18, 1838; d. Sept. 20, 1840.
     4  FRANCIS LOWELL, b. Oct. 25, 1840.
670  669 · 5  WILLIAM W., b. Jan. 27, 1845; m. Aug. 28, 1873, Annie
          F. Stonley.
     6  HARRIET M., b. July 4, 1848.

———————

669  670 (VIII.) WILLIAM W. PRATT (son of VII. William), b. Jan.
          27, 1845; m. Aug. 28, 1873, Annie F. Stonley, of Attle-
          boro.

# JOSEPH PRATT, OF WEYMOUTH.

---

The last Will and Testament of Joseph Pratt of Weymouth of the County of Suffolk in New England as followeth.

In the Name of God Amen, the fifth day of March in the year of our Lord 1719. I Joseph Pratt of Weymouth in the County of Suffolk in New England, Husbandman, being through the decay and decease of Old Age weak in Body but of perfect mind and memory thanks be given unto God, therfore calling to mind the mortality of my Body and knowing it is appointed for men once to dye. Do make and ordain this my last Will and Testament, That is to say. Principally and First of all I give and commend my Soul into the hand of God that gave it hoping through the merits death and passion of my Savior Jesus Christ to have full and free pardon and forgiveness of all my sins and to Inherit Everlasting Life, and my body I commit to the Earth to be decently buried at the discretion of my Executor hereafter named, nothing doubting but at the General resurection I shall receive the same Again by the mighty power of God and as touching such worldly Estate wherewith it hath pleased God to bless me in this life, I give demise and dispose of the same in the following manner and form. That is to say.

FIRST, I will that all those Debts or Duties as I Do owe in right and conscience to any manner of Person or Persons whatsoever shall be well and truly contented and paid or ordained to be paid in convenient time after my Decease by my Executor hereafter named.

ITEM. I give and bequeath to Sarah my dearly beloved Wife all my movables and household goods and a good convenient maintenance so that she may live comfortably upon the Income of my Estate to be brought in unto her by my Executor hereafter named, during her Natural life.

ITEM. I do give to my Son Joseph Pratt Ten Shillings besides what I have formerly given unto him —

ITEM. I do give unto my son John Pratt Ten Shillings if he should ever come hither again.

ITEM. I do give unto my son William Pratt five Shillings besides what he hath had of my Estate already.

ITEM. I do give unto my Son Ephraim Pratt five shillings besides what he hath had of my Estate already.

ITEM. I do give unto my son in Law Aron Pratt and to the children born of the Body of my late daughter Sarah Pratt deceased his late Wife Ten Shillings to be equally divided amongst them.

ITEM. I do give unto my Daughter Experience Battle Eight Pounds besides what she hath already had of my Estate.

ITEM. I do give unto my Daughter Hannah Hinds five pounds besides what she hath had in bringing up one of her Daughters and whatsoever else out of my Estate formerly.

ITEM. I do give to my Son Samuel Pratt whom I likewise constitute make and ordain my only and Sole Executor of this my last Will and Testament, all and Singular my Housing Lands Messuages and Testaments in Weymouth and all my Meadow Land by him and his assigns freely to be possessed and enjoyed, and my Will is that my Executor shall pay all the above said Legacies and I do hereby utterly Disallow revoke and Disannul all and every other former Testaments Wills & Legacies Bequests and Executors by me in any ways before this time named Willed & Bequeathed Ratifying and Confirming this and no other to be my last Will and Testament.

In Witness whereof I have hereunto set my hand and Seal the day and year above written.

*Joseph pratt.* (Seal.)

Signed Sealed Published Pronounced and Declared by the said Joseph Pratt as his last Will and Testament In the presence of us the Subscribers, Viz.

EDWARD BATE.
JOHN REED.
JOSHUA TORREY.

Exam: ℞
JOHN BOYDELL, Reg.

671 (II.) JOSEPH PRATT, of Weymouth (son of I. Matthew), b. June 10, 1637; d. Dec. 24, 1720; m. May 7, 1662, Sarah Judkins, b. 1638; d. Jan. 14, 1726.

He was the youngest son, and lived with his parents until about the time of his marriage. His name frequently occurs in the Town Records, in which are found his birth, marriage and death.

In 1666 and 1673 he was a fence viewer. 1657 he cut 600 shingles for his house; 1681 appointed to cut 5 cords of wood a year for the Pastor; 1682 on a committee to rebuild the Meeting House; 1685 a way-warden; 1689 a surveyor; 1693 named a "freeholder"; 1706 surveyor of highways; 1709 chosen to lay off land adjoining his own; 1710, 87 rods of land laid out for Joseph Pratt, senior, bounded by land, owned by himself and Samuel Whitmarsh, who married Hannah, the daughter of Mathew Pratt (his niece).

He appears, by the records, to have been prominent, not only in the town affairs, but in the church.

His will is dated March 5, 1719 (Boston Probate), in which he names his children in the following order.

Children:

| | | | |
|---|---|---|---|
| 679 | 672 | 1 | JOSEPH, b. Feb. 2, 1665. |
| 1007 | 673 | 2 | JOHN, b. May 17, 1668. |
| 678 | 674 | 3 | WILLIAM. |
| 1100 | 675 | 4 | EPHRAIM. |
| 677 | 676 | 5 | SARAH, b. May 31, 1664. |
| | | 6 | EXPERIENCE, m. Battle. |
| | | 7 | HANNAH, m. Hines. |
| | | 8 | SAMUEL, was a surveyor, 1734. Weymouth Records: Land granted, 1710, to Samuel Pratt, son of Joseph Pratt. |

676 677 (III.) SARAH PRATT, of Hingham (dau. of II. Joseph), b. May 31, 1664; d. July 22, 1706; m. Aaron Pratt, son of Phinehas Pratt. He m. (2) Sept. 4, 1707, Sarah Cummings (Wright), a widow; she d. Dec. 25, 1752. He d. 1735, aged 81 years.

His children were:

1 HENRY, settled in Newton.
2 DANIEL, " " Needham.
3 AARON, " " Cohasset.
4 JOHN, " " Taunton (Rehoboth).
5 JONATHAN, " " Cohasset.
6 MOSES, " " Boston.

7 SARAH.
8 MERCY.
9 ELIZABETH.
10 HANNAH.
11 NATHANIEL, m. MacFarlane, of Hingham; d. in Cuba.
12 PHINEHAS, m. Mary Lincoln, of Hingham; moved
  toward Worcester. His descendants went to Connecticut.
13 BENJAMIN.

---

78 (III.) WILLIAM PRATT, of Weymouth (son of II. Joseph),
  b. ——; d. ——; m. Experience King.

 Children:
1 JOANNA, b. Sept. 23, 1692.
2 WILLIAM, b. Oct. 3, 1695.
3 ISAAC, b. Feb. 20, 1700; surveyor, 1729.
4 EXPERIENCE, b. April 3, 1703.
5 ANN, b. March 30, 1705.

---

79 (III.) JOSEPH PRATT, of Bridgewater (son of II. Joseph),
  b. Feb. 2, 1665; d. Jan. 14, 1765; m. (1) Sarah Benson,
  of Hull, by whom he had twenty children. He m. (2)
  Ann Richards, of Weymouth, Dec. 14, 1721; she d.
  March 21, 1766, aged 93 years, without issue.

He lived in Weymouth, where he held such town
offices as fence-viewer, surveyor of highways, etc.,
*being styled Junior* in the town records. In 1704-5, he
removed to Bridgewater with his cousin William Pratt,
where he again held positions of trust in the town
affairs, being on the Grand Jury, Feb. 17, 1720, and a
selectman, 1739.

He sold a mill at Abington, 1704 (probably being
interested with Matthew Pratt, his cousin, in business).

The Boston News Letter of January 31, 1765, states
as follows: "On the fourteenth of this month died at
Bridgewater Joseph Pratt, aged 100 years. A man
of good character and religious profession. He had
twenty children by his first wife, but none by his
second, who still survives him, about 90 years of age."

He was called "Little-leg Joe" on account of one
leg being a trifle short.

His will, dated March 13, 1755, names (in the order given) the following children, the rest probably deceased.

Children:

| | | | |
|---|---|---|---|
| 686 | 680 | 1 | JOSEPH, d. 1753. |
| 715 | 681 | 2 | NATHANIEL, b. Nov. 23, 1701; d. 1749. |
| 849 | 682 | 3 | BENJAMIN, b. 1693. |
| 900 | 683 | 4 | SOLOMON. |
| 979 | 684 | 5 | DAVID, b. 1708. |
| 1006 | 685 | 6 | SAMUEL. |
| | | 7 | SARAH, d. before 1755; m. Ebenezer Snow, 1723. |

---

680 386 (IV.) JOSEPH PRATT, of Bridgewater (son of III. Joseph), b. ——; d. ——, 1753; m. (1) Dec. 9, 1712, Lydia Leonard; m. (2) Alice Hayward, April 5, 1749, dau. of Deacon Thos. Hayward; she d. Oct. 13, 1803, aged 96 years. On her grave-stone is found the following epitaph:

"By long experience I have known
God's sovereign power to save;
At his command I venture down
Securely to the grave."

He was surveyor of highways and a tithing-man, 1720.

Children:

| | | | |
|---|---|---|---|
| | | 1 | JOSEPH, a soldier in the war of 1700. |
| 690 | 687 | 2 | JONATHAN, b. 1720; m. Nov. 11, 1740, Elizabeth French. |
| 692 | 688 | 3 | JOB. |
| 694 | 689 | 4 | LYDIA, b. Oct. 6, 1713; d. June 29, 1741; m. Benj. Mohuren, Dec. 33, 1731. |
| | | 5 | SUSANNAH, m. Jas. Richards, May 15, 1740. |
| | | 6 | HANNAH, b. 1722; d. Sept. 26, 1764. |
| | | 7 | TABITHY, m. Seth Hayward, Sept. 6, 1748. |
| | | 8 | CHARITY, m. Jeremiah Washburn, April 24, 1754. |
| | | 9 | DELIVERANCE, m. Amasa Rickard, March 12, 1759. |
| | | 10 | ABIGAIL, m. Edward Curtis, 1759. |

---

687 690 (V.) JONATHAN PRATT (son of IV. Joseph), b. 1720; d. March 13, 1775; m. Nov. 11, 1740, Elizabeth French, dau. of Ebenezer French. He resided at Bridgewater. She d. Dec. 21, 1794, aged 74 years. The following is on his grave-stone:

> "All, young and old, that come this way,
> Remember this your house of clay;
> Acknowledge nature to be just,
> When you are summoned to the dust."

Children :

1   JONATHAN, b. July 6, 1741.
2   LUCY, b. Jan. 26, 1743.
3   EBENEZER, b. Dec. 21, 1744; d. Feb. 7, 1745.
4   EBENEZER, b. Dec. 17, 1745; d. May 28, 1750.
696  691   5   CORNELIUS, b. Feb. 3, 1748.
6   ELIZABETH, b. Jan. 25, 1751; m. Andreas Vinacca, March 10, 1778.
7   JEREMIAH, b. Jan. 24, 1753; m. Ann Bolton, Nov. 27, 1777.
8   EBENEZER, b. Nov. 13, 1757; m. Charity Besse, 1780.

---

688  692  (V.)  JOB PRATT (son of IV. Joseph), b. at Bridgewater, 1729; d. Nov. 6, 1786; m. Feb. 1, 1757, Mary Washburn, dau. of Josiah, d. Jan. 30, 1793. Estate valued £183. 8s. 11d.

Children :

1   SARAH, b. June 23, 1758; m. Barnabas Blossom, April 20, 1777.
703  693   2   JOB, b. 1766; d. June 3, 1853.
3   LYDIA, m. Azor Howe, 1787.

---

689  694  (V.)  LYDIA PRATT (dau. of IV. JOSEPH), b. Oct. 6, 1713; d. June 20, 1741; m. Dec. 23, 1731, Benj. Mehuren.

Children :

1   SARAH, b. June 9, 1732.
2   HEZEKIAH, b. March 24, 1734.
3   LUCY, b. March 25, 1736.
4   BENJAMIN, b. July 13, 1739.
5   ISAAC, b. June 15, 1741.

---

691  695  (VI.)  CORNELIUS PRATT, of Bridgewater (son of V. Jonathan), b. Feb. 3, 1748; d. Sept. 21, 1822; m. Martha Leonard, dau. of Jonathan, b. 1763; d. 1845. He was a Lieutenant.

Children:

1 JONATHAN, m. Deborah Hathaway, April 27, 1817.
699 696 2 LEONARD, b. 1791; d. Nov. 6, 1870.
700 697 3 EBENEZER, b. Feb. 7, 1797; d. May 17, 1880.
4 BETSEY, b. 1793; d. Dec. 26, 1794.
5 MARTHA, m. Jabez Vaughan, 1817.
712 698 6 CORNELIUS.
7 LUCY, m. Thomas Cushman.

---

696 699 (VII.) LEONARD PRATT, of Bridgewater (son of VI. Cornelius), b. ——, 1791; d. Nov. 6, 1870; m. Dec. 3, 1818, Clarissa, dau. of Sylvanus and Eunice Leonard, b. 1797, d. June 22, 1863.

Children:

1 DEBORAH H., b. Feb. 10, 1820; d. May 15, 1844.
2 MARTIN, b. Sept. 10, 1821; d. July 13, 1844.
3 LEONARD, b. July 30, 1824; d. Dec. 10, 1843.
4 CLARISSA, b. June 19, 1826; m. Oct. 31, 1862, Thos. B. Bradford.
710 700 5 SYLVANUS, b. Aug. 23, 1828; d. Dec. 6, 1866; m. Jan. 1866, F. Fuller.
702 701 6 SILAS, b. Sept. 21, 1831.
7 JOSEPH A., } b. April 18, 1839; { m. Nettie Thayer, 1877,
8 MARY K., } { went to Brooklyn.

---

701 702 (VIII.) SILAS PRATT, of Bridgewater (son of VII. Leonard), b. Sept. 21, 1831; m. Nov. 25, 1865, Emily F. Fuller, dau. of Nathan and Sarah S.; she d. May 19, 1870, aged 26 years. He m. (2) Levesta N. Fuller, Nov. 6, 1873.

Children:

1 ELTON L., b. Oct. 29, 1866.
2 EMILY M.
3 HERBERT AUGUSTUS, Dec. 11, 1877.
4 EVERETT BRADFORD, May 4, 1880.

---

693 703 (VI.) JOB PRATT, of Middleboro (son of V. Job), b. ——, 1766; d. June 3, 1853; m. Mary ——, 1789.

Children:

1 HANNAH, b. June 27, 1790.

    2  BETSEY, b. April 27, 1792.
    3  ELIHU, b. July 30, 1794.
    4  JOHN, b. Sept. 13, 1705. He m. (2) Elizabeth ——.
    5  DENNIS, b. May 26, 1797.
    6  MAHALA, b. June 4, 1811.
    7  CYRUS W., b. March 30, 1813.
04  8  REUBEN DEXTER, b. April 9, 1815.
    9  WILLIAM HATHAWAY, b. Oct. 30, 1818; m. Zilpah B.
          Curtis, May 28, 1837.

       Child:
       Wm. H., b. Feb. 3, 1855; d. Dec. 24, 1855.

——————

05 (VII.) REUBEN D. PRATT, of Middleboro (son of VI. Job),
          b. April 9, 1815; d. ——; m. Sarah W. ——. He re-
          sided in Taunton.

     Children:
     1  ELIZABETH J., b. May 6, 1842; m. Jan. 15, 1868, Chas.
          H. Rider.
     2  ADELBERT T., b. 1837; m. March 22, 1868, Emily M.
          Drake.

——————

06 (VII.) EBENEZER PRATT, of Bridgewater (son of VI.
          Cornelius), b. Feb. 7, 1797; d. May 7, 1880; m. May
          23, 1824, Olive S. Wood, still living (1887) in her 92d
          year.

     Children:
07   1  EBENEZER A.
     2  OLIVE S., b. June 22, 1831; m. April 25, 1854, Edwin
          Thompson, of Halifax.
08   PHILANDER, b. Feb. 3, 1825.

——————

09 (VIII.) EBENEZER A. PRATT, of Bridgewater (son of VII.
          Ebenezer), b. ——; m. Charlotte A. Soule.

     Children:
     1  EDWIN LEONARD, b. Nov. 22, 1800.
     2  LYMAN AUSTIN, b. Oct. 26, 1803.

00  710 (VIII.) SYLVANUS PRATT, of Bridgewater (son of VII. Leonard), b. Aug. 23, 1828; d. Dec. 6, 1866; m. Jane F. Fuller.

Child:

EDITH FRANCIS, b. Aug. 8, 1864; d. Dec. 26, 1866.

---

06  711 (VIII.) PHILANDER PRATT, of Bridgewater (son of VII. Ebenezer), b. Feb. 3, 1825; m. Sarah Leonard, June 9, 1850; she d. 1862. He m. (2) Bethia Spooner, April 6, 1864.

Children:

1 AMANDA F., m. Rev. Frank L. Higgins.
2 SARAH ABBIE, b. Dec. 17, 1852; m. Sept. 8, 1883, Fred M. Leonard.
3 HERBERT E., b. Sept. 28, 1857; d. Oct. 3, 1875.
4 LUCY OLIVE, b. Nov. 24, 1868.

---

06  712 (VII.) CORNELIUS PRATT, of Bridgewater (son of VI. Cornelius), b. ——; m. March 26, 1823, Lucina Thompson, of Halifax.

Children:

1 CORNELIUS, d. young.
14  713      2 OTIS, b. 1827.

---

13  714 (VIII.) OTIS PRATT, of Halifax (son of VII. Cornelius), b. ——, 1827; m. Emily Wood, 1850.

Children:

1 EMILY J., b. April 24, 1853; d. Oct. 2, 1873; m. Samuel O. Gurney, of Abington, Nov. 28, 1872.
2 LUCINA F., b. Aug. 1, 1855.
3 CORNELIUS, b. Oct. 13, 1859.

---

81  715 (IV.) NATHANIEL PRATT (son of III. Joseph), b. Nov. 23, 1701; d. ——, 1749; m. (1) Jan. 15, 1733, Sarah Snow, or Allen; she d. 1743; m. (2) Hannah, dau. of Lot Conant, Nov. 5, 1745.

Children by first wife:

717 716    1   SETH PRATT, b. June 21, 1729; d. Dec. 30, 1795.
           2   ANNA, m. John Packard, Oct. 7, 1760.

716 717 (V.)   SETH PRATT, Deacon (son of IV. Nathaniel), b. 1729; d. Dec. 22, 1795; m. Hannah Washburn, 1752; she b. Sept. 17, 1733; d. Aug. 26, 1834; she was a dau. of Captain Joseph Washburn, of Bridgewater. He is named as the residuary logatee and Executor of his Grandfather (III.) Joseph's will. For many years he was a selectman of Bridgewater, and a Deacon.

The following epitaph was placed on the stone, marking his grave in the Old Burying Ground at Bridgewater:

" Help Lord: for the godly man ceaseth; for the faithful fail from among the children of men."

Children :

725 718    1   NATHANIEL, b. Feb. 1, 1754; d. May 21, 1828.
795 719    2   JOSEPH, b. April 1, 1756; d. Jan. 8, 1835, at Brogwell, Canada.
           3   NEHEMIAH, b. Nov. 20, 1757; d. Aug. 3, 1778.
796 720    4   SIMEON, b. Sept. 16, 1759; d. Sept. 19, 1848.
           5   SETH, b. Sept. 8, 1761; d. young, at sea, 1796.
           6   SALLY, b. July 21, 1763; d. Aug. 12, 1778.
           7   HANNAH, b. Feb. 2, 1766; d. July 25, 1778.
831 721    8   CHLOE, b. Feb. 25, 1768; d. April 20, 1832.
838 722    9   SYLVANUS, b. May 20, 1770; d. Jan. 11, 1833.
843 723   10   JOANNAH, b. April 9, 1772; d. June 11, 1857.
844 724   11   ASA, b. April 23, 1774; d. Dec. 13, 1831.
         12   NEHEMIAH, b. Jan. 27, 1781; d. Feb. 18, 1784.

718 725 (VI.)   NATHANIEL PRATT (son of V. Seth), b. Feb. 1, 1754; d. May 21, 1828; m. Nov. 12, 1777, Elizabeth Washburn, b. Jan. 11, 1756; d. July 4, 1828; dau. of Ezekiel Washburn.

Children :

740 726    1   SALLY, b. Nov. 25, 1779; d Dec. 1, 1853.
745 727    2   HANNAH, b. Sept. 27, 1781; d. Oct. 28, 1851.
761 728    3   BETSEY, b. Sept. 19, 1783; d. Dec. 14, 1865.
          4   ENOCH,    } b. Sept. 21, 1786; { d. July 18, 1788.
764 729    5   ELIJAH,    }               { d. June 23, 1858.

|   |   |   |   |
|---|---|---|---|
|   |   | 6 | ALBERTINA, b. Nov. 4, 1788; d. April 15, 1866. Unmarried. |
| 733 | 730 | 7 | SETH, b. April 28, 1790; d. Nov. 21, 1879. |
| 787 | 731 | 8 | CHLOE, b. June 30, 1792; d. July 9, 1864. |
| 792 | 732 | 9 | NATHANIEL, b. April 9, 1795; d. April 25, 1842. |

---

730 733 (VII.) SETH PRATT (son of VI. Nathaniel), b. April 28, 1790; d. Nov. 21, 1879; m. Nov. 17, 1816, Lucinda Conant, b. Nov. 22, 1793, dau. of Deacon John Conant, d. Sept. 22, 1877.

Children:

| 737 | 734 | 1 | SETH, b. May 15, 1818; m. Dec. 23, 1839, Rachel Alden. |
|---|---|---|---|
| 738 | 735 | 2 | EDWIN, b. Jan. 18, 1820. |

---

735 736 (VIII.) EDWIN PRATT, of Bridgewater (son of VII. Seth), b. Jan. 18, 1820; m. Oct. 1846, Ann, dau. of Caleb Christian and Roxolana Dunbar.

Children:

1 FRANCES ANN, b. June 13, 1850; d. April 18, 1853.
2 FREDERIC C., b. June 3, 1857; m. March 3, 1882, Minnie A. Swift, b. March 9, 1859.
3 FRANK HEWITT, b. Dec. 15, 1859; d. May 15, 1870.

---

734 737 (VIII.) SETH PRATT (son of VII. Seth), b. May 15, 1818; m. Dec. 19, 1839, Rachel, b. March 30, 1818; d. May 5, 1886, dau. of Hosea Alden and Martha Howard of Randolph.

Children:

| | | 1 | WARREN B., b. July 16, 1841; d. July 5, 1842. |
|---|---|---|---|
| 739 | 738 | 2 | GUSTAVUS, b. Dec. 8, 1842. |

---

738 739 (IX.) GUSTAVUS PRATT (son of VIII. Seth), b. Dec. 8, 1842; m. Sept. 10, 1867, Sylvia T., dau. of Wm. Shockley and Delia Taber, of New Bedford.

Children:

1 GUSTAVUS W., b. May 31, 1869.
2 MARION, b. Feb. 24, 1873.
3 EDWARD T., b. Aug. 12, 1881.

726    740 (VII.) SALLY PRATT (dau. of VI. Nathaniel), b. Nov. 25,
              1779; d. Dec. 1, 1853; m. April 13, 1779, Isaac Swift,
              b. Nov. 22, 1779; d. Dec. 1, 1853; son of Jirah Swift
              and Lucy Keith.

       Children :

       1  SALLY SWIFT, b. Aug. 6, 1797.
       2  MELVIN SWIFT, b. Feb. 19, 1801.
       3  VAN RENSSELLAER, b. March 31, 1812.

------

727    745 (VII.) HANNAH PRATT (dau. of VI. Nathaniel), b. Sept.
              27, 1781: d. Oct. 28, 1851; m. Sept. 26, 1801, Seth
              Conant, b. 1780, son of John Conant and Deborah
              Conant (cousins).

       Children :

       1  ENOCH PRATT, b. March 6, 1803; d. Aug. 12, 1822.
       2  HANNAH, b. April 7, 1805.
       3  HEZEKIAH, b. Oct. 16, 1808.
       4  ALVIN, b. July 31, 1811; d. Oct. 21, 1820.
       5  LOUDIA, b. April 24, 1814; d. Oct. 22, 1835.
       6  SARAH ANN, b. July 12, 1816.
       7  SETH WILDER, b. March 16, 1822.  Killed in the Battle
              of the Wilderness, May 5, 1864.

------

728    761 (VII.) BETSEY PRATT (dau. of VI. Nathaniel), b. Sept. 19,
              1783; d. Dec. 14, 1865; m. David Waterman, b. April
              1, 1781; d. March 24, 1808, son of Elisha Waterman
              and Martha Benson, of Halifax.  She m. (2) Daniel
              Hudson, and (3) Calvin Keith, both of E. Bridgewater.

       Children :

       1  ANTHONY W., b. Oct. 18, 1804; d. April 17, 1862.
       2  LEONARD C., b. Jan. 18, 1815.

------

729    764 (VII.) ELIJAH PRATT (son of VI. Nathaniel), b. Sept. 21,
              1786; d. June 28, 1858; m. Jan. 7, 1813, Naoma Wade,
              b. Dec. 16, 1786, dau. of Robert Wade and Molly
              (Edson), of E. Bridgewater; d. March 22, 1862.

Children :

| | | | |
|---|---|---|---|
| 780 | 765 | 1 | BETSEY W., b. Sept. 11, 1813. |
| | | 2 | SUSAN L., b. March 27, 1815. |
| 785 | 766 | 3 | ENOCH, b. Sept. 12, 1817 ; d. Aug. 13, 1864. |
| 786 | 767 | 4 | LOUISA A., b. July 23, 1820. |

765 780 (VIII.) BETSEY W. PRATT (dau. of VII. Elijah), b. Sept. 11, 1813 ; m. Dec. 22, 1836, Periz F. Andrews, b. Feb. 20, 1813, in Livermore, Me.

Children :

1 SUSAN L., b. May 20, 1839.
2 SARAH F., b. Dec. 17, 1842.
3 AZUBA S., b. April 1, 1844.
4 EDGAR F., b. Feb. 2, 1847.
5 ELMER P., b. Feb. 2, 1850.
6 ELIJAH P., b. May 8, 1854.

766 785 (VIII.) ENOCH PRATT, of Bridgewater (son of VII. Elijah), b. Sept. 12, 1817 ; d. Aug. 13, 1864 ; m. Hannah A., dau. of John Maxum and Susan Pratt, of Wareham.

Children :

1 ENOCH W., b. April 13, 1845 ; d. Dec. 25, 1846.
2 NAOMI S., b. Aug. 29, 1847 ; m. June 4, 1866, Charles Stubbs.
3 ENOCH W., b. Aug. 8, 1849.
4 ATTOSA E., b. Feb. 19, 1851.
5 CELIA M., b. July 17, 1753 ; m. Sept. 29, 1869, Nahum Benson.
6 HANNAH L., b. March 20, 1855.
7 MARTHA N., b. Dec. 2, 1859.
8 LIZZIE E., b. April 30, 1858 ; d. Dec. 15, 1865.

767 786 (VIII.) LOUISA ANN PRATT, of Bridgewater (dau. of VII. Elijah), b. July 23, 1820 ; m. Aug. 30, 1841, Simeon Jordan, of Marshfield, b. Jan. 13, 1819.

Children :

1 SIMEON F., b. March 24, 1843 ; m. Aug. 1868, Harriet Washburn.
2 LOUISA A., b. June 6, 1849 ; d. Jan. 31, 1865.
3 SYDNEY L., b. April 1, 1856.
4 ANN L., b. July 19, 1860.

731 787 (VII.) CHLOE PRATT (dau. of VI. Nathaniel), b. June 30, 1792; d. July 9, 1864; m. April 18, 1813, Alvan Crossman, of Taunton, b. Feb. 1788; d. Dec. 1819; m. (2) Nahum Mitchell, b. Aug. 27, 1785, of E. Bridgewater, son of Bradford Mitchell, and resided at Raynham.

Children by first husband:
1  WILLIAM B., b. Oct. 3, 1813.
2  JULIANNA, b. Dec. 3, 1815.
3  An Infant, b. Aug. 24, 1818; d. Aug. 25, 1818.

---

732 792 (VII.) NATHANIEL PRATT (son of VI. Nathaniel), b. April 9, 1795; d. April 25, 1842; m. Lucy Thomas, b. March 21, 1788; d. June 6, 1856, dau. of Briga Thomas, of Marshfield.

Children:
1  SARAH D., b. May 18, 1818; d. Nov. 26, 1823.
2  ELIZABETH T., b. Aug. 24, 1819; d. Dec. 11, 1819.
794 793 3  NATHANIEL W., b. Jan. 19, 1821.
4  AUGUSTA, b. Sept. 22, 1825; d. Sept. 16, 1826.
5  AUGUSTA, b. March 20, 1828; m. Dec. 7, 1851, George Boylston, b. Aug. 1, 1825.

---

793 794 (VIII.) NATHANIEL W. PRATT (son of VII. Nathaniel), b. Jan. 19, 1821; d. ——; m. (1) June 10, 1843, Mary A. Boyd, of Boston, b. 1826; d. Dec. 1, 1857; m. (2) Sept. 16, 1860, Margaret W. Wardell, b. 1830, at Newcastle, Eng.

Children by first wife:
1  GEORGE H., b. Aug. 16, 1845.
2  NATHANIEL J., b. Jan. 6, 1848.
3  CHARLES A., b. March 20, 1852.

By second wife:
4  EMELINE W., b. June 30, 1861.

---

719 795 (VI.) JOSEPH PRATT (son of V. Seth), b. April 1, 1756; d. Jan. 8, 1835; m. Lucy French, of Conway, Vt.; he, after the death of his wife, removed to Chazy, in the upper part of New York State. He d. at Brogwell, Canada, 1835.

Children :

1 Francis.                3 Joseph.
2 Julia.                  4 Lucinda.

---

720 706 (VI.) SIMEON PRATT, Captain (son of V. Seth), b. Sept. 16, 1759; d. Sept. 25, 1848; m. Nov. 17, 1791, Sarah Willis, dau. of Judge Benjamin Willis and his wife Sarah, widow of Nathaniel Bradford, and daughter of Thomas Spooner, of Plymouth. Sarah d. Jan. 22, 1847, aged 79.

He was in the Revolutionary War, voluntarily enlisting when nearly two years younger than the age at which he could legally have been drafted.

He was with the troops under Washington during the investiture of Boston; was also stationed on Rhode Island, and at Fort William in Boston Harbor.

He was (for that period), a well educated and accomplished man, teaching school in the winter seasons, and working his farm in summer; being a good singer, a performer on the flute, and a genial, quick-witted companion withal, was much esteemed in the social circles of his day.

He was a keen politician of the Federalist school when party feelings ran high, and filled several offices in his town (Bridgewater) with acceptance.

Most of the above, as regards personal characteristics, I learned from the late venerable Judge Wilkes Wood, they having been quite intimate in their early manhood.                                    W.P.

Children :

802 797   1 Simeon, b. April 27, 1792; d. Feb. 25, 1876, at Halifax, Mass.

800 798   2 Charles, b. May 17, 1794; d. Dec. 29, 1863, at Pawtucket, R. I.

816 799   3 Henry Willis, b. June 6, 1797; d. Feb. 16, 1849, at St. Charles, Ill.

825 800   4 Sarah Spooner, b. April 9, 1803; d. Dec. 16, 1846, at Bridgewater, Mass.

830 801   5 Benjamin Willis, b. April 9, 1803; d. May 6, 1871, at Danville, Pa.

---

797 802 (VII.) SIMEON PRATT (son of VI. Simeon), b. April 27, 1792; d. Feb. 25, 1876; m. Nov. 15, 1815, at Pembroke, now Hanson, Alice Vinal Waterman, dau. of Nath-

aniel Waterman and Alice Vinal. His wife b. May 19, 1798, in Boston; d. July 16, 1855.

He was engaged during the business years of his life in iron founding at Freetown, Mass., Providence and Pawtucket, R.I.

He was one of those manufacturers who were instrumental in establishing what was known for many years as the "Old Colony List of Prices," an early form of protective union, which has since ripened into the "trusts" of the present day.

His later years were much occupied with genealogical researches, a fondness for which he inherited from his mother, dau. of Judge Benjamin Willis. These investigations were directed not only in the line of his own family, but also in the families of Bradford, Spooner, Willis, Waterman, Ware and Conant; this book contains some of the results of his labors.

Children:

805  803   1  WILLIAM, b. Sept. 10, 1816, at Halifax.
800  804   2  AROLINE PEABODY, b. Feb. 26, 1820, at Freetown.
           3  ELLEN, b. Nov. 27, 1823, at Providence; m. Oct. 15, 1863, John A. Carr, of Boston.

803  805  (VIII.) WILLIAM PRATT, DR. (son of VII. Simeon), b. Sept. 10, 1816; m. Sept. 27, 1843, Ann Elizabeth Eddy, dau. of Nathaniel Eddy and Abagail Andros, of Middleboro; she b. April 6, 1817.

He was for many years a dentist in Baltimore, Md., and is believed to be the first who successfully constructed a complete artificial roof to the mouth, and vibrating palate attached thereto. Failing health compelled the abandonment of his profession. Turning his efforts towards improvements in fire-arms, he was Superintendent of the Burnside Armory in Providence, R.I., during the civil war, and invented quite a number of improvements in arms and machines for their production. Was appointed aid to Gov. Jas. Y. Smith of R.I., with rank of Colonel.

Children:

1  ANN ELIZABETH, b. Nov. 4, 1845; d. March 1, 1862.
2  ALICE MAUD, b. July 25, 1849; d. March 29, 1869.
3  NATHANIEL WATERMAN, b. Jan. 31, 1852: m. June 10, 1880, Carrie Virginia Deudney, b. May 22, 1857, dau. of William Deudney and Fanny Wiggins of Rondout, N.Y.

Member of The Am. Inst. Mechanical Engineers, Am. Inst. of Mining Eng., Am. Naval Institute, etc.; lives in Brooklyn, N.Y.; Treasurer of The Babcock & Wilcox Boiler Co. of New York, and owner in the same. Is known at home and abroad from inventions in his special and other departments of Mechanical Engineering.

Children:

1 *August Goubert*, b. March 31, 1881.
2 *Arthur Dewbury*, b. Oct. 26, 1882.
3 *Penny Dewbury*, b. May 16, 1884.

---

994 996 (VIII.) AROLINE P. PRATT (dau. of VII. Simeon), b. Feb. 26, 1829; m. June 23, 1852, John Morton Soule, b. Sept. 16, 1819; son of Jabez Soule and Susannah Richmond, of Halifax.

Children:

1 SUSAN RICHMOND, b. May 12, 1853; d. Sept. 6, 1853.
2 CHARLES WATERMAN, b. Nov. 27, 1844; d. Dec. 2, 1862, at Newbern, N.C.
3 SUSAN RICHMOND, b. Nov. 15, 1846.
4 ALICE WATERMAN, b. Oct. 3, 1849.
5 MARY ALLERTON, b. Dec. 26, 1853.

---

796 996 (VII.) CHARLES PRATT, Captain (son of VI. Simeon), b. May 7, 1794; d. Dec. 26, 1853, at Pawtucket, R.I.; m. Oct. 16, 1821, Livonia Pope, b. Aug. 5, 1796, dau. of Freeman Pope, of Fairhaven, and Hannah Thayer, of Weymouth. His wife b. in Bridgewater.

He was one of the earliest recievers in New England of the theological teachings of Swedenborg, and to the close of his life an earnest advocate of the religion derived from them. He was a man of much culture, and of very logical habits of thought, a fine musician, and a man of singularly handsome and commanding presence.

Children:

1 CHARLES FREEMAN, b. Aug. 26, 1822; d. Oct. 26, 1823, in Bridgewater.
2 GEORGE, b. Oct. 24, 1823; d. Dec. 11, 1826, in Bridgewater.

| 813 | 810 | 3 | FRANCIS, b. March 1, 1825. |
| | | 4 | LIVONIA, b. Feb. 22, 1827; d. Feb. 27, 1829, in Swansea. |
| | | 5 | MARIA, b. Jan. 28, 1829; d. in Endfield; m. —— Green. |
| 814 | 811 | 6 | SARAH, b. July 6, 1831, in Endfield. |
| | | 7 | SARAH JANE, b. June 15, 1832. |
| 815 | 812 | 8 | EIMIAH, b. Feb. 22, 1839, in Bridgewater. |
| | | 9 | LOIS, b. Oct. 30, 1841; d. March 1, 1842, in Pawtucket. |

810  813 (VIII.) FRANCIS PRATT (son of VII. Charles), b. Feb. 22, 1827; d. ——; m. (1) June 16, 1849, Francis Tillinghast, b. May 15, 1828; d. April 3, 1853, dau. of Nicholas Tillinghast and Mary Jerold, of Pawtucket, R.I. He m. (2) June 6, 1860, Mary Elizabeth, b. 1829, dau. of Gideon South and Mary Whittier, of Pawtucket.

Children by first wife:

1  EMILY, b. Feb. 26, 1850.
2  CHARLES, b. Oct. 17, 1851.
3  MARY, b. March 3, 1853.

By second wife:

4  FRANCIS WHITTIER, b. Feb. 3, 1861; d. Sept. 13, 1861.
5  WILLIAM, b. May 27, 1863.
6  ANNA WENDELL, b. April 23, 1868.

811  814 (VIII.) SARAH PRATT (dau. of VII. Charles), b. July 6, 1831, in Endfield; m. Feb. 3, 1853, Smith W., son of Bela Clapp and Cynthia Carr, of Westboro.

Children:

1  MARIA, b. June 30, 1854; d. July 4, 1855.
2  CHARLES, b. Aug. 3, 1856; d. Dec. 11, 1870.

812  815 (VIII.) EDGAR PRATT (son of VII. Charles), b. Feb. 22, 1839, in Bridgewater; m. Jan. 23, 1868, Laura J., dau. of Rev. Chas. E. Titus, of Taunton; she b. 1845.

Children:

1  EDNA MARTHA, b. Nov. 3, 1869; d. April 14, 1871.
2  CHARLES EDGAR, b. March 24, 1873.

799 816 (VII.) HENRY W. PRATT (son of VI. Simeon), b. June 6, 1797; d. Feb. 16, 1849, at St. Charles, Ill.; m. Nov. 21, 1821, Clarinda (b. in Bridgewater, Oct. 23, 1799; d. Aug. 3, 1845, at St. Charles, Ill.), dau. of Daniel and Mary Leonard, of Bridgewater.

Henry Willis Pratt followed the business, for many years, of putting up and running machinery, mostly saw, lath, and shingle mills. On the 12th of January, 1830, before daylight in the morning, while clearing the sawdust away from under the circular saw of the shingle-machine he was then running at Halifax, Mass., he had his right hand taken off, leaving only the thumb and one joint of the forefinger. He went back into the same mill in June, and with that mutilated hand did vastly more than his share of manual labor for seventeen years.

Children:

819 817   1   WILLIAM HENRY, b. Sept. 6, 1822, at Bridgewater.
      2   HARRISON, b. Oct. 11, 1824; d. Oct. 9, 1825.
      3   LUCIUS, b. April 11, 1829; d. April 13, 1830.
      4   EDWIN LEONARD, } b. Feb. 11, 1831; { d. Sept. 9, 1833.
822 818   5   ELMIRA,                   { d. Jan. 25, 1832.

---

817 819 (VIII.) WILLIAM H. PRATT (son of VII. Henry), b. Sept. 6, 1822; m. Feb. 3, 1849, at Chicago, Ill., Elizabeth Matilda (b. in Halifax, Eng., April 3, 1823), of St. Charles, Ill., dau. of John S. Christian and Matilda Rainsforth. He, Christian, was born in camp, 1801, and was brought up on the Isle of Man. His father was a soldier in the English Army, and had his nose split at the battle of Waterloo.

William H. Pratt has done much toward gathering data relating to the genealogy of the Pratts. He is a prominent scientist of the West, being the Curator of the Davenport Academy of Natural Sciences, and one of its trustees. A man of great energy, and highly respected.

Children:

834 820   1   ELLA LOUISA, b. Dec. 29, 1849, at Tremont, Ill.
      2   LUCY MATILDA, b. May 3, 1851, at Tremont, Ill.
      3   MARY ELMIRA, b. Aug. 20, 1853; d. Sept. 5, 1862.
      4   FRANKIE LAURA, b. May 6, 1856, at Peoria, Ill.
823 821   5   CHESTER LOAMMI, b. Oct. 17, 1858, at Davenport, Ia.

818  822 (VIII.) ELMIRA PRATT (dau. of VII. Henry W.), b. Feb. 11, 1831; d. Jan. 25, 1882; m. Sept. 18, 1850, Isaac Wilson, Jr., of La Salle Co., Ill.

Children:

1  WILLIAM HENRY, b. Oct. 5, 1852.
2  EVA, b. Feb. 13, 1856.
3  CLARA, b. May 6, 1859; d. May 7, 1859.
4  ALONZO,  } b. Jan. 1, 1861; { d. Jan. 8, 1861.
5  MELISSA, }                  { d. Jan. 11, 1861.

818  823 (IX.) CHESTER L. PRATT, of Edmunds County, Dak. (son of VIII. William H.), b. Oct. 17, 1858; m. July 27, 1882, at Kansas City, Mo., Jennie Chandler, an adopted daughter of Hugh Garrett; she b. Sept. 30, 1864. He is now (1887) Register of Deeds, Edmunds Co., Dak.

Children:

1  CHESTER WILLIAM, b. March 8, 1885, at Ipswich, Dak.
2  GERTRUDE, b. Dec. 9, 1886, at Ipswich, Dak.

820  824 (IX.) ELLA LOUISA PRATT (dau. of VIII. William H.), b. Dec. 29, 1849; m. Sept. 14, 1871, George W. Jenkins, of Davenport, Ia. He is now (1887) an Attorney at Law at Aberdeen, Dak.

Children:

1  GEORGE, b. Aug. 16, 1872.
2  CHESTER, b. March 20, 1875.

800  825 (VII.) SARAH S. PRATT (dau. of VI. Simeon), b. April 9, 1803; d. Dec. 16, 1846, at Bridgewater; m. June 4, 1829, Capt. Jabez (b. March 20, 1797), son of Lieut. Samuel Harden, and Silence Fuller, of Bridgewater. He m. (2) widow Baker A. Josselyn.

Children:

1  GEORGE PRATT, b. July 29, 1830.
2  BENJAMIN H., b. March 23, 1833.
3  ALICE, b. Jan. 17, 1835; m. April 24, 1855, Albert K. Washburn.
4  ALBERT, b. Feb. 23, 1842; m. Elizabeth T. Jordan.

801  830 (VII.) BENJAMIN W. PRATT (son of VI. Simeon), b.
April 9, 1803; d. May 6, 1871, at Danville, Pa.; m.
May 23, 1832, at Halifax, Joannah Thompson Lucas
(b. April 17, 1809), dau. of Isaiah Lucas and Joannah
T. Waterman.

Children:

1 BENJAMIN HORATIO, b. Aug. 11, 1834, at Taunton;
m. May 9, 1866, Fanny A. Taylor, of Syracuse, N.Y.
He resides at Elmira, N.Y.
2 HENRY MARSHALL, b. Dec. 20, 1836, at Taunton; d.
Aug. 11, 1838, at Brooklyn, N.Y.
3 JOANNAH, b. May 17, 1842, at Williamsport, Pa.; d.
Dec. 11, 1848, at Lycoming, Pa.
4 AUGUSTA, b. March 25, 1844, at Lycoming, Pa.; m. at
Danville, Pa., Nov. 15, 1866, Robert A. Hall.
5 ADELAIDE, b. March 25, 1844.
6 GEORGE COX, b. Feb. 28, 1846; d. Sept. 1847, at Danville, Pa.
7 WILLIAM MAGILL, b. Aug. 25, 1852, at Danville, Pa.


721  831 (VI.) CHLOE PRATT (dau. of V. Seth), b. Feb. 25, 1768;
d. April 20, 1852; m. 1793, Jeremiah Conant, b. June
28, 1758; d. Jan. 21, 1825; son of John Conant and
Abigail Pratt.
He was a descendant of Roger Conant, who came
to New England in 1623, and lived in Plymouth,
Nantucket, Cape Ann, and Salem.

Children:

1 SETH, b. Oct. 3, 1796.
2 OPHER, b. Nov. 19, 1798; d. March 17, 1842.
3 MARSHALL, b. Jan. 5, 1801; 1801; m. Sept. 1, 1835,
at Pomfret, Vt., Roxana Darling, b. Oct. 1806. He
was Principal of the Normal School at Bridgewater.
4 LUCIA, b. March 5, 1803; d. Nov. 18, 1822.
5 ACHOAH, b. March 28, 1805; d. June 28, 1832.
6 THOMAS, b. Aug. 6, 1807.


722  838 (VI.) SYLVANUS PRATT (son of V. Seth), b. May 20,
1770; d. Jan. 11, 1833; m. June 26, 1803, Experience
Alden, b. Feb. 25, 1780, dau. of Oliver Alden and
Experience Leonard, of Bridgewater.

Children:

841  839  1 EXPERIENCE, b. July 21, 1804; m. Benjamin P. Pope;
              d. June 10, 1837.
842  840  2 MARY, b. May 6, 1809; m. Benjamin Crooker.

839  841 (VII.) EXPERIENCE PRATT (dau. of VI. Sylvanus), b.
         July 21, 1804; d. June 10, 1837; m. Benjamin P. Pope,
         of Bridgewater.

Children:

1 MARTHA A., b. July 13, 1825; m. George Perkins, of
  Bridgewater.
   Children:
   1 *Solomon*, b. Feb. 1, 1851.
   2 *Mattie L.*, b. Dec. 4, 1861.
2 LAURA, b. March 21, 1827; d. April 14, 1868; m. May
  15, 1853, Aaron Perkins, b. Feb. 28, 1830.
   Children:
   1 *Simeon*, b. Feb. 23, 1855.
   2 *Nellie M.*, b. Sept. 6, 1856; d. Jan. 12, 1860.
   3 *Manfred*, b. Feb. 9, 1858; d. Jan. 19, 1860.
   4 *Frank P.*, b. May 9, 1860.
   5 *Lizzie P.*, b. Nov. 1862.
3 SYLVANUS P., b. Dec. 1830; m. Jan. 28, 1858, Hannah
  Bonson, b. Oct. 6, 1834.
   Child:
   *Mary P.*, b. March 2, 1860.
4 NAHUM, b. Jan. 27, 1833; m. Mary E. Stetson.
5 HULDAH, b. Jan. 2, 1835; m. Alfred H. Perkins.

840  842 (VII.) MARY PRATT (dau. of VI. Sylvanus), b. May 6,
         1809; m. Benjamin Crooker, b. Jan. 11, 1807.

Children:

1 BENJAMIN T., b. June 27, 1833.
2 LUCIUS C., b. Nov. 18, 1838.
3 ELMER H., b. Dec. 4, 1841.
4 MARY E., b. July 30, 1846.
5 ANN F., b. Aug. 18, 1849.

723  843  (VI.) JOANNAH PRATT (dau. of V. Seth), b. April 9, 1772; d. June 11, 1857; m. (1) March 31, 1791, Adam Bessee, b. Feb. 7, 1770; d. 1793. He was a son of Nehemiah Bessee of Wareham; m. (2) 1797, Isaac Keith of Easton, a lineal descendant of Rev. James Keith, the first minister of Bridgewater, settled Feb. 18, 1664; he was b. Sept. 1, 1773; d. Dec. 1, 1843.

Children by first husband :

1  MARSHALL, b. Sept. 24, 1792; d. Oct. 23, 1842.
2  JOANNAH, b. May 8, 1793; d. Jan. 4, 1848.

Children by second husband :

3  PAMELIA, b. May 13, 1798; d. March 25, 1831.
4  EDWIN, b. Sept. 27, 1800; d. Dec. 19, 1860.
5  MARIETT, b. March 21, 1804.
6  PHILO, b. Sept. 8, 1806.
7  ASA PRATT, b. Dec. 12, 1808; d. Jan. 3, 1865.
8  HARRIETT, b. March 13, 1813; d. Jan. 1, 1854.

---

724  844  (VI.) ASA PRATT (son of V. Seth), b. April 23, 1774; d. Dec. 15, 1831; m. March 21, 1799, Lydia Sprague, b. Aug. 24, 1777; d. June 18, 1848.

Children :

847  845  1  HARRIET MILLER, b. Aug. 25, 1800.
848  846  2  LUCANNA TUCKER, b. March 6, 1804.

---

845  847  (VII.) HARRIET M. PRATT (dau. of VI. Asa), b. Aug. 25, 1800; m. (1) Sept. 18, 1821, John E. Howard, b. April 21, 1793; d. Aug. 21, 1854; he was a son of Hon. Daniel Howard, of West Bridgewater; m. (2) June 25, 1862, Benjamin B. Howard, of New Bedford.

Children :

1  HARRIET A., b. April 20, 1825; d. July 25, 1852; m. Oct. 28, 1847, Artemus Hale, b. Nov. 26, 1822; d. Dec. 30, 1853; he was a son of Hon. Artemus Hale, of Bridgewater.

Children :

1  *Caroline A.*, b. Feb. 18, 1850.
2  *Ellen*, b. July 16, 1852.

    2  WILLIAM R., b. May 15, 1837; d. March 20, 1828.
    3  JOHN E., b. July 7, 1830; m. Oct. 18, 1852, Ann
      Mitchell.

      Children :
      1  *An infant*, d. young.
      2  *Francis H.*, b. Aug. 22, 1855.
      3  *Frederic B.*, b. June 21, 1860.

    4  ELLEN E., b. Oct. 10, 1841; d. Feb. 6, 1842.

---

846- 848  (VII.) LUCANNA T. PRATT (dau. of VI. Asa), b. March 6,
    1804; m. April 1, 1822, Maj. Cushing Mitchell, of
    East Bridgewater; b. 1785; d. April 8, 1872.

    Children :
    1  LYDIA C., b. April 5, 1824; d. Sept. 16, 1824.
    2  SARAH H., b. May 1, 1831; d. Dec. 19, 1831.
    3  LUCANNA T., b. June 23, 1833; d. Oct. 17, 1833.

---

682  849  (IV.) BENJAMIN PRATT (son of III. Joseph), b. ——,
    1693; d. ——, 1762; m. Sarah (b. 1796), dau. of
    Henry Kingman, June 24, 1719; she d. Dec. 20,
    1767.

    Children :
853  850  1  BENJAMIN, b. 1719; d. about 1765; m. Lydia Harlow,
      1741.
853  851  2  NATHAN, d. 1750; m. Sarah Harlow, Oct. 15, 1745.
.51  852  3  JOHN, m. Martha Mehuren.
    4  BETHIA, m. Josiah Mehuron, Oct. 21, 1769.
    5  SUSANNA, b. 1738; d. Dec. 17, 1764.
    6  SILENCE, m. John Maxum, Sept. 15, 1748.
    7  ANN, m. Azariah Hayward, Aug. 28, 1768.

---

851  853  (V.) NATHAN PRATT (son of IV. Benjamin), b. ——;
    d. —— 1750; m. Sarah Harlow, Oct. 15, 1745; she
    m. (2) —— Perkins.

    Children :
    1  SARAH.
    2  ABIGAIL, m. Benjamin Benson, Sept. 27, 1770.
    3  BENJAMIN, m. Jan. 16, 1788, Olive Perkins.

852 854 (V.)  JOHN PRATT, of Bridgewater (son of IV. Benjamin), b. —— ; d. —— ; m. Martha Mehuren, dau. of Hugh.

Children :

1 MARTHA, b. June 18, 1750; d. Sept. 28, 1858.
2 OLIVE, b. Sept. 13, 1751; m. Lazarus Hathaway, Dec. 1, 1774.
3 LEVI, b. April 1, 1754; m. March 20, 1777, Mary Hathaway, of Middleboro.
4 JOHN, b. June 18, 1757; d. June 25, 1757.
5 BATHSHEBA, b. Sept. 22, 1759.
6 MARY, b. June 13, 1760.

---

850 855 (V.)  BENJAMIN PRATT (son of IV. Benjamin), b. ——, 1719; d. about 1765; m. Dec. 22, 1741, Lydia Harlow of Middleboro; she d. Aug. 4, 1807, aged 85 years.

He lived in South Bridgewater, on Titicut River near Woodward's Bridge, where he built a number of vessels of from 40 to 50 tons burthen, he being the captain of one of them and his son Benjamin of another. With these vessels they carried on a trading business between North Carolina and the West Indies, in cedar lumber, having bought a cedar swamp for that purpose. This they continued to do for several years, until he died in North Carolina, with three of his sons, of yellow fever (as is supposed). He was a man of good character and great enterprise.

Children :

1 BENJAMIN, b. April 25, 1745; d. of yellow fever in North Carolina.
2 CALVIN, b. April 29, 1749; d. of yellow fever in North Carolina.
3 NATHAN, b. April 3, 1751; d. of yellow fever in North Carolina.
860 856  4 WILLIAM, b. April 4, 1746 or 47.
947 857  5 LUTHER, b. Sept. 29, 1763; m. March 7, 1790, Theodorah Leonard.
960 858  6 NATHANIEL.
7 LYDIA, b. Jan. 29, 1753; m. Manasseh Tucker.
8 HANNAH, b. April 3, 1757; m. L. Shaw of Middleboro.
9 BETSEY or BETTY, b. Oct. 19, 1761.
851 859  10 SALLY or SARAH, b. Dec. 20, 1759.

(VI.) WILLIAM PRATT (son of V. Benjamin), b. April
6, 1746; d. June 4, 1808, aged 62 years; m. Mary
King, of Raynham, b. 1744; d. 1816, aged 72 years.

Few men of the age in which he lived possessed
his enterprising spirit, business tact, and energy of
character. He was a man of strong Christian principles, and died as he had lived, in the hope of
immortality. He left a large property. It is recorded
of him that at the age of twenty, hearing of the death
of his father and brothers in North Carolina, he went
there, and sold the vessels and cedar swamp which
they had owned, and after settling all their business,
he bought a horse, armed himself with a brace of
pistols for protection against robbers and rode home,
bringing with him a considerable sum of money, re-
sulting from the settlement of the property in North
Carolina. He lived in Titicut Parish, called North
Middleboro, where he bought a farm of one Boyce,
who bought of Chicatanbut, an Indian sachem. He
built a large house about 1782, and added to his
farm from time to time, until he owned nearly 400
acres. He built a number of vessels, and was the
captain of one of them for a few years. By permit
of the General Court, with Captain Edson he erected
a dam across the Great River, where he built on the
south side a grist mill, a saw mill, and a linseed-oil
mill (Captain Edson built several mills on the
opposite side of the dam). He kept a store, had a
blacksmith shop, also a shoe shop, near his house.
Besides these various occupations, he carried on
farming extensively. For many years he was captain
of the Militia Company of North Middleboro, and
on the receipt of the news that the English had
landed at New Bedford and set fire to the town, he
immediately marched his company to that place, for
its defence. He was a true patriot and a warm
supporter of his country's rights and the Declaration
of Independence. He was active in defence of his
country during the entire war of the Revolution.
His estate was valued at $18,410.99.

Children :

1   CALVIN, b. April 18, 1774; d. Oct. 10, 1821.
2   ISAAC, b. March 6, 1776.
3   SALLY, b. Dec. 26, 1778.
4   ENOCH, b. July 31, 1781.

889  865    5  GREENLEAF, b. May 13, 1783.
920  866    6  BENJAMIN, b. May 11, 1785.
921  867    7  WILLIAM, b. June 8, 1788.
922  868    8  ZEBULON K., b. Feb. 4, 1791.

---

861  869 (VII.) CALVIN PRATT, of Bridgewater (son of VI. William), b. April 18, 1774; d. Oct. 10, 1821; m. Jan. 23, 1790, Clarissa Keith, dau. of Lieut. Solomon and Louisa Keith, of Bridgewater, b. Jan. 23, 1777; d. Jan. 18, 1846.

He was a Justice of the Peace, a Representative to the General Court for several terms, a Captain of the Militia. In business he was very industrious and enterprising, and accumulated a large fortune.

Children:

1  GEORGE W., b. Feb. 2, 1800; killed in California about 1757; unmarried.
2  HAMDEN KEITH, b. Feb. 21, 1804; d. Nov. 27, 1882; m. Sept. 9, 1829, Sarah, dau. of Benjamin and Abigail Toby, and removed to Binghamton, N.Y.

    Children:

    1  *Benjamin*, lives in St. Louis.
    2  *Sarah*.

875  870    3  CALVIN B., b. April 15, 1806; m. Nov. 28, 1833, Mary T. Perkins.
          .4  WILLIAM H., b. July 6, 1808; d. in Binghamton; unmarried.
            5  SALLY KEITH, b. Oct. 4, 1801; d. June 8, 1886; m. Feb. 8, 1827, Jonathan Washburn, of South Bridgewater.

    Child: *Susan W.*

873  871    6  CHRISTIANA, b. Jan. 8, 1811; m. Nahum Washburn.
874  872    7  HENRY C., b. Dec. 15, 1814; d. Feb. 12, 1884.
            8  CLARISSA S., b. Oct. 18, 1818; m. May 17, 1842, Albert Washburn; d. March 29, 1843.

---

871  873 (VIII.) CHRISTIANA PRATT, of Bridgewater (dau. of VII. Calvin), b. Jan. 8, 1811; m. Nahum Washburn, b. ——— d. ———; she is now (1887) living in Bridgewater. He was a prosperous dentist for many years at South Bridgewater, widely known and highly respected.

Children:

1   CHRISTIAN, b. April 22, 1838; m. Salome Keith.
1   NAHUM, b. July 30 1839.
8   CLARA S., b. April 15, 1845.
4   GEORGE, b. April 22, 1850.

---

4 (VIII.) HENRY C. PRATT [COL.] (son of VII. Calvin), b. Dec. 15, 1814; d. Feb. 12, 1884; m. Mary Clita.

Col. Henry C. Pratt was a graduate of the Bridge-water Academy and the West Point Military Academy (from the latter in 1836). He served in the Mexican War under General Scott, and was in active service in the War of the Rebellion, and continued in the Army until retired in 1881.

Children:

1   MARY, m. General Small.
2   HENRY C., d. in Mexico, 1887; m. Bessie Conger, of Hot Springs.
3   SEDGEWICK, m. Martha W. Keith, of Bridgewater.
4   CLARA.
5   CHESTER.
6   EDDIE.

---

5 (VIII.) CALVIN B. PRATT (son of VII. Calvin), b. April 15, 1806; d. April 23, 1862; m. Mary T., dau. of Jacob and Mary Perkins, of South Bridgewater, Nov. 28, 1833; she b. Oct. 25, 1809; d. June 5, 1875.

He was a successful and respected physician of South Bridgewater.

Children:

1   MARY B., b. Sept. 15, 1834; d. March 5, 1874; m. Joseph E. Carver, Nov. 29, 1855.
2   HENRY T., b. Aug. 24, 1836; m. Sept. 11. 1867, Lucia Hooper; no children.
3   SARAH K., b. May 4, 1839; unmarried.
4   CLARA S., b. March 4, 1841; d. April 6, 1841.
5   CALVIN, b. March 24, 1842.
6   JONATHAN W., b. Feb. 9, 1854; He is the physician in charge of the Massachusetts General Hospital in Boston.

876  877  (IX.) CALVIN PRATT (son of VIII. Calvin B.), b. March
24, 1842; m. June 19, 1866, Adelaide Edstrom of New
York. He is a physician, having a large practice in
Bridgewater.

Children :

1  CALVIN BARTON, b. March 17, 1867.
2  EMILY LOUISE, b. June 12, 1870.
3  MARY BARTON, b. April 7, 1875.
4  ELISE ADELAIDE, b. April 26, 1882.

---

802  878  (VII.) ISAAC PRATT (son of VI. William), b. March 6,
1776; d. Dec. 3, 1864, at North Middleboro; he m.
May 19, 1804, Naomi Keith, dau. of Agatha (Bryant)
and Jeremiah Keith of Bridgewater; she was b. Sept.
11, 1785, and d. Jan. 28, 1867, and was much beloved
by all who knew her, on account of her generosity
and noble character.

The Boston Evening Traveller of Dec., 1864, refers
to Isaac Pratt as follows : —

"Our readers in Plymouth County will notice with
regret the announcement of the decease of the venerable
Isaac Pratt, of North Middleboro, who died on the 3d inst.
at the advanced age of eighty nine years. The active
business efforts of the deceased were for a time given to
the introduction and development of the nail manufacture, but he passed the great portion of his long life
upon his well-cultivated farm, in agricultural pursuits.
He was industrious, frugal and unostentatious, benevo-
lent and hospitable, a patron of educational and theological interests, a kind, hearty neighbor, a devout Christian
and public-spirited citizen. For more than seventy years
he was an exemplary member of the Congregational
Church. Although he adhered to the tenets of his faith
with a steadfastness characteristic of his Puritan ancestry,
he was neither bigoted, dogmatical, or ascetic; he was
conservative, but liberal in his views. * * * Mr. Pratt
will long be remembered as a fine type of a class now rapidly passing away — the sturdy, honest, liberty-loving
farmers of the early days of the Republic."

Children :

836  879  1  JANE GURNEY, b. March 16, 1805.
887  880  2  ENOCH, b. Sept. 10, 1808.
888  881  3  SUSANNA KEITH, b. Jan. 15, 1811.
907  882  4  ISAAC, b. June 27, 1814.
5  JEREMIAH K., b. Jan. 23, 1817; d. Feb. 26, 1823.

916  883    6  DAVID G., b. Dec. 19, 1819 ; d. Nov. 23, 1848.
917  884    7  NATHAN FREDERIC CASWELL, b. July 28, 1822 ; d. Dec.
               22, 1878.
            8  MARY P., b. Oct. 18, 1827 ; d. Jan. 1, 1829.

879  886 (VIII.) JANE GURNEY (dau. of Isaac), b. March 16, 1806 ;
               d. Oct. 29, 1884 ; m. George L. Oakes, a merchant of
               Boston, Mass., March 13, 1831 ; Mr. Oakes d. at
               North Middleboro, Feb. —, 1851 ; she afterwards
               resided at her father's house in Titicut, until her
               mother died. They had no children.

880  887 (VIII.) ENOCH PRATT (son of VII. Isaac), b. Sept. 10, 1808 ;
               m. Aug. 1, 1837, Louisa Martin, dau. of Samuel Hyde,
               of Baltimore, Md. They have had no children.

               He was in business in Boston until twenty-one
               years of age, and had at that time established a
               reputation for sagacity and business integrity be-
               yond his years. In 1831 he removed to Baltimore,
               and founded the firm of Pratt & Keith, in the iron
               business, followed by Enoch Pratt & Brother.

               In all his business Mr. Pratt has made a most
               remarkable success, becoming in a few years one of
               the wealthy merchants of Baltimore, a leader among
               the business men of his city in large enterprises.
               His property is estimated at several millions.

               His adopted city will always remember him for his
               noble gift of more than one million dollars to build
               and furnish the Enoch Pratt Free Library and its
               branches.

               Mr. Pratt has been a Director of the National
               Farmers and Planters' Bank for nearly fifty years,
               a Director and Vice-President of the Philadelphia,
               Wilmington and Baltimore Railroad Company for
               thirty years, a Director of the Savings Bank of Balti-
               more, one of the Board of Finance of the city, also
               a director of many charitable and industrial institu-
               tions. Mr. Pratt also endowed the Pratt Free School
               of Middleboro.

881  888 (VIII.) SUSANNAH KEITH PRATT (dau. of VII. Isaac), b.
               Jan. 15, 1811 ; m. Joshua B. Tobey, of Wareham, Oct.
               12, 1835 ; he was b. Feb. —, 1807 ; d. Dec. 25, 1870.

He was the president of the Tremont Nail Company, and the largest owner of its stock; also the president of the Wareham National Bank, besides being interested in many other corporations and branches of trade, in which he accumulated a very large fortune. He was the most successful merchant that Wareham has produced.

Children:

1  GIRARD CURTIS, b. Oct. 16, 1836; graduated from Harvard College, July 19, 1858. He is the president of the Wareham National Bank, also a director of The Boston Safe Deposit and Trust Company, and of the Pemberton Mills; he is also president and principal owner of the Tremont Nail Company.

2  HORACE PRATT, b. Jan. 4, 1838; graduated from Harvard College, July 19, 1858. He is the treasurer and general manager of the Tremont Nail Company.

3  THEODORE FEARING, b. March 31, 1840; d. ——.

4  GEORGE OAKES, b. Oct. 27, 1841; m. July 12, 1871, Blanche H. Waterman.

Children:

1  *Virgil*, d. young.
Two others living.

———

865  889 (VII.) GREENLEAF PRATT (son of VI. William), b. May 13, 1782; d. May 8, 1824, aged 42 years; m. Lucy Edson, b. Feb. 25, 1788; d. June 12, 1828; she was dau. of Polycarpus Edson, of Bridgewater.

He was a man of uncommon physical strength, of great decision of character, of stirring enterprise and activity, devoted chiefly to the culture of his farm, large-hearted, of generous hospitality, public-spirited, and an acknowledged leader among men.

In the war of 1812 he commanded a militia company, and was stationed at Plymouth. He succeeded to the homestead of his father William, and was a favorite son. When the church edifice was being erected, in 1806, an undertaking of a good deal of magnitude for that day, the father, who was on his dying bed, called for Greenleaf, and expressed the deepest anxiety lest he should meet with some accident. A strong personal attachment existed between himself and Zachariah Eddy of Middleboro, followed by frequent interchange of visits; the one was as distinguished for his law attainments as the other for his knowledge of and interest in agriculture, and the fruits of their study and experience were mutually helpful; this bond of union was strengthened by the dearest family ties, for each took his wife from the same family, which gave an unequalled domestic charm to their whole life. Everything moved under his watchful eye; the forests were levelled, lands were broken up and enriched, long lines of stone wall were built enclosing the fields, the store-houses were filled, oxen and cattle were in the stalls, and when the huge doors of his massive barn swung on their hinges it was interesting to witness the groaning loads as they moved in from the harvest.

In mature life, Mr. Pratt admitted the claims of a personal Saviour, and united with the Congregational Church in his native village. Ever active before in the support of public worship and in works of Christian benevolence, his purpose and hope were now peculiarly bright and firm. He died in the prime of his life, honored and lamented by all about him, and with his wife and several of the children, lies in the church-yard cemetery, his burial place near by his birthplace.

Children:

|     |     |   |                                                              |
|-----|-----|---|--------------------------------------------------------------|
|     |     | 1 | MARCIA EDSON, b. July 29, 1810; d. Aug. 7, 1825.             |
| 823 | 800 | 2 | LOUISA MARIA, b. Feb. 7, 1812; d. April 11, 1876.            |
| 897 | 801 | 3 | CHARLES KING, b. Aug 1, 1814.                                |
|     |     | 4 | A son, b. Dec. 28, 1816; d. one day old.                     |
|     |     | 5 | LUCY EDSON, b. June 30, 1818; d. Feb. 12, 1822.              |
| 900 | 802 | 6 | FRANCIS GREENLEAF, b. Jan. 30, 1821.                         |

---

800  803 (VIII.) LOUISA MARIA PRATT (dau. of VII. Greenleaf), b. Feb. 7, 1812; m. Lucius Junius Eddy, April 29, 1834; d. in Fall River, April 11, 1876.

Children:

1 CALEB FRANCIS, b. in Amherst, Mass., July 20, 1836; m. Georgiana Winslow, Nov. 29, 1860; resides in West Newton, and has a summer place in Middleboro.

He is a large dealer in coal at West Newton; also, with his son has an extensive hay and grain business in Boston, under the name of C. F. and G. W. Eddy & Co.

Children :

1  *George W.*, b. May 12, 1862.
2  *Louisa M.*, b. Dec. 20, 1863.
3  *Lillian*, b. Dec. 17, 1865.
4  *Clinton L.*, b. May 9, 1868.
5  *Frederick W.*, b. Dec. 27, 1869.
6  *Frank S.*, b. Sept. 27, 1871.
7  *Bertha,*  } b. Feb. 23, 1876.
8  *Bessie,*
9  *Clifford R.*, b. Nov. 25, 1877.
10  *Marion*, b. Sept. 29, 1879.
11  *Katharine Cleveland*, b. June 14, 1882.
12  *Ruth Winslow*, b. Oct. 14, 1883.

2 SARAH ELIZABETH, b. in Rockaway, N.J., Jan. 12, 1838; m. Dec. 13, 1865, George Parsons. He is a capitalist, having large interests in railroads and real estate. They reside in New York City, and have a summer home in Kennebunk, Me.

Children :

1  *Henry*, b. Nov 1, 1866.
2  *May Eddy*, b. May 18, 1868.
3  *Joseph*, b. Sept. 17, 1869.
4  *Charlotte*, b. April 21, 1871.
5  *William Usher*, b. Oct. 24, 1873.
6  *Mary Abby*, b. May 31, 1878.
7  *Louisa*, b. Jan. 17, 1880.

3 JOHN JACKSON, b. in Rockaway, N.J., May 2, 1840; m. Oct. 18, 1867, Katharine Cleveland, of Cleveland, O. No children.

Mr. Eddy is cashier of the National Exchange Bank, Boston, and resides at West Newton.

4 GEORGE STETSON, b. Jan. 22, 1843; m. (1) Emeline A. . Jones, Nov. 7, 1870; she d. Dec. 19, 1876. He m. (2) Mary E. Thompson, of New Britain, Conn., Aug. 6, 1879.

He graduated at Harvard Medical College, with honor, and went abroad for study in the hospitals. During the War he was a surgeon in the Navy, and has since had a very large practice in the city of Fall River.

Child by first wife:

1  *George S.,* b. Aug. 9, 1873.

Children by second wife:

2  *Joseph Thompson,* b. May 13, 1880.
3  *Lucina,* b. Dec. 4, 1882.
4  *Mary Eleanor,* b. May 13, 1884.

---

691  897 (VIII.) CHARLES KING PRATT (son of VII. Greenleaf), b. Aug. 1, 1814; m. June 1, 1841, Cordelia Williams, of Raynham.

Having accumulated a considerable fortune as a merchant in Fall River and Nantucket, he retired to Bridgewater, where he now resides.

Children:

1  CORDELIA WILLIAMS, m. Frank B. Keene, of Nantucket.
2  CHARLOTTE FRANCES, m. Joseph H. Church of Taunton, Jan. 20, 1876, and there resides.

Child:

1  *Charles W. Church,* b. May 30, 1888.

904  897a  3  CHARLES GREENLEAF, b. Nov. 1, 1852.
905  898   4  HERBERT, b. March 9, 1854.
906  899   5  WALLACE, b. June, 1856.

---

892  900 (VIII.) FRANCIS GREENLEAF PRATT (son of VII. Greenleaf), b. Jan 30, 1821; m. Sept. 8, 1846, Charlotte Elizabeth, dau. of Zachariah Eddy, of Middleboro.

He graduated at Amherst College 1840; teacher at New Bedford, 1840–41; Principal of Bridgewater Academy, 1841–43; member of Union Theological Seminary, New York City, 1844–45; graduated at Andover Theological Seminary, 1846; Pastor South Malden (now Everett) Congregational Church, 1849–58; preached at Peacedale, R.I., 1860–61; Resident at Eddyville, Mass., 1860–88.

Children:

1  ZACHARIAH EDDY, b. May 13, 1848; d. at Dover, N.H., April 9, 1850.
2  FRANCIS GREENLEAF, b. Aug. 8, 1850; member of the firm of Perry Mason & Company, publishers of "The Youth's Companion," Boston.

3 GEORGE WINTHROP, b. in Everett, Feb. 22, 1855; graduate of Normal School, Bridgewater, and of Phillips Academy, Andover, entering Harvard University, and leaving at the end of his Sophomore year on account of illness. He was for three years in the Editorial Department of the Boston Daily Advertiser.

4 A daughter, b. and d. May 11, 1858.

---

894 a 904 (IX.) CHARLES GREENLEAF PRATT, of Bridgewater (son of VIII. Charles K.), b. Nov. 1, 1852; m. June 20, 1883, Emma H. Hawley, of Bath, Me., b. April 20, 1855.

He has been engaged in the dry goods business many years.

Children:

1 ALICE, b. April 27, 1884.
2 MARION, b. March 27, 1888.

---

898 905 (IX.) HERBERT PRATT, of Bridgewater (son of VIII. Charles K.), b. March 9, 1854; m. April 22, 1885, Alice G. Copeland, of Brockton, b. Oct. 12, 1855. He is engaged in the dry goods business in Boston.

Child:

LILLIAN WARREN, b. Oct. 17, 1886.

---

899 906 (IX.) WALLACE M. PRATT, of Bridgewater (son VIII. Charles K.), b. June, 1856; m. Nov. 24, 1881, Ellen K. Keith, of Bridgewater. He is postmaster and has a general store in Scotland, Bridgewater.

Child:

HENRY WALLACE, b. Aug. 17, 1882.

---

882 207 (VIII.) ISAAC PRATT, (son of VII. Isaac), b. June 27, 1814; m. June 9, 1840, Hannah, dau. of Benjamin and Abby K. (Whitman) Thompson.

Mr. Pratt is a large capitalist and owner of real estate the city of Boston and suburbs, and has resided at Allston, for many years. Educated at the common school and Bridgewater Academy, at the age of 16 he entered his father's counting-room, where he remained until 1834; then for one year with Warren Murdock of Boston; was then connected with Benjamin L. Thompson, Long Wharf, becoming a partner in the firm in 1836; the business being chiefly the manufacture of nails, and dealing in hops. In 1866 he was elected a director in the Atlantic National Bank of Boston, and in 1869 its President, which position he now (1888) holds. He is also a director in the National Bank of Wareham, Mass. Mr. Pratt has been connected with several other enterprises, holding high positions in their management, and was in 1875 elected a representative to the Legislature from the Brighton and Newton Districts.

Children :

| | | | |
|---|---|---|---|
| 912 | 908 | 1 | ELLEN JANE OAKES, b. March 27, 1841. |
| 913 | 900 | 2 | ISAAC LOWELL, b. Oct. 18, 1843. |
| 914 | 910 | 3 | DAVID GURNEY, b. Nov. 7, 1848. |
| 915 | 911 | 4 | EDMUND THOMPSON, b. July 5, 1852. |
| | | 5 | MARLAND LANGDON, b. Dec. 3, 1857. |

---

908  912  (IX.) ELLEN JANE OAKES PRATT (dau. of VIII. Isaac), b. March 27, 1841; m. Sept. 23, 1863.

Children :

1  IDA BIGELOW, b. Dec. 21, 1864; d. Feb. 18, 1865.
2  HORATIO HARRIS, b. Aug. 16, 1866.
3  LESLIE PRATT, b. Dec. 30, 1869.
4  ELLEN HILDRETH, b. Nov. 29, 1871.

---

909  913  (IX.) ISAAC LOWELL PRATT (son of VIII. Isaac), b. Oct. 18, 1843; m. Emily L. Cutter, of Boston, Feb. 27, 1866.

He was a clerk in his father's office at 16 years of age, where he remained seven years, when he started in business for himself as agent for the Bridgewater Iron-Works, having for a partner Wm. B. Stetson, with whom he remained about eleven years. In 1881 he bought out the firm of W. G. Roby & Co., 52 Fulton St., Boston, where he now carries on a large business in metals.

Children:

1 LOWELL TYLER, b. Feb. 12, 1867.
2 STELLA, b. Feb. 4, 1870.
3 JOHN THOMPSON, b. April 6, 1871.
4 EMILY, b. Aug. 1, 1872.

---

910 914 (IX.) DAVID GURNEY PRATT (son of VIII. Isaac), b. Nov. 7, 1848; m. Nov. 26, 1873; Marion Grace Pratt, dau. of Thomas J. Pratt, of Titicut.

He was Boston agent for the Bridgewater Iron Works for several years; is a Trustee of the Pratt Free School in Middleboro, and is a Mason.

No children.

---

910 915 (IX.) EDMUND THOMPSON PRATT (son of VIII. Isaac), b. July 5, 1852; m. Oct. 16, 1878, Susanna K. Pratt, dau. of Thomas J. and Dordania K. Pratt of North Middleboro, Mass.

He was for several years selling agent of the Weymouth Iron Company. Has large interests in Boston real estate, and is a director in the Atlantic National Bank of Boston.

Child:

EDMUND, b. Feb. 18, 1883.

---

883 916 (VIII.) DAVID GURNEY PRATT (son of VII. Isaac), b. Dec. 12, 1819; He was partner of his brother Enoch Pratt in Baltimore in the iron business; d. Nov. 23, 1848, after a voyage to South America for his health, which had been for some time failing.

---

884 917 (VIII.) NATHAN FREDERIC CASWELL PRATT (son of VII. Isaac), b. July 28, 1822; d. Dec. 22, 1878.

He went to Boston at an early age, and was for a long time connected with the iron business there. Returning to North Middleboro, he lived with his father, and after the latter's death resided on the homestead.

863 918 (VII.) SALLY PRATT (dau. of VI. William), b. Dec. 26, 1778; d. ——; m. Sept. 13, 1801, Jeremiah, son of Jeremiah and Agatha Keith, and brother of Naomi, wife of Isaac Pratt.

Children:

1 MARY KEITH, m. Darius Weston, of Middleboro.
2 NAHUM, m. —— Williams, of Raynham.
3 NAOMI, m. William Eaton, of Middleboro.
4 JARED, m. Lucinda Eaton, of Middleboro.
5 SARAH.

---

864 919 (VII.) ENOCH PRATT, REV. (son of VI. William), b. July 31, 1781; d. ——, 1860; m. (1) April 27, 1809, Mary, dau. of Deacon Joseph Field, of Boston. She died suddenly, 1826, aged 44. He m. (2) Dec. 11, 1827, Mercy L., dau. of Capt. Joseph Snow, of Brewster. She d. March 13, 1839. He m. (3) April 18, 1840, the widow Lucy Alley, dau. of Deacon Brady Jenkins, of Barnstable.

He graduated at Brown University, Providence, R.I., 1803, and afterwards studied Theology with Dr. Kirkland in Boston. His first pastorate began Oct. 28, 1807, at the West Church in Barnstable, remaining there about thirty years, when he removed to Brewster, and continued to preach, supplying vacant pulpits, and as agent for Bible Societies, distributing the Scriptures through the country. He was in the ministry fifty-two years.

Children by first wife:

1 ELIZABETH F., b. March 4, 1811; m. S. S. Morris, of Newark, N.J., 1837.

Children:

1 Adelaide, m. Chas. Weeks, Oct. 3, 1863.
2 Clariene, m. Chas. Litchfield, of Brooklyn.
3 Elodra, m. Harriet Davis, of Albany, N.Y.

2 MARY R., b. Sept. 5, 1813; m. Ellison Congor, of Newark, N.J., Dec. 22, 1835.

Children:

1 Mary, d. 1863.
2 Emma, m. Jas. S. Creamer, of New York city.
3 Fanny, m. Leroy C. Emery.
4 Clara, d. Jan. 29, 1874.

3 SOPHIA B., b. May 4, 1819; m. Dr. Harlan Pillsbury, of Lowell, Mass., Sept. 7, 1842.

Children :

1 *George.*  2 *Edmund.*  3 *Samuel.*

4 JOSEPH W., b. April 25, 1821; went to California.

Children by second wife :

5 JOSEPHINE R. S., b. Nov. 6, 1828; d. 1830.
6 ENOCH H., b. Dec. 31, 1829; went to Marysville, California.
7 FRANCIS G., b. Nov. 14, 1831; d. 1833.
8 SARAH C., b. March 14, 1833; m. Walter Curtis, M.D.
9 FREDERIC S., b. Sept. 14, 1836; m. Phebe Smith, of Milburn, N. J.

Children by third wife :

10 GEORGE G., b. May 6, 1842.
11 CHARLES K., b. Feb. 8, 1844; d. Sept. 5, 1853.
12 IDA HYDE, b. Sept. 26, 1846; d. Jan. 2, 1847.

---

366 920 (VII.) BENJAMIN PRATT (son of VI. William), b. May 11, 1785; d. ——, 1833; m. (1) ——, 1809, Avis, dau. of Capt. James Shaw, of Paris, Me., where he settled as a farmer. He m. (2) in 1813–4, Almira Packard.

Child of Avis :

1 SIMEON AVIS, d. 1811.

Children of Almira :

2 AVIS KING, b. June 3, 1815; m. Charles Bemis.
3 ENOCH HARLOW, b. June 2, 1817; settled in Brookfield.
4 SERVETUS.
5 EMELINE, m. Henry Porter.
6 ZEBULON, settled in Chelsea, Mass.
7 BENJAMIN.
8 MARY, b. June 11, 1822.
9 SARAH, b. Dec. 21, 1823.

---

367 921 (VII.) WILLIAM PRATT (son of VI. William), b. June 8, 1787; d. Feb. 1, 1849, aged 62; m. Polly Keith, dau. of Captain Seth Keith of Bridgewater; she b. ——, 1786; d. Sept. 28, 1874.

He was a farmer and trader.

Children :

924 922     1   ALBERT G., b. July 24, 1811.
            2   WILLIAM, b. June 12, 1813; d. about 1854, on his way
                home from California.

927 923     3   ANTHONY S., b. July 20, 1815; m. 1840, Susan L.
                Holmes.
            4   POLLY or MARY K., b. Aug. 15, 1817; m. (1) Sampson
                King, 1839.

                Child :

                *Uriah S.*, b. 1839.
                   She m. (2) 1841, Charles H. Alden.

                Children :

                1  *Martha*, b. 1847.    2  *Sarah W.*, b. 1851.

            5   CASSANDRA, b. Dec. 25, 1820; m. Seth Washburn,
                Nov. 29, 1839.

                Children :

                1  *Ann.*              3  *Lucy.*
                2  *Seth B.*           4  *Edward.*

            6   MARIA LOUISA, b. May 13, 1834; d. Nov. 11, 1851.
            7   BETSEY, b. Feb. 6, 1826; m. (1) —— Perkins; m. (2) a
                brother of her first husband.
            8   JANE MINERVA, b. May 30, 1830; m. Gilman Keith
                and had two children.
            9   ALBERT K., b. Oct. 8, 1823; d. 1846.

            ———

922  924 (VIII.) ALBERT G. PRATT, of Bridgewater (son of VII.
                William), b. July 24, 1811; d. July 27, 1860: m. March
                5, 1834, Elizabeth White Parsons, of Middleboro, dau.
                of Loring and Betsey W.; she d. Oct. 12, 1882, aged
                68 years 11 months and 7 days.

                He was a prosperous farmer.

                Children :

            1   ALBERT HAMILTON, b. May 6, 1835; d. Nov. 5, 1880;
                unmarried.
            2   WILLIAM LORING, b. Nov. 8, 1836; m. Sept. 26, 1865,
                Harriet A. Russell; they are living in Lynn; no
                children.

931 925     3   FREDERIC GERARD, b. Aug. 18, 1839.
930 926     4   HARRISON O., b. Sept. 28, 1843; d. Oct. 29, 1874.
            5   FRANCANA E., b. June 24, 1841; m. Dec. 24, 1860,
                Luke Reed, of Middleboro; he d. July 10, 1861; no
                children.

6  AUGUSTA M., b. Sept. 29, 1845; d. an infant.
7  FLORA M., b. Jan. 13, 1848; m. Feb. 8, 1870, Edward
   P. Padelford.
   Child:
   *Gilbert H.*, b. Dec. 8, 1871.
8  IDA W., b. Feb. 19, 1850; m. Feb. 19, 1880, Cyrus
   White, of Jamaica Plain, Boston.

---

923  927 (VIII.) ANTHONY S. PRATT, of Bridgewater (son of VII.
              William), b. July 20, 1815; d. April 25, 1869; m. Jan.
              1, 1840, Susan L. Holmes, of Bridgewater.
              Children:
              1  SUSAN S., Jan. 6, 1841; m. Mark Phillips of East
                 Bridgewater.
929  928      2  ENOCH, b. Oct. 4, 1843.

---

928  929 (IX.) ENOCH PRATT, of Bridgewater (son of VIII. An-
              thony S.), b. Oct. 4, 1843; m. Lucretia E. Perkins of
              Middleboro, Nov. 18, 1874, and moved to Middleboro.
              He is a successful boot and shoe manufacturer at
              Titicut.
              Child:
              1  MIRIAM E., b. March 20, 1876.

---

926  930 (IX.) HARRISON O. PRATT, of Middleboro (son of VIII.
              Albert G.), b. Sept. 28, 1843; d. Dec. 31, 1874; m. Sept.
              14, 1869, Corda E., dau. of Elijah E. and Elizabeth
              (Hall) Perkins.
              Child:
              1. HARRY S., b. March 4, 1874.

---

925  931 (IX.) FREDERIC GERARD PRATT, of Middleboro (son
              of VIII. Albert G.), b. Aug. 18, 1839; d. May 14, 1870;
              m. Nov. 3, 1869, Ellen Washburn of Bridgewater.
              He moved to Jersey City, N.J., and d. there.
              Children:
              1  ELLEN LEORA, b. Sept. 20, 1870.
              2  EDITH FORRESTER, b. April 11, 1872.

868 932 (VII.) ZEBULON K. PRATT (son of VI. William), b. Feb. 4
1791; d. May 5, 1859; m. Feb. 22, 1815, Susanna, dau.
of Jeremiah and Agatha Keith, and sister of Naomi
Keith, wife of Isaac Pratt, and Jeremiah Keith, husband of Sally Pratt; she (Susanna) b. Jan. 29, 1796;
d. Jan. 11, 1857.

He owned and successfully managed a large farm;
was twice a member of the Massachusetts Legislature; a mason, and was highly respected as a citizen.
He died at St. Peter, Minn., May 5, 1859.

Children :

939 933   1  ZEBULON, b. Jan. 8, 1816.
942 934   2  PHILIP C., b. April 19, 1818; d. July 24, 1850, in
           California.
943 935   3  BENJAMIN F., b. Sept. 20, 1820; d. Feb. 8, 1870.
         4  SUSAN E., b. Feb. 14, 1823; d. Feb. 25, 1823.
944 936   5  THOMAS J., b. Sept. 10, 1826.
945 937   6  JEREMIAH K., b. Nov. 24, 1829.
946 938   7  MARTIN VAN BUREN, b. April 21, 1835.

---

933 939 (VIII.) ZEBULON PRATT, of Bridgewater (son of VII.
Zebulon K.), b. Jan. 8, 1816; m. April 5, 1842, Matilda Hathaway; she d. May 22, 1880, aged 58.

He was for many years engaged in the book business, and accumulated a large property; he resided
formerly at Titicut, but removed to Bridgewater
some twenty years ago.

Children :

  1  SUSAN M., b. Oct. 26, 1843; m. Nov. 11, 1862, Jared F.
     Alden of Middleboro. Three children.
  2  EMMA A., b. Jan. 14, 1846; unmarried.
  3  BETSEY H., b. Sept. 28, 1850; m. Nov. 10, 1869,
     George M. Loach, of Raynham. She d. ——.
     Children :

     1  *Frank A.*, b. 1870.
     2  *Walter M.*, b. 1873.
     3  *Corn M.*, b. 1875.
     4  *Sadie*, b. April 19, 1877.

  4  CORA A., b. Feb. 19, 1854; d. young.
941 940   5  ADRIAN Z., b. May 6, 1856.
  6  LUCY A. S., b. Nov. 16, 1858; m. Dec. 14, 1881, Henry
     M. Lane, of Taunton. They live at Evanston, Ill.

940 941 (IX.) ADRIAN Z. PRATT, of Bridgewater (son of VIII. Zebulon), b. May 6, 1856: m. Nov. 24, 1881, Jennie Mabel Copeland. He is in business at Bridgewater.

Children:
1 Esther M., b. Oct. 29, 1880.
2 Emma A., b. May 2, 1882.
3 Lucy M., b. July 12, 1886.
4 Zebulon, b. 1887.

---

934 942 (VIII.) PHILIP C. PRATT (son of VII. Zebulon K.) b. April 19, 1818; d. July 24, 1850, in California; m. June 20, 1839, Keziah L. Hathaway.

Children:
1 Philip H., b. 1839; d. 1841.
2 Arthur J., b. 1844.

---

935 943 (VIII.) BENJAMIN F. PRATT (son of VII. Zebulon K.), b. Sept. 20, 1820; d. Feb. 8, 1870; he was not married. He was engaged with his brother Zebulon in the book trade; and afterwards went to St. Peter, Minn., where he dealt in real estate.

---

936 944 (VIII.) THOMAS J. PRATT (son of VII. Zebulon K.), b. Sept. 10, 1826; m. Sept. 15, 1848, Dordania K. Pratt dau. of Otis Pratt. In early life he was in the book business with his brothers. He inherited the old homestead and has resided there for many years.

Children:
1 Marion Grace, b. Feb. 24, 1852; m. David G. Pratt.
2 Susanna K., b. April 23, 1858: m. Edmund T. Pratt.

---

937 945 (VIII.) JEREMIAH K. PRATT, of Middleboro (son of VII. Zebulon K.), b. Nov. 24, 1829; m. May 17, 1858, Annie M., dau. of Otis and Catherine Pratt, and sister of Dordania K. Pratt.

He has been engaged in the selling of books in Pittsburg and in other cities, with his brothers for many years, and has been very successful, having acquired a large property.

Children :

1  FREDERICK STANTON, b. April 15, 1859; d. Oct. 29, 1874.
2  BENJAMIN F., b. July 17, 1863; m. June 12, 1888, Amelia, dau. of Stephen Davis, of Campello.
3  CHESTER THOMAS, b. March 25, 1866; d. Feb. 29, 1876.
4  NORMAN, b. July 12, 1870.
5  ELLEN PERCY, b. May 31, 1871; d. April 8, 1876.
6  GEORGE N., b. May 4, 1876; d. Sept. 12, 1877.

---

938  946  (VIII.) MARTIN VAN BUREN PRATT (son of VII. Zebulon K.), b. April 21, 1835; m. (1) June 13, 1865, Susan E., dau. of Solomon Alden, of Bridgewater; she d. 1867. He m. (2) July 5, 1871, Rebecca Wing, dau. of Henry and Sally Dyer.

He has been associated with his brothers in the sale of books during the winter seasons, residing in the summer at Titicut.

Children by Susan E. :

1  EMILY ALDEN, d. young.
2  MARTIN, b. May 5, 1867.

Children by Rebecca :

3  JOSEPH HENRY, b. Dec. 5, 1872.
4  An infant, d. in 1875.
5  CHESTER MAYO, b. Jan. 6, 1878.

---

867  947  (VI.) LUTHER PRATT, of Maine (son of V. Benjamin), b. Sept. 29, 1763, in Bridgewater, Mass.; d. 1818; m. March 7, 1790, Theodorah Leonard; she d. 1818. They moved to Paris, Maine.

Children :

1  BETSEY, m. Jacob Winslow.
962  948  2  LEONARD, m. Sally Gibson.
3  POLLY.
963  949  4  CALVIN, b. May 17, 1797; m. Deborah Barrows.
5  MARTIN, d. 1827.
6  SALLY, b. 1801; m. —— Ricker, of Poland.
7  ELIZA, b. Aug. 12, 1804; m. Nov. 4, 1825, Ansel Cushman, of Hebron.
8  NANCY, b. 1806; m. Stephen Mitchell.

858 950 (VI.) NATHANIEL PRATT (son of V. Benjamin), b. ——;
m. Lucy Shaw, and removed to Paris, Maine, then a
wilderness, but now the shire town of Oxford County.

Children:

1 NATTY (NATHANIEL)
2 NATHAN.
3 SERENA (CYRENE), m. David Andrews.
4 LUCY, b. July 17, 1797; m. Wm. Cummings.
5 LYDIA, b. April 15, 1801; m. (1) Moses Cummings;
(2) Daniel Cummings.
6 ABIGAIL, m. David Andrews.

859 951 (VI.) SARAH PRATT (dau. of V. Benjamin), b. Dec. 20,
1759; d. Aug. 1836; m. Feb. 1779, Judge Samuel Paris,
and removed to Hebron, Me.   He b. Aug. 31, 1755;
d. Sept. 1847.

When they moved to Maine, the spot on which they
settled was an unbroken wilderness, but was subsequently incorporated as a town.  He, by great industry
and honesty, acquired a prominent position in the
community.  He served in the Revolutionary War
both on land and sea; was the first representative of
the town to the General Court of Massachusetts, and
was repeatedly re-elected.  In 1805 he was appointed
one of the Judges of the Court of Common Pleas.  In
1812, a Presidential Elector.

Child: .

ALBION K., b. Jan. 1788; m. 1810, Sarah Whitman.
He became a very prominent citizen, holding some
of the highest offices in the gift of the town, state,
and national government.

948 952 (VII.) LEONARD PRATT, of Paris, Me. (son of VI. Luther),
b. ——; d. 1826; m. Sarah Gibson, of Waterford, Me.
She m. (2) Thomas Dunham, of Hebron, Me.

Children:

1 MARY JANE, m. (1) Ether Dooring; (2) Robert Skillings.
2 SARAH, d. young.

9 953 (VII.) CALVIN PRATT, of Paris, Me. (son of VI. Luther), b. May 17, 1797; d. May 15, 1871; m. Oct. 22, 1799, Deborah, dau. of Ansel Barrows, of Granby, Vt.

> Her father lived in a log hut when he came to Paris. She survived her husband, and was living (1884) with her son at West Paris.

Children:

5 954   1 OLIVER LEONARD, b. May 2, 1820.
     2 THEODORA LEONORA, b. April 20, 1822; m. Richard H. Jordan, of Bethel.
     3 HANNAH ELLIOT, b. March 31, 1829; m. John C. Warren.

------

4 955 (VIII.) OLIVER L. PRATT, of West Paris, Maine (son of VII. Calvin), b. May 2, 1820; m. May 10, 1841, Elizabeth Fuller, of Woodstock, dau. of Lewis and Betsey (Dunham).

Children:

8 956   1 ANSEL BARROWS, b. May 1, 1842.
9 957   2 LLEWELLYN, b. Nov. 12, 1849.
     3 MARY ANGELINE, b. Jan. 18, 1854; m. Julian F. Young.

------

6 958 (IX.) ANSEL BARROWS PRATT, of West Paris, Mo. (son of VIII. Oliver L.), b. May 1, 1842; m. (1) Elizabeth Cotton, of Woodstock, dau. of John; m. (2) widow Nuttie Barnum.

Children:

     1 LIZZIE AGNES, b. Dec. 31, 1866.
     2 ELIZA JANE, b. June 12, 1873, at Ashland, Mass.

------

57 959 (IX.) LLEWELLYN PRATT, of West Paris, Me. (son of VIII. Oliver L.), b. Nov. 12, 1849; m. Nov. 8, 1871, Pauline Murdock, dau. of Eliab C.

Children:

     1 SARAH MAUDE, b. Oct. 10, 1872.
     2 LEONARD MURDOCK, b. Aug. 30, 1879.

683 960 (IV.) SOLOMON PRATT, of Bridgewater (son of III. Joseph), b. ——, 1696; d. July 26, 1757; m. Jan. 27, 1719, Sarah Johnson, dau. of Isaac. He was a Deacon.

Children:

    1  SARAH, b. Nov. 22, 1721; m. Nathan Perkins, April 2, 1752.

    2  ABAGAIL or ABIEL, b. Dec. 3, 1724; m. John Conant, March 3, 1745-6.

    3  MARY, b. March 6, 1727; m. Thos Perkins, Jr., April 5, 1748.

964 961   4  SOLOMON, b. Feb. 20, 1729.

965 962   5  EBENEZER, b. March 3, 1731; m. Jan. 19, 1758, Abial, widow of John Alger, dau. of John Johnson; he m. (2) Aug. 8, 1760, Bulah Washburn. He settled in Middleboro.

    6  HANNAH, b. Sept. 12, 1733; m. Timothy Hayward, July 16, 1767.

978 963   7  ISAAC, b. May 15, 1736; m. Catherine Caswell, Sept. 5, 1758.

    8  DANIEL, b. March 3, 1741; m. Mary Patten of Connecticut. He d. 1778, a soldier.

---

961 964 (V.) SOLOMON PRATT, of Bridgewater (son of IV. Solomon), b. Feb. 20, 1728-9; d. ——; m. Dec. 3, 1761, Mary Keith, of Bridgewater; d. Nov. 7, 1764, dau. of John Keith. He m. (2) Abigail, dau. of James Hooper, June 11, 1767.

Children:

    1  MARY, b. Sept. 15, 1762; m. Ebenezer Perkins, 1782.

    2  SOLOMON, b. Oct. 26, 1764; d. Dec. 13, 1764.

    3  NANCY, b. ——; m. Timothy Conant, 1788.
And others.

---

962 965 (V.) EBENEZER PRATT (son of IV. Solomon), b. March 3, 1731; d. ——; He b. at Bridgewater, but removed to Middleboro. He m. Jan. 19, 1758, Abiel, widow of John Alger, dau. of John Johnson. She d. Sept. 30, 1759. He m. (2) Aug. 8, 1760, Bulah Washburn.

Children:

    1  MARGARET, b. Oct. 8, 1758; d. Sept. 8, 1800.

    2  JOHN, b. May 30, 1760.

3  OLIVE, b. June 14, 1762.
4  LUCY, b. April, 20, 1764; d. April 2, 1790.
968  966    5  EBENEZER, b. May 16, 1766; m. Elizabeth Norcutt,
May 4, 1787.
6  LEWIS, b. March 19, 1768.
7  THOMAS, b. Nov. 7, 1771.
969  967    8  THOMAS, b. March 15, 1775; d. May 22, 1804.

---

966  968  (VI.) EBENEZER PRATT, of Middleboro (son of V.
Ebenezer), b. May 16, 1766; d. before 1820; m. May 4,
1757, Elizabeth Norcutt.

Children:

1  SELEUDAH, b. May 16, 1787.
2  THOMAS, b. April 19, 1789 (Plymouth Records); a
soldier in 1813.
3  EBENEZER, b. Aug. 25, 1791.
4  BETSEY, b. May 4, 1794.
5  SAMUEL, b. Aug. 22, 1796.
6  JAMES, b. Aug. 6, 1798.
7  DANIEL, b. Jan. 7, 1801.
8  WYBRIA, b. Aug. 4, 1803.
9  BENONI.
10  ANDREW, b. Jan. 1813; d. Jan. 12, 1866 (unmarried).

---

967  969  (VI.) THOMAS PRATT, of Middleboro (son of V. Ebenezer), b. March 15, 1775; d. May 22, 1864, of extreme
old age; m. Lydia Macomber, Sept. 13, 1798; d. Dec.
11, 1856; aged 77 years and 9 months.

Children:

1  OLIVE, b. Oct. 29, 1799; d. Sept. 4, 1800.
2  LYDIA, b. July 5, 1801.
3  THOMAS, b. Jan. 11, 1803; d. Dec. 4, 1809.
973  970    4  SIMEON MACOMBER, b. Oct. 2, 1805.
5  OLIVE, b. March 11, 1808; m. Oct. 21, 1834, Darius
Wentworth, and went to Bridgewater.
6  EUNICE, b. March 24, 1810; d. May 27, 1811.
7  LOUISA JANE, b. May 11, 1812.
972  971    8  THOMAS ADDISON, b. Nov. 19, 1814; m. Ruth C. Bradford.

971  972  (VII.) THOMAS ADDISON PRATT, of Middleboro (son of VI. Thomas), b. Nov. 19, 1814; m. Ruth C. Bradford. He owns a farm near Middleboro Four Corners.

Children:

1  EUNICE ADLEY, b. March 5, 1837.
2  MARY AMABELLA, b. Feb. 20, 1841; m. May 10, 1863, Joseph Morrison.

---

970  973  (VII.) SIMEON M. PRATT, of Middleboro (son of VI. Thomas), b. Oct. 2, 1805; m. (1) Betsey Leach, Sept. 5, 1837; m. (2) Irene S. Bradford.

He is a prosperous farmer, living near his brother Thomas A.

Children:

1  BETSEY LEACH, b. March 17, 1839.
2  IRENE BRADFORD, b. Oct. 26, 1844; d. Oct. 2, 1859.
976  974  3  SIMEON L., b. May 16, 1847.
977  975  4  LUTHER BRADFORD, b. Dec. 2, 1850.
5  IRENE BRADFORD, b. Sept. 22, 1866.

---

974  976  (VIII.) SIMEON L. PRATT, of Middleboro (son of VII. Simeon M.), b. May 16, 1847; m. Dec. 17, 1869, Mary J. Banks, of Ireland, dau. of Thomas and Elizabeth, b. 1850. He m. (2), Oct. 23, 1880, Bertha S. B. Savory, of Cleveland, Ohio.

He is a farmer, and lives on the old homestead.

Children of Mary J. :

1  ADAM, b. Dec. 18, 1870.
2  IRENE S., b. June 15, 1876.

Children of Bertha:

3  BERTHA, b. Nov. 26, 1880.
4  GERTRUDE B., b. Jan. 28, 1882.
5  ALABRANTOE, b. Feb. 19, 1883.
6  ALMEDA, b. July 13, 1884.
7  LEWIS, b. Oct. 14, 1885.
8  A daughter, b. Dec. 1886.

77 (VIII.) LUTHER BRADFORD PRATT, of Middleboro (son of VII. Simeon M.), b. Dec., 1850; m. Nov. 25, 1875, Lizzie C. Swift, of Sandwich.

Child:

1  ERNEST SUMNER, b. April 30, 1885.

---

78  (V.) ISAAC PRATT, of Middleboro (son of IV. Solomon), b. May 15, 1736; d. ——; m. Sept. 5, 1758, Katharine Caswell.

Children:

1  SARAH, b. Jan. 7, 1759.
2  KATHARINE, b. Nov. 14, ——; m. Jan. 17, 1781, Jeremiah Thayer.
3  SERDINE, b. Aug. 16, ——.
4  LUVINE, b. July 23, 1764.
5  LOIS, b. Feb. 24, 1766.
6  HANNAH, b. March 28, 1768,
7  BETHIA } b. March 27, ——.
8  LUCY }

---

79  (IV.) DAVID PRATT (son of III. Joseph 2d), b. 1708; d. 1799; m. (1) April 30, 1722, Joannah Allen, and settled in East Bridgewater. He m. (2), widow Anna (Bryant) Leonard, Jan. 31, 1738.

Children by first wife:

1  JEREMIAH, b. May 16, 1722.
2  REBECKAH, b. Oct. 31, 1724; m. Elisha Allen, 1745.
3  JOANNAH, b. Oct. 26, 1726; m. Phineas Conant, Sept. 26, 1749.
4  DORCAS, b. March 16, 1729; m. James Lovell, Nov. 28, 1754.
90  5  DAVID, b. Sept. 29, 1730; m. Abigail Bondage.
6  DEBORAH, b. May 16, 1732; m. Dec. 10, 1751, Josiah Orcutt.
81  7  ABNER, b. Nov. 4, 1734; m. Aug. 28, 1764, Martha (Byram) Carey.

Children by second wife:

8  RUTH, b. Nov. 24, 1740; m. May 27, 1762, Obadiah Bates.
9  MARTHA, b. July 10, 1742.

1001 962    10   PETER, b. April 10, 1746; m. Amy ——.
           11   ANN, b. Nov. 24, 1747.
           12   THOMAS, b. Oct. 15, 1750; m. —— Morton, and settled at Titicut.

---

980 983   (V.)   DAVID PRATT, of E. Bridgewater (son of IV. David), b. Sept. 29, 1730; d. Jan. 1, 1810; m. April 12, 1753, Abigail Bowditch, b. 1730; d. Aug. 5, 1783, dau. of Wm. Bowditch. He m. (2) July 5, 1784, widow Phebe Atwood (Gloyd), of Abington; she d. Oct. 28, 1817, aged 70. He was a farmer, and quite prominent.

Children:

         1   MARY, b. Feb. 21, 1756; m. 1783, Joshua Pratt.
987 984      2   OLIVER, b. Sept. 9, 1757; d. Jan. 20, 1832.
         3   JEREMIAH, b. July 14, 1760 (moved away).
         4   WILLIAM, b. March 22, 1763.
         5   ALLEN, b. March 14, 1866; d. June 2, 1843. He m. and settled in the ministry at Westmoreland, N.H., where he preached fifty years. His dau. Persis, b. May 9, 1794; m. Moses Dudley.
988 985      6   DAVID, b. 1787; d. 1817.
990 986      7   ISAAC, b. 1790.

---

984 987   (VI.)   OLIVER PRATT, of East Bridgewater (son of V. David), b. Sept. 9, 1757; d. Jan. 20, 1832; m. (1) May 17, 1787, Susanna Lowden, dau. of Nathaniel; she d. 1802, aged 36. He m. (2) July 22, 1803, Rebecca Ford; she d. Dec. 1, 1821, aged 61. He m. (3) May 19, 1823, Thankful Ford; she d. Jan. 27, 1844, aged 77. He was a farmer.

Children:

         1   ALLEN, b. ——; a mariner and shipmaster.
         2   SUSANNA, 1794; d. June 22, 1816.

---

985 988   (VI.)   DAVID PRATT, of East Bridgewater (son of V. David), b. 1787; d. Sept. 30, 1817; m. Nov. 23, 1815, Mary Hobart, dau. of Seth; she d. Jan. 24, 1824. He was a farmer and carpenter.

Child:

1003 969       DAVID, b. April 15, 1817.

986 990 (VI.) ISAAC PRATT, of East Bridgewater (son of V. David), b. May 9, 1790; d. Jan. 27, 1875; m. 1813, Nancy Pratt, of Carver; she b. Feb. 4, 1789; d. April 11, 1871.

He was a selectman and assessor for many years; a farmer and very prominent in the town, serving in the legislature several sessions.

Children:

993 901  1 GEORGE H., b. April 18, 1813.
908 902  2 OLIVER, b. Dec. 30, 1816.
         3 NANCY, b. Nov. 20, 1819; d. young.

---

991 993 (VII.) GEORGE H. PRATT, of East Bridgewater (son of VI. Isaac), b. April 18, 1813; m. 1833, Sarah D. Prouty, b. Feb. 25, 1811. He is a farmer, and has been prosperous.

Children:

         1 Nancie W., b. Nov. 12, 1834; m. Jan. 1, 1871, Lemuel Pratt.
         2 MARY F., b. Feb. 3, 1841; m. June 11, 1859, Marshall N. Humble.
996 994  3 ISAAC S., b. April 27, 1843.
         4 MARIA A., b. May 22, 1848; m. May 22, 1870, Asa W. Whitman.
997 995  5 GEORGE H., b. April 9, 1850.
            MANNELLA H., b. April 12, 1852; m. July 11, 1874, Samuel J. Blois.

---

994 996 (VIII.) ISAAC S. PRATT, of East Bridgewater (son of VII. George H.), b. April 27, 1843; m. Dec. 24, 1873, Ida M. Blois.

Child:

         1 MINNIE G., b. March 16, 1876.

---

995 997 (VIII.) GEORGE H. PRATT, Jr., of East Bridgewater (son of VII. George), b. April 9, 1850; m. (1) Jan. 25, 1871, Lydia S. Somers; she d. Sept. 26, 1875. He m. (2) April 9, 1878, Abby M. Thayer.

Children:

         1 HARRY, d. young.
         2 HENRY B., b. July 26, 1879.

(VII.) OLIVER PRATT, of East Bridgewater (son of VI. Isaac), b. Dec. 31, 1816; m. (1) Jan. 1, 1844, Louisa F. Pool, of East Bridgewater; she d. Sept. 6, 1850; m. (2) Jan. 1, 1855, Lydia Atwood Whitmarsh, b. May 2, 1825, dau. of Lot Whitmarsh, of East Bridgewater.

He is a successful farmer, has been prominent in town affairs, and held two military commissions granted by Gov. Edward Everett, viz., Ensign, Sept. 10, 1836, and Captain, April 6, 1839.

Children of Louisa:

1  OLIVER A., b. Aug. 20, 1844; d. Sept. 14, 1844.
2  ELLEN LOUISA, b. Aug. 8, 1846; m. Alfred W. Barrows.
3  ALICE JANE, b. June 5, 1848; m. Simeon Sharp, Jan. 2, 1868.
4  EDGAR OLIVER, b. Aug. 31, 1850; m. Kate Hodgkins.

   Children:

   1  *Edgar Merton.*
   2  *Maud L.*
   3  *Clarence.*

Children of Lydia:

5  ROSA LEE, b. March 17, 1864.
6  ABBIE FRANCES, b. July 11, 1866.

----

(V.) ABNER PRATT, of Bridgewater (son of IV. David), b. Nov. 4, 1734; d. ——; m. (1) Aug. 28, 1764, Martha (Byram) Carey, dau. of Dr. Joseph Byram, and widow of Henry Cary. He m. (2) widow Anna Leonard.

Children:

1  NATHAN, b. 1765; m. Lois Fuller, Oct. 7, 1787.
2  SUSANNA, b. 1768; m. James Richards, 1798.

----

(V.) PETER PRATT, of Bridgewater (son of IV. David), b. April 10, 1746; m. Amy ——.

Children:

1  SAMUEL, b. 1775.
2  REBECCA, b. 1777.
3  MOLLY, b. 1779.

1000 1002  (VI.) NATHAN PRATT, of South Bridgewater (son of V. Abner), b. 1765; m. Oct. 7, 1787, Lois Fuller.

Child:
1  LOIS, b. Dec. 9, 1799.

---

989 1003  (VII.) DAVID PRATT, of East Bridgewater (son of VI. David), b. ——; m. Sept. 3, 1838, Mary M. Weld, of Maine; b. 1816; d. July 4, 1863.

Children:
1  ALONZO H., b. June 4, 1839; d. Jan. 22, 1863; unmarried.
2  MARY ELLA,     } b. April 19, 1850; } m. Alma D.
3  MENDALL ADAMS,  Howe, of East Bridgewater.

Child:
*David Burton*, b. March 23, 1884.

1005 1004  4  ALLEN P., b. Dec. 11, 1846.
           5  ABBY FRANCES, b. Dec. 31, 1857; m. March 17, 1874, William Glover.

---

1004 1005 (VIII.) ALLEN P. PRATT, of East Bridgewater (son of VII. David), b. Dec. 11, 1846; m. Sept. 23, 1866, Lorinda Rumsey, b. 1849.

Children:
1  ALONZO ALLEN, b. May 31, 1869.
2  MANNA GERTRUDE, b. Jan. 12, 1874.
3  LOLA DEFOREST, b. July 14, 1879.

---

685 1006  (IV.) SAMUEL PRATT (son of III. Joseph), b. ——; d. ——; m. Bethia Byram, Dec. 30, 1720, and settled in East Bridgewater; she d. 1774, aged 65. The family moved westward.

Children:
1  MAHITABEL, m. (1) David French; (2) 1752, Benjamin Price.
2  SAMUEL.
3  PAUL.

4 SILAS.

5 BETHIA, b. 1747; m. Jan. 14, 1768, William Daniels, of Abington.

6 SARAH, b. April 23, 1731.

---

673 1007 (III.) JOHN PRATT, of Weymouth (son of II. Joseph), b. May 17, 1668; d. ——; m. Mercy Newcomb.

Children:

1 JOHN, b. March 8, 1692; d. young.
1009 1008   2 JOHN, b. May 26, 1696.

---

1008 1009 (IV.) JOHN PRATT (son of III. John), b. May 26, 1696; d. June 12, 1769; m. Feb. 23, 1724, Jael Beals, b. 1706; d. Jan. 9, 1770.

Children:

1 MERCY, b. Sept. 27, 1724; d. May 26, 1789; m. May 1, 1744, Jacob Smith.
2 HANNAH, b. May 1, 1726; m. —— Lindsley.
3 JOHN, b. Sept. 25, 1727; d. Sept. 26, 1727.
4 LYDIA, b. Sept. 22, 1728; d. April, 1817; m. Dec. 21, 1749, James H. Lewis.
1014 1010   5 JOHN, b. Oct. 4, 1730; d. June 28, 1786.
1031 1011   6 NEHEMIAH, b. Oct. 22, 1732; d. Nov. 9, 1793.
7 MARY, b. June 28, 1735; d. Oct. 27, 1801; m. Feb. 7, 1754, Daniel Blanchard.
1032 1012   8 JOSIAH, b. April 19, 1738; d. July 10, 1800.
1033 1013   9 EZRA, b. March 25, 1740; d. Nov. 7, 1807.

---

1010 1014 (V.) JOHN PRATT (son of IV. John of III. John), b. Oct. 4, 1730; d. June 28, 1786; m. (1) Aug. 27, 1752, Martha White, dau. of Mathew and Martha (Vinson), b. Dec. 24, 1730; d. April 5, 1755; m. (2) Oct. 17, 1756, Sarah Bayley, dau. of Rev. James and Sarah, b. June 16, 1735.

Child of Martha:

1 HANNAH, b. Aug. 5, 1753.

Children of Sarah:

1022 1015   2 JOHN, b. Dec. 18, 1757; m. (P.) Sept. 3, 1775, Sarah Bicknell.

3  JAMES, b. Jan. 13, 1760.
1017 1016   4  ISAAC, b. May 25, 1763; d. Feb. 19, 1841.
5  LEAH, b. Nov. 24, 1764.
6  MICAH, m. Jan. 9, 1786, Deborah Bicknell.

———

1016 1017  (VI.) ISAAC PRATT (son of V. John), b. May 25, 1763; d. Feb. 19, 1841; m. Jan. 29, 1787, Sarah Vinson, d. Aug. 31, 1815, aged 51.

Children:

1  POLLY, b. Sept. 28, 1787; d. Oct. 23, 1801.
1025 1018   2  JAMES, b. Dec. 30, 1790; d. Dec. 7, 1832; m. 1818, Sally Hawes.
1020 1019   3  ISAAC, b. May 12, 1792; d. Nov. 3, 1840; m. 1817, Charlotte Cushing.
4  SALLY, b. Sept. 20, 1794; d. Oct. 10, 1830.
5  LYDIA, b. Feb. 13, 1797; d. Aug. 10, 1815.
6  RACHEL, b. Aug. 28, 1799; d. March 28, 1816.
7  MICAH, b. Sept. 9, 1801; d. April 10, 1830.
8  JOHN, b. April 2, 1804; d. Aug. 10, 1822.

———

1019 1020  (VII.) ISAAC PRATT (son of VI. Isaac and Sarah), b. May 12, 1792; d. Nov. 3, 1840; m. (P.) July 19, 1817, Charlotte Cushing.

Children:

1  ISAAC VINSON, b. May 29, 1818.
2  ELBRIDGE, b. Nov. 17, 1820; d. July 27, 1834.
3  ELIZABETH, b. Nov. 13, 1823.
4  CHARLOTTE, b. Nov. 23, 1825.
5  EMILY, b. June 28, 1827.
6  JOHN WESLEY, b. Dec. 9, 1829; m. Oct. 23, 1853, Hannah I. Turner, of Abington.
7  SARAH, b. Nov., 1830.
8  CAROLINE, b. Feb., 1833.
1024 1021   9  ELBRIDGE SANDFORD, b. Oct. 1835; m. June 5, 1861, Ellen L. Pratt, dau. of Chester D.
10  ROSAMOND STUDLEY, b. Nov. 1837; d. Dec. 26, 1864, single, in Taunton.
11  JOSHUA CUSHING, b. Aug. 10, 1841; d. Sept. 19, 1843.

1015 1022 (VI.) JOHN PRATT, of Weymouth (son of V. John and Sarah Bayley), b. Dec. 18, 1757; d. ——; m. (P.) Sept. 3, 1775, Sarah Bicknell.

Child:

1030 1023     WILLIAM, b. April 3, 1777.

---

1021 1024 (VIII.) ELBRIDGE S. PRATT, of Chicago, Ill. (son of VII. Isaac), b. Oct., 1835; m. Ellen Louise Pratt, dau. of Chester D. Pratt, of Weymouth, b. Dec. 16, 1843.

Children:

1 WALTER S., b. July 1, 1863; m. Emma Farncy, of Chicago.
2 HARRY ELBRIDGE, b. 1869.
3 LOUISA ELLEN.
4 CHESTER ALONZO.

---

1018 1025 (VII.) JAMES PRATT, of Weymouth (son of VI. Isaac). b. Dec. 30, 1790; d. Dec. 7, 1832; m. (P.) Feb. 5, 1818, Sally Hawes.

Children:

1 LYDIA M., d. June 29, 1832.
2 SARAH VINSON.
3 MARY ANN, b. 1822; d. Oct. 20, 1867.
4 ELROTA.
5 AUGUSTA.
1027 1026  6 JAMES BAILEY, d. July 7, 1857.

---

1026 1027 (VIII.) JAMES B. PRATT (son of VII. James), b. ——; d. July 7, 1857; m. May 22, 1853, Melvina F. Holbrook, dau. of Abner and Abigail.

Children:

1 ABBY ELLA, b. July 26, 1854; m. May 4, 1883, James Quinn.
1029 1028  2 JAMES B., b. March 2, 1857.

29 (IX.) JAMES BAILEY PRATT (son of VIII. James B.), b. March 8, 1857; m. Dec. 19, 1876, Lucinda Bicknell French, dau. of Samuel and Lucinda B. (Salisbury).

Child:

WILLIAM PORTER, b. April 27, 1877.

———

30 (VII.) WILLIAM PRATT, of Weymouth (son of VI. John and Sarah), b. April 3, 1777; d. ——; m. Nancy ——.

Children:

1 NANCY RICE, b. Nov. 2, 1819.
2 SARAH ANN, b. Aug. 28, 1821.
3 MARY, b. Jan. 12, 1823.
4 MARGARET, b. April 18, 1826.
5 WILLIAM PERKINS, b. Aug. 29, 1828; d. Dec. 15, 1859.

———

31 (V.) NEHEMIAH PRATT (son of IV. John), b. Oct. 22, 1732; d. Nov. 9, 1793; m. June 24, 1753, Mary (in marriage record), Sarah (in birth record) Pratt, d. Oct. 5, 1767; m. (2) (P.) Oct. 22, 1768, m. Jan. 7, 1769, Ruth Torrey, of Abington.

Children of Mary:

1 LOIS or LOVIS, b. Sept. 19, 1753.
2 NEHEMIAH, b. March 21, 1755.
3 MARY, b. Oct. 17, 1756.
4 LYDIA, b. Aug. 28, 1759; m. March 26, 1778, Ezekiel Clapp.
5 DAVID, b. June 23, 1761.
6 ABIGAIL, b. Feb. 20, 1764.

Children of Ruth:

7 OLLA, b. April 10, 1770.
8 LEVI, b. Aug. 2, 1772.
9 BEULAH, b. July 7, 1776.
10 PATTY WILLIAMS, b. Nov. 27, 1782.
11 THOMAS, b. Oct. 22, 1784.
12 THEODORE.

———

32 (V.) JOSIAH PRATT, of Weymouth (son of IV. John), b. April 10, 1738; d. July 10, 1800; m. Aug. 20, 1759, Mary Bayley dau. of Rev. James and Sarah, b. Oct. 17, 1742; d. Jan. 11, 1816.

Children :

1 OLIVE, b. Jan. 16, 1760.
2 JOSIAH, b. Sept. 1, 1761.
3 MARY, b. July 12, 1763; d. April 11, 1836; m. 1796,
    John Newton, of Abington.
4 HANNAH, b. Oct. 17, 1766.
5 LOIS, b. Oct. 18, 1773; d. Aug. 10, 1810.

---

1013 1033 (V.) EZRA PRATT, of Weymouth (son of IV. John), b.
March 25, 1740; d. Nov. 7, 1807; m. (P.) March 29,
1766, Abigail Clark, of Braintree, d. April 8, 1822,
aged 77.

He was a very large land-owner, and a prosperous
farmer.

Children :

           1 SUSA, b. Jan. 19, 1770; d. Dec. 3, 1836.
           2 LUCY, b. May 5, 1772; d. May 20, 1847.
           3 CHLOE, b. Aug. 16, 1774; d. 1857; m. 1800, David
             Holbrook.
           4 SARA, b. April 30, 1776; d. Jan. 22, 1802.
1037 1034 5 BELA, b. Dec. 30, 1777; d. June 20, 1843.
1062 1035 6 ASA, b. March 15, 1780; d. Dec. 16, 1805.
1066 1036 7 JACOB, b. Dec. 23, 1781; d. Aug. 23, 1828.
           8 HANNAH, b. Jan. 27, 1784; d. Dec. 16, 1858.
           9 LYDIA, b. Aug. 2, 1789; d. Feb. 6, 1858.

---

1034 1037 (VI.) BELA PRATT, of Weymouth (son of V. Ezra), b.
Dec. 30, 1777; d. June 20, 1843; m. Feb. 28, 1801,
Sophia Western Lyon, of Halifax, Mass., b. Oct. 23,
1780; d. Nov. 5, 1841.

He was an extensive builder and contractor.
Among the most noted edifices erected by him were
the only stone church in Marblehead, 1824; Bird
Island Light, Buzzard's Bay, 1819; and a church in
Boston, 1823; the latter was for some time occupied
by Wellington Brothers as a store on Chauncy Street,
but it was taken down in 1885, and a chapel built of
the freestone in Auburndale. He built for his residence the first stone house in Weymouth.

He was found dead in the field, with his scythe
beside him and his scythe-rifle in his hand.

Children:

1041 1038    1   EZRA, b. Sept. 22, 1801; d. April 10, 1874; m. 1824, Everline L. Vining.

          2   ELIZA T. b. May 17, 1803; m. March 19, 1832, Jacob Laud, Jr.; he d. July 6, 1883.

1047 1039    3   MIXOT, b. Jan. 8, 1805; m. March 22, 1829; d. March 29, 1878.

          4   LOIS, b. Aug. 10, 1806; d.——; m. Oct. 23, 1821, Ellis Weeks.

          5   ABIGAIL CLARK, b. Aug. 6, 1808; d. April 16, 1877; never married.

1055 1040    6   BELA LYON, b. Oct. 28, 1810; d. 1844; m. Oct. 4, 1830, Nabby B. Tirrell.

          7   LUCY, b. Oct. 24, 1812; m. Dec. 1, 1846, Rev. Wales Lewis.

          8   SOPHIA WENTERN, b. Nov. 24, 1814; m. Nov. 29, 1832, Jeremiah Towle; d. Jan. 8, 1869.

          9   MARIA LOUISA THERESA, b. Jan. 25, 1816; d. April 20, 1818.

        10   MARIA LOUISA THERESA, b. Dec. 20, 1818; m. Sept. 1, 1837, Thomas Chandler.

        11   MARY JANE, b. Jan. 12, 1820; m. Dec. 30, 1840, Enos D. Raymond.

        12   ADELINE W., b. March 17, 1823; d. Oct. 25, 1865; m. March 9, 1845, William W. Raymond; d. Oct. 25, 1865.

        13   OLIVE ISABELLA BROADHEAD, b. Jan. 5, 1825; d. Jan. 18, 1856; May 1, 1842, Jos. Ford French.

———

1038 1041 (VII.) EZRA PRATT, of Weymouth (son of VI. Bela), b. Sept. 22, 1801; d. April 10, 1874; m. Everline L. Vining, dau. of Bela and Content (Pratt), Oct. 19, 1824; she b. March 25, 1805; d. Jan. 7, 1868.

He was a stone contractor.

Children:

          1   HENRY MARTIN, b. March 22, 1827; d. March 23, 1827.

1046 1042    2   THEODORE CONSTANTINE, b. Jan. 3, 1829.

1052 1043    3   EZRA GRANVILLE, b. July 4, 1833.

1053 1044    4   BELA EDWARD, b. Oct. 1, 1844.

1054 1045    5   WILLIAM HENRY NEWTON, b. July 10, 1849.

———

1042 1046 (VIII.) THEODORE C. PRATT, of Weymouth (son of VII. Ezra), b. Jan. 3, 1829; m. 1855, Emeline Augusta Reed, dau. of Elbridge G. and Mary Ann, of Sterling, b. Feb. 23, 1834.

Children :

1  MELISSA ANN, b. March 14, 1856.
2  EUGENE NEANDER, b. July 31, 1860 ; d. Oct. 7, 1865.
3  ELLA BOARDMAN, b. March 9, 1862 ; d. Oct. 7, 1865.
4  ALBERT WALLACE, b. Sept. 3, 1864 ; d. Oct. 13, 1865.
5  LESTER CHANNING, b. April 15, 1873.

    Is an Orthodox Minister, settled at Auburn, N.H. ;
    educated at Worcester Academy, Amherst College,
    and Andover Theological Seminary ; formerly of
    Orford, Tilton and Hampstead, N.H.

---

1039 1047 (VII.)  MINOT PRATT, of Concord (son of VI. Bela), b. Jan.
                  3, 1805 ; d. March 29, 1878 ; m. March 22, 1829, Maria
                  Jones Bridge, b. March 27, 1806, in Boston. She is the
                  sister of Mrs. Alvin Adams, wife of the late Alvin
                  Adams, proprietor of Adams Express.

                  He was printer of the Christian Register for eight
                  years, was afterwards a prominent member of the
                  Brook Farm Community and was an active worker
                  in the temperance cause, being a frequent contri-
                  butor to local papers. He was an acknowleged
                  authority in botany, and at the time of his death was
                  a farmer.

                  Children :

              1   HENRY MINOT, b. Feb. 22, 1830, at Hingham ; d. Aug.
                  29, 1830.
1050 1048     2   FREDERICK GRAY, b. April 2, 1831, at Hingham.
1051 1049     3   JOHN BRIDGE, b. June 15, 1833, at Boston ; d. Nov.
                  28, 1870, at Maplewood.
              4   CAROLINE HAYDEN, b. Nov. 9, 1836, at Boston ; d.
                  July 10, 1866, at Concord. She was a teacher in the
                  Blind Asylum.
              5   THEODORE PARKER, b. Aug. 2, 1842 at Brook Farm,
                  West Roxbury ; d. March 20, 1850 at Concord,
                  Mass.

---

1048 1050 (VIII.)  FREDERICK GRAY PRATT (son of VII. Minot), b.
                   April 2, 1831 ; m. Jan. 16, 1853, Sarah Maria Emery,
                   b. March 4, 1833, at Dryden, N.Y. ; d. Aug. 21, 1879, at
                   Concord, Mass.

                   Child :

                   HENRY MINOT, b. Dec. 23, 1853, at Meadville, Pa.

1049 1051 (VIII.) JOHN BRIDGE PRATT (son of VII. Minot), b. June
     15, 1833; d. Nov. 28, 1870, at Maplewood, Mass.; m.
     May 23, 1860, Annie Bronson Alcott, b. March 16,
     1831, at Philadelphia. She was the daughter of A.
     Bronson Alcott, one of the most distinguished of
     the Concord philosophers, and is a sister of the late
     Louisa M. Alcott, the writer.

     Children :

     1 FREDERICK ALCOTT, b. March 28, 1863, at Chelsea;
       m. Feb. 8, 1888, Jessica Cate, dau. of Luther G., at
       Wakefield.
     2 JOHN SEWALL, b. June 24, 1865, at Roxbury.

———— ————

1043 1052 (VIII.) EZRA GRANVILLE PRATT (son of VII. Ezra), b.
     July 4, 1843, in Weymouth; m. (1) Celestia Jackson
     Nov. 15, 1866, dau. of Ezra S. Jackson and Maria
     Osborn; d. Sept. 12, 1876; m. (2) Henrietta R. Spear,
     Dec. 18, 1879, dau. of Seth and Elizabeth (Bowker).

     He removed from Weymouth to Quincy, where he
     practised law, and is now (1888) an Associate Judge
     of the District Court of East Norfolk.  He is exten-
     sively engaged in and about Boston in the general
     practice of law, in which he has been very successful.
     He has been at the head (Grand Dictator) of the So-
     ciety of the Knights of Honor of Massachusetts,
     numbering almost 11,000 members, and representative
     to the Supreme Lodge.
     To him is due the credit of gathering nearly all
     the information respecting the Weymouth Pratts,
     which the compiler has put together in this work.

———— ————

1044 1053 (VIII.) BELA EDWARD PRATT, of Brockton, Mass. (son
     of VII. Ezra), b. Oct. 1, 1844; m. Dec. 30, 1869, Ida
     W. Cushing, dau. of William N. and Caroline A.
     (White); she d. Oct. 3, 1871, aged 23; He m. (2) Abbie
     Thayer, Dec. 14, 1870.

     Child :

     CARRIE EVERLINE, b. Sept. 29, 1870.

**1045 1054 (VIII.) WILLIAM H. N. PRATT,** of Boston (son of VII. Ezra), b. July 10, 1849 at Weymouth; m. Nov. 10, 1871, Mary Granville Salisbury, b. April 5, 1851, dau. of Henry T., of Taunton, Mass.

He is a large wholesale dealer in jewelry, of the firm of Floyd, Pratt and Rounds, Washington Street, Boston.

Children:

1 MORTIMER AUGUSTUS, b. Sept. 26, 1872.
2 NORMAN TWOMBLY, b. Aug. 23, 1877.
3 EVERLINE VINING, b. Oct. 17, 1886.

**1040 1055 (VII.) BELA LYON PRATT,** of Weymouth (son of VI. Bela), b. Oct. 28, 1810; m. 1830, Nabby Bates Tirrell.

He was a local preacher in the M. E. Church, and prominent in all church work, filling during his short life all the offices in the church of his choice with great acceptance.

In the anti-slavery movement he was among the very first to take a pronounced position, and came out boldly for the abolition of human slavery; and was the first candidate for election as representative to the General Court from the town of Weymouth.

In the cause of temperance, also, he was one of the first to take hold and move in the great reformation which began almost at the same time as the anti-slavery crusade.

In every moral and religious reform his name was always found in the front rank.

Children:

1058 1056 1 CHARLES HENRY, b. Dec. 26, 1830.
1061 1057 2 GEORGE, b. Oct. 12, 1832.
3 MINOT, b. Aug. 20, 1834; d. Oct. 22, 1857.
4 ELLEN SOPHIA, b. Aug. 10, 1836: m. Andrew J. Garey, Nov. 18, 1853.
5 ADELINE WILSON, b. May 31, 1839; m. Nathan D. Canterbury, Nov. 15, 1859.
6 SUSAN JANE F., b. Jan. 25, 1841; d. April 6, 1870; m. Warren Stetson, of Braintree.

**1056 1058 (VIII.) CHARLES HENRY PRATT,** of Weymouth (son of VII. Bela L.), b. Dec. 26, 1830; m. Oct. 16, 1850, Elzira N. Rice, dau. of William and Margaret N. (Pratt).

He is a prominent leather-merchant of Weymouth, his business being the cutting of "uppers," etc., for boots and shoes, of which he has made a specialty, and has by great energy been very successful.

Child:

1060 1059     WILLIAM HENRY, b. Nov. 23, 1851.

---

1059 1060  (IX.)  WILLIAM HENRY PRATT, of Weymouth (son of VIII. Charles H.), b. Nov. 23, 1851; m. March 18, 1874 at Westfield, Annie Frances Treat, dau. of Oliver and Satera (Adams).

Child:

ANNIE, b. May 2, 1881; d. May 2, 1881.

---

1057 1061 (VIII.) GEORGE PRATT, of Norwich, Conn. (son of VII. Bela L.), b. Oct. 12, 1832; d. June 4, 1875; m. July 31, 1858, Sarah Victoria Whittlesey, dau. of Orramel and Charlotte Maconda Whittlesey, of Salem, Conn.

He was such a remarkably brilliant and prominent man, that the following has been copied from the Norwich Bulletin, of June 7, 1875.

"When a prominent citizen falls in the community, full of years, ripened in character, with his life-work complete, he must be in a measure known and read of all men; his qualities and peculiar traits have become familiar, especially in the less bustling years of advanced and ripened age. When, however, one dies in his prime, while still taxed with the struggle of success, preoccupied with the cares of mid-career, not yet fully developed nor having attained to all the responsibilities of which he is capable, the measure of his loss is fully realized only by those who stood nearest him. Such a man was George Pratt, in whom we mourn a life-long friend, and by whose death Norwich loses a citizen already of great usefulness, and of yet more abundant promise.

He graduated at Yale College in 1857, having a high personal and literary standing in a class of more than average ability. He acquired his education at his own expense; his early training in self-reliant, economical and industrious habits having admirably prepared him to advance his own way, not only in his student years but throughout his life. He could, indeed, be fairly called a self-made man. He was ignorant of the art of wasting time, and had an utter distaste for all forms of dissipation, so that he maintained an unblemished moral character in college, and acquired those habits of assiduous, painstaking study which have distinguished him ever since. After graduation he taught for a short time, and began the study of law in New York State. Subsequently, however, he entered the law office of the Hon. John T. Wait, then in Norwich, Iowa, where he pursued his studies till his admission to the Bar in 1850.

He was elected to represent Salem in the General Assembly in 1860, and in the same year removed to this city, where he opened a law office, and has continued to reside ever since. By his native ability and steady application to business he soon began to rise in his profession, and continued to progress, till at the time of his death, he stood among the foremost members of the Norwich Bar.

For several years he had been employed as attorney by the city, and was Corporation Counsel at the time of his death.

In 1864, 1865 and 1869, he represented Norwich in the General Assembly. He was on several of the most important committees, and was always active in pushing business — courting labor, — and being thoroughly informed upon every question which he introduced to the house. He was the author of several important measures, among which the Registry Law may be mentioned, and was, on both occasions when the question came up, one of the most ardent advocates of the impartial suffrage amendment. He was an earnest Republican.

He was a public-spirited citizen, was connected with some of the most important business corporations of the State, also the public schools, libraries, etc. He was a trustee of the Otis Library.

He was actively engaged in religious matters, having been for years a warden of Trinity Church, and superintendent of the Sunday School.

Of decided literary tastes, he always had some special line of study, and contributed to various magazines and newspapers. Among his subjects were church history, history of the colonial times, and political economy.

He was thoroughly domestic in his tastes, his home being a very happy one, and upon it he lavished a large share of his time and income.

If Mr. Pratt's life has been a successful one, it has been owing more to starling qualities and principles beneath the surface of his character than to those traits which were so easily apparent. He has been little aided by adventitious circumstances, but he is a fair example of a man who by strict adherence to the homely and wholesome maxims which too many young men neglect or despise, has gained a legitimate reward.

The loss of such a man is a calamity to the entire community — and indeed in the present case will be more widely felt, for in some respects Mr. Pratt was more highly appreciated in other parts of the State than at home — though the sharpness of bereavement can only be fully experienced by those who stood nearest his heart.

NOTE. — Notices of a similar character to the above appeared in many other newspapers of the State.

Children:

1   ALICE MACONDA, b. Sept. 20, 1860; m. Joseph D. Boardman April 20, 1882; living in Knoxville, Tenn.

2   ORHAMEL WHITTLESEY, b. Aug. 8, 1862; in Kansas City, Mo. (1887).

3   GERTRUDE, b. Dec. 11, 1864.

4   BELA LYON, b. Dec. 11, 1867; student at Yale Law School (1887).

5   SUSIE WARREN, b. Nov. 30, 1869; d. April 3, 1873.

6   MINOT TULLY, b. Nov. 21, 1872.

---

1035  1062  (VL)   ASA PRATT (son of V. Ezra), b. March 15, 1780; d. Dec. 16, 1865; m. (P.) April 3, 1802, Lydia Lyon, of Halifax, Mass.; she d. May 7, 1816, aged 36; m. (P.) (2) Rebecca Loach, Oct. 20, 1818.

He resided at East Bridgewater, and was a shoe-maker.

Children of Lydia:

1078  1063   1   SELDEN, b. July 11, 1803; m. Mary Ann Fisher; m. (2) Jane.

2   SALLY or SARAH, b. Feb. 21, 1805; m. Jos. Hawes; she d. Oct. 2, 1836.

1079  1064   3   ABNER C., b. Feb. 15, 1806; m. Priscilla Loach, 1839.

4   IRENE, b. Oct. 18, 1809; m. Nov. 13, 1831, Winslow Jackson.

1076  1065   5   HENRY, b. March 10, 1811; d. Aug. 14, 1864, in Georgia.

6   LYDIA CUSHMAN, b. July 14, 1816.

Children of Rebecca:

1077  1066   7   JOTHAM C., b. Sept. 13, 1819.

8   REBECCA L., b. Dec. 9, 1821; m. Lucius Harden.

1080  1067   9   DAVID H., b. Feb. 5, 1824; m. Marcus Harden.

10   CHLOE H., b. Aug. 1826; d. Aug. 1826.

168 (VI.) JACOB PRATT, a farmer of Weymouth (son of V. Ezra), b. Dec. 23, 1781; d. Aug. 23, 1828; m. Dec. 24, 1802, Hannah Loring of Hingham, b. June 6, 1783.

    He was killed by a lever becoming unfastened on a load of stone.

Children:

    1 DOLLY S., b. Oct. 20, 1803; m. Nov. 17, 1824, William Young of Scituate.

    2 LAURA, b. June 10, 1805.

169    3 LORING, b. March 3, 1807; m. Oct. 31, 1830, Laura Vining.

    4 ADMERIA, b. April 25, 1809; m. David Bates, of Abington.

    5 HANNAH, b. May 23, 1811.

    6 LOUISA, b. April 7, 1813; d. June 16, 1815.

170    7 GEORGE WASHINGTON, b. April 10, 1815.

171    8 CHESTER D. b. May 9, 1817.

172    9 JACOB, b. Nov. 16, 1820.

    10 LOUISA A., b. May 22, 1823; lives in Woburn; unmarried.

---

173 (VII.) CHESTER D. PRATT, of Weymouth (son of VI. Jacob, b. May 9, 1817; m. Sept. 3, 1843, Louisa P. Hobart, of Hingham, b. May 10, 1824. Shoe manufacturer, now (1887) a farmer.

Children:

    1 ELLEN LOUISA, b. Dec. 16, 1843; m. Elbridge S. Pratt, son of Isaac.

174    2 ALONZO CHESTER, b. April 16, 1846.

    3 FANNIE HOBART, b. March 5, 1849; m. J. Stanley Tanner.

    4 ABBY FLORENCE, b. Sept. 5, 1855; m. Thomas T. Morrill.

---

175 (VIII.) ALONZO C. PRATT, of Weymouth (son of VII. Chester D.), b. April 16, 1846; m. Nov. 16, 1870, Clara J. Fogg, of Braintree. Commission merchant, of Boston.

Children:

    1 FLORENCE ETHEL, Aug. 6, 1873.

    2 WILLIAM DELANO, b. Feb. 9, 1875.

1065 1076 (VII.) HENRY PRATT, of East Bridgewater (son of VI.
Asa), b. March 10, 1811; d. Aug. 14, 1864, in Georgia.
He m. May 25, 1851, Elizabeth Merriam, of East
Bridgewater.

Children:

1　EMELINE, b. Jan. 29, 1852; m. G. H. Campbell.
2　DANIEL H., b. Nov. 29, 1854.
3　WILLIAM, b. Feb. 13, 1856; d. Feb. 18, 1856.

---

1066 1077 (VII.) JOTHAM C. PRATT, of East Bridgewater (son of
VI. Asa, of East Bridgewater), b. Sept. 13, 1819; m.
July 3, 1842, Laura A. Harden, of E. Bridgewater.

Children:

1　WILBER or WALTER.
2　FREDERIC BARNARD, b. Feb. 3, 1849; d. July 9, 1866.
3　ALICE HORTON, b. April 13, 1851.
4　ANTOINETTE P., b. Jan. 18, 1858; d. Feb. 27, 1864.

---

1063 1078 (VII.) SELDEN PRATT (son of VI. Asa), b. July 11, 1803;
m. (1) Sarah Ann Hathaway, Aug. 6, 1831; d. Sept. 25,
1834; m. (2) Jane Ford, May 2, 1835.

Children:

1　ASA, b. Oct. 31, 1832; d. 1832.
2　LUCY JANE, b. July 18, 1834; d. Dec. 5, 1834.
3　LUCY JANE, b. June 2, 1840.
4　ASA, b. Feb. 12, 1851.

---

1064 1079 (VII.) ABNER C. PRATT, of Halifax (son of VI. Asa), b.
Feb. 15, 1800; m. June 14, 1833, Priscilla Leach; she
d. Aug. 10, 1852, aged 54. He d. July 2, 1872.

Children:

1　THOMPSON L., b. April 17, 1836.
2　SELDEN, b. March 21, 1838.
3　LYDIA C., b. Nov. 2, 1842; m. July 19, 1863, Charles
R. Bishop.

1067 1080 (VII.) DAVID H. PRATT, of Halifax (son of VI. Asa), b. Feb. 5, 1824; m. Mary S. Harden, Nov. 18, 1847. He works at South Abington.

Children:

1   ELLA F., b. Dec. 23, 1849; m. Daniel Sullivan, July 6, 1879.
2   WALTER SCOTT, b. Sept. 2, 1848.

---

1070 1081 (VII.) GEORGE WASHINGTON PRATT, of Weymouth (son of VI. Jacob), b. April 10, 1815; m. (1) Oct. 6, 1833, Lucy Burrell; she d. April 1, 1847. He m. (2) Elizabeth McCready, Aug. 31, 1847.

Farmer. Superintendent for eight years of the Town-Farm of Weymouth. He now (1887) lives in Hingham, near the South Weymouth line.

Children of Lucy:

1   HELEN M., b. Feb. 28, 1834; m. Geo. W. Hobbs, of Charlestown, Mass.

1085 1082   2   CHESTER D., b. Sept. 15, 1838; m. and lives in Hyde Park, Ill.

3   LUCY AMANDA, b. Aug. 8, 1840; m. Benj. Hinckley, of Woburn.

4   HANNAH LORING, b. Dec. 26, 1841; m. John H. Hancock. He is in the Custom House, Boston.

5   GEORGE W., b. Aug. 2, 1843; m. Flora White; lives in Acton.

6   ELIZABETH W., b. Aug. 6, 1845; d. Aug. 24, 1874.

7   CHARLES HENRY, b. March 19, 1847; m. March 18, 1868, Rhoda N. Moore.

Child of Elizabeth:

1084 1083   8   FREDERICK ARTHUR, b. July 13, 1853; m. Jan. 15, Lydia A. Vining, b. April 8, 1847.

---

1083 1084 (VIII.) FREDERICK A. PRATT, of Hingham (son of VII. George W.), b. July 13, 1853; m. Jan. 15, 1878, Lydia A. Vining, b. April 8, 1847.

Children:

1   HOWARD VINING, b. May 15, 1879.
2   LIZZIE AROLINE, b. Nov. 10, 1882.
3   HELEN MARIA, b. June 27, 1885.

1082 1085 (VIII.) CHESTER D. PRATT, of Chicago, Ill. (son of VII. George W.), b. Sept. 15, 1838, at Weymouth, Mass.; m. 1867, Sallie L. Downey, of Clear Spring, Md.

He entered Thetford Academy, Vt., in 1857, and graduated in 1859. From there he went to Dartmouth College, but did not finish his course of studies at that institution, having enlisted, 1861, in the First Mass. Cavalry, and served with honor in the War of the Rebellion, being discharged on account of disability. He then studied law in Boston, and was admitted to the bar in 1866, after which he removed to Linn County, Mo., where he married, and practiced his profession until he went to Chicago, in 1876, where he now resides. A lawyer of considerable prominence and a worthy representative of the ability for which the descendants of the first Mathew Pratt are noted.

Children:

1    ANNIE CONRAD, b. July 5, 1869; d. March 27, 1870.
2    LUCY BURRELL, b. Oct. 12, 1870.
3    ELIZABETH LORING, b. April 27, 1872.
4    MARY DOWNEY, b. Feb. 12, 1877.
5    MABEL STEARNS, b. Jan. 27, 1885.

---

1069 1086 (VII.) LORING PRATT, of Weymouth (son of VI. Jacob), b. March 3, 1807; m. Oct. 31, 1830, Laura Vining, b. April 17, 1809; d. March, 1883. Farmer.

Children:

1    ANNA CORDELIA, b. Aug. 8, 1831; m. July 1, 1851, F. S. Torrey.
1092 1087   2   JACOB LORING, b. Aug. 6, 1835.
3    LYDIA MARIA, b. Jan. 27, 1838; unmarried.
1090 1088   4   PRESTON, b. Oct. 29, 1844; m. Dec. 31, 1872.
1091 1089   5   CHARLES STUART, b. Feb. 10, 1854.

---

1088 1090 (VIII.) PRESTON PRATT (son of VII. Loring), b. Oct. 29, 1844; m. Malvina C. Farrow, Dec. 31, 1872, at Scituate, dau. of Allen and Rachel B. No children. Farmer.

---

1089 1091 (VIII.) CHARLES STUART PRATT, of Boston (son of VII. Loring), b. Feb. 10, 1854; m. Nov. 11, 1877, Ella Farman, dau. of Rev. T. and Hannah Farman.

Ho graduated with first honors from South Weymouth High School, removed to Boston, and, since their establishment in 1875 and 1877, with his wife, has edited the Magazines "Wide Awake" and "Babyland"; is author of "Bye-O-Baby Ballads," published in 1886 by D. Lothrop & Co., and "Baby's Lullaby Book," now in press with L. Prang & Co., and various magazine stories and poems. Mrs. Pratt is author of "Good-For-Nothing Polly," a book for boys, honored with republication abroad, "How Two Girls Tried Farming, a personal experiment, "A White Hand," a novel, and half a dozen volumes for young people, published by D. Lothrop & Co., also contributor to "The Atlantic Monthly," Harper's Magazine," etc.

Child :

RALPH FARMAN, b. July 7, 1878.

---

1067 1092 (VIII.) JACOB L. PRATT, of Strong, Mo. (son of VII. Loring), b. Aug. 6, 1835; m. June 14, 1876, Lucy Church Soule. He is a Congregational clergyman.

Children :

1 GEORGE LORING, b. June 17, 1877.
2 ELBERT STEARNS, b. Feb. 12, 1879.

---

1072 1093 (VII.) JACOB PRATT, of Chelsea (son of VI. Jacob), b. Nov. 16, 1820; m. Nov. 22, 1847, Frances Pearson Larkin, b. March 11, 1825.

Children :

1097 1094    1 FREDERICK SERENO, b. Sept. 9, 1848.
1098 1095    2 JACOB, b. Nov. 17, 1850.
            3 ALBERT LARKIN, } b. Aug. 31, 1852.
1099 1096    4 ALFRED LORING, }
            5 EMMA FRANCES, b. Nov. 23, 1860.
            6 ELIZABETH LOUISE, b. April 13, 1863.

---

1094 1097 (VIII.) FREDERICK S. PRATT, of Chelsea (son of VII. Jacob), b. Sept. 9, 1848; m. (1) Jan. 3, 1872, Mary Louise Young; she d. Nov. 11, 1872. He m. (2) Oct. 8, 1877, Carrie Fish.

Children :
1  HARRY FREDERICK, b. Aug. 20, 1878.
2  BESSIE FRANCES, b. June 14, 1880.

———

1095 1098 (VIII.) JACOB PRATT, Jr., of Chelsea (son of VII. Jacob),
           b. Nov. 17, 1850; m. Sept. 30, 1875, Mary Gilbert.

Children :
1  GILBERT HOMER, b. June 30, 1876.
2  FLORENCE MARY, b. June 8, 1884.

———

1096 1099 (VIII.) ALFRED L. PRATT, of Chelsea (son of VII. Jacob),
           b. Aug. 31, 1852; m. Dec. 27, 1878, Ellen M. Murphy.

Children :
1  ALFRED STEARNS, b. May 7, 1879.
2  HELEN BRADFORD, b. Dec. 26, 1881.

———

675 1100 (III.) EPHRAIM PRATT, of Weymouth (son of II. Joseph),
           b. ———; d. about 1745. He m. Phebe ———; she d.
           Dec. 2, 1736.

           He possessed considerable land in Weymouth; was
           elected Surveyor of Highways, 1724; Tithing-man,
           1725; (at this latter election the town voted to pay
           one shilling for every old crow's head, and six-pence
           for young ones. Also two-pence for old blackbirds'
           heads); Fence-viewer 1729-1732, and other offices
           were held by him subsequently. His will is dated
           Feb. 9, 1740, in which he leaves property valued at
           £191. 8d. 0s.

           Children :
1104 1101  1  EPHRAIM, b. June 15, 1698; d. May 20, 1769.
           2  PHEBE, b. March 20, 1700; m. Jan. 18, 1719, Zach.
              Shaw.
1111 1102  3  JOSEPH, b. Sept. 1703.
1115 1103  4  JOHN, b. March 1, 1705.
1114 1102a 5  MARY, b. June 28, 1711; m. Daniel Pratt.

———

1101 1104 (IV.) EPHRAIM PRATT, of Weymouth (son of III. Eph-
           raim), b. June 15, 1698; d. ———; m. 1728, Lydia
           Burrell.

Among other offices, he was elected Surveyor of Highways, 1736. May 13, 1734: "Ephraim Pratt, Jr., shall have that piece of land that he has fenced in at the north end of his land at the place called Honey Hill, there being a steep ledge of Rocks which will serve the making a considerable deal of fence, that ledge of Rocks to be his bounds." (This may identify his location in Weymouth).

Child:

1106 1105      EPHRAIM, b. 1741; d. Jan. 30, 1799.

---

1105 1106 (V.)      EPHRAIM PRATT, of Weymouth (son of IV. Ephraim), b. 1741; d. Jan. 30, 1799; m. Jan. 19, 1760, Lucy Porter, of Abington.

Children:

1116 1107    1   JOSEPH, b. Dec. 8, 1760; d. July 26, 1809.
         2   PETER, b. July 16, 1763.
1125 1108    3   ASA, b. Dec. 12, 1766; m. Sally Lovell.
1110 1109    4   EPHRAIM, b. July 13, 1769; d. Feb. 18, 1850.
         5   LYDIA, b. May 9, 1772.
         6   LUCY, b. Dec. 12, 1778; m. Nov. 8, 1794, Noah Stowell.
         7   ELIZABETH, b. Oct. 27, 1785.

---

1109 1110 (VI.)      EPHRAIM PRATT (son of V. Ephraim), b. July 13, 1769; d. Feb. 18, 1850; m. Hannah Gardner, Jan. 1, 1805; she d. Sept. 18, 1870.

Children:

         1   EPHRAIM, b. 1807; d. March 12, 1830; m. Hannah W. Lewis, Oct. 11, 1829.
         2   LUCY.
         3   NATHANIEL, d. Oct. 1, 1869.

---

1102 1111 (IV.)      JOSEPH PRATT (son of III. Ephraim), b. March 20, 1700; m. Jan. 23, 1729, Rachel Lincoln.

Children:

1113 1112    1   JOSEPH, b. Dec. 20, 1729.
         2   DEBORAH, b. Sept. 3, 1731.
         3   MEHITABLE, b. Aug. 15, 1733.
         4   DORCAS, b. June 4, 1736; d. Feb. 12, 1796.
         5   PHEBE, b. Sept. 21, 1738.

1112 1113  (V.) JOSEPH PRATT (son of IV. Joseph of III. Ephraim),
           b. Dec. 20, 1729; d. ——; m. (1) Jan. 30, 1756, Molly
           Beal, dau. of Wm. and Hannah (Smith), b. Feb. 7,
           1736; d. 1736; m. (2) Hannah; m. (3) Sarah.

           Children :
           1  Noah, b. Dec. 27, 1755; son of Molly.
           2  David, b. Dec. 29, 1759; son of Hannah.
           3  Elizabeth, b. Dec. 9, 1765; dau. of Sarah.


1102a 1114 (IV.) MARY PRATT (dau. of III. Ephraim), b. June 28,
           1711; d. April 16, 1781; m. Daniel Pratt, Nov. 1, 1739.
           He b. 1707; d. Nov. 6, 1797.  He was the grandson of
           II. Samuel.

           Children :
           1  Daniel, b. July 29, 1740; d. Sept. 1, 1740.
           2  Hannah, b. Feb. 9, 1742; d. Feb. 15, 1742.
           3  Mary, b. Sept. 12, 1743; d. Feb. 4, 1768.
           4  Meriam, b. Oct. 22, 1745.
           5  Ichabod, b. April 8, 1748; d. May 4, 1822.
           6  Samuel, b. Jan. 26, 1751; d. May 22, 1830.


1103 1115  (IV.) JOHN PRATT, of Weymouth (son of III. Ephraim),
           b. May 1, 1705; m. Jan. 3, 1734, Mary Gurney.

           Children :
           1  Sylvanus, b. Aug. 10, 1735.
           2  Mary, b. Jan. 28, 1739.
           3  Hannah, b. April 9, 1743.
           4  Joanna, b. Jan. 20, 1747.


1107 1116  (VI.) JOSEPH PRATT (son of V. Ephraim and Lucy), b.
           Dec. 8, 1760; d. July 26, 1809; m. Mercy Shaw, Sept.
           21, 1783.

           Children :
           1  Sophia, b. Jan. 13, 1785; m. Seth Curtis.
           2  Selah, b. June 29, 1787; m. —— Tower.
1119 1117  3  Charles, b. Oct. 8, 1792; d. Dec. 4, 1864.
1121 1118  4  Jason, b. March 2, 1798.
           5  Jane, b. Dec. 18, 1799; m. Aug. 15, 1818, Cornelius
              Tirrell.
           6  Almira, b. July 11, 1804; m. Abram Pratt, of Ran-
              dolph.

1117  1119 (VII.) CHARLES PRATT, of Weymouth (son of VI. Joseph and Mercy), b. Oct. 8, 1792; d. Dec. 4, 1864; m. Sally Burrell.

He was a manufacturer of boots and shoes, and kept a general store in South Weymouth.

Children:

1  CHARLES H., b. May 24, 1816; d. July 9, 1837.
2  SALLY B., b. Dec. 18, 1817; m. Arad T. Linfield.
3  EMILY, b. March 31, 1820; d. Nov. 3, 1824.
4  BETHIA F., b. July 31, 1822; m. Martin Thomas.
5  BELINDA, b. Feb. 13, 1825; d. Nov. 12, 1825.
6  QUINCY, b. Oct. 15, 1827; d. May 13, 1828.
7  SUSAN E., b. May 12, 1829; d. April 12, 1880; m. Benjamin R. Dean, March 30, 1856.

1124  1120  8  GEORGE D. C., b. Aug. 25, 1831.
9  QUINCY S., d. young.
10  HENRY F., b. March 21, 1837; m. Jan. 25, 1866, Caroline H. White. No children.

———————————

1118  1121 (VII.) JASON PRATT, of Weymouth (son of VI. Joseph and Mercy), b. March 2, 1798; d. Dec. 6, 1882; m. Dec. 29, 1825, Betsey Lovell.

He was a man of considerable prominence in Weymouth, where he manufactured, and kept a store. At one time he was captain of the Franklin Guards. He was in the Legislature three terms, and held other positions of trust in the gift of the people.

Noted for his strict integrity and attention to business, he accumulated considerable property. He resided at what is called Lovell's Corner.

Children:

1  BETSEY JANE, b. Sept. 9, 1826; d. Dec. 9, 1845.
1123  1122  2  FRANKLIN DEXTER, b. July 27, 1832.
3  MARY E., b. Oct. 7, 1835; m. Richard Loud.

———————————

1122  1123 (VIII.) FRANKLIN DEXTER PRATT, of Weymouth (son of VII. Jason), b. July 27, 1832; m. Nov. 22, 1855, Lydia Beals Holbrook, dau. of Asa and Lucitta; she b. July 5, 1835; d. May 15, 1883.

He now (1887) resides at Lovell's Corner, Weymouth, having retired from active business, in which he was very successful, being one of the most prominent men of the town.

Children :

   1  FRANK PORTER, b. Sept. 16, 1861 ; d. Dec. 30, 1880.
   2  EDWIN TRUFANT, b. Oct. 19, 1865 ; d. April 29, 1884.

---

1120 1124 (VIII.) GEORGE DE WITT CLINTON PRATT, of Weymouth (son of VII. Charles), b. Aug. 25, 1831 ; m. Feb. 12, 1856, Sarah Cleverly, of Abington, where he resides. He is one of the State Detectives.

Child :

CHARLES HENRY, b. Jan. 21, 1858.

---

1108 1125 (VI.) ASA PRATT, of Weymouth (son of V. Ephriam and Lucy), b. Dec. 12, 1766 ; d. Nov. 28, 1824 ; m. Nov. 8, 1789, Sarah Lovell, dau. of Yardly and Sarah (Nash), b. Aug. 16, 1766 ; d. March 9, 1829. (T. F. Cleverly states that he d. Dec. 5, 1824, and she d. March 5, 1829.)

Children :

   1  SARAH, b. March 28, 1790 ; d. May 30, 1870 ; m. —— Daly.
   2  CHARLOTTE, b. Dec. 28, 1791 ; d. Sept. 30, 1870 ; m. (1) —— Brown ; m. (2) —— Myrick.
1136 1126  3  ASA, b. June 20, 1794 ; d. Nov. 29, 1864.
   4  PETER, b. Sept. 29, 1796 ; d. Aug. 22, 1818, at New Orleans.
1129 1127  5  CORNELIUS, b. March 2, 1799 ; d. June 13, 1879.
   6  LUCY, b. April 12, 1802.
1137 1128  7  COTTON, b. April 1, 1805 ; d. Jan. 3, 1876 ; m. Sarah —— He was a sea-captain.

---

1127 1129 (VII.) CORNELIUS PRATT, of Weymouth (son of VI. Asa), b. March 2, 1799 ; d. June 13, 1879 ; m. April 13, 1823, Rebecca Badger Leach, of Weymouth, b. Sept. 28, 1801 ; d. Feb. 5, 1874. He is styled a captain.

Children :

1133 1130  1  BENJAMIN FRANKLIN, b. June 28, 1824.
   2  WILLIAM PERKINS, b. Jan. 24, 1830 ; m. July 20, 1867, Sophia Dorchester ; they reside in Virginia City, Nev. No children.

3 ELIZA LEACH, b. Jan 30, 1833; m. George H. Pratt.

31    4 JOSIAH HUMPHREY, b. July 5, 1835.

---

32 (VIII.) JOSIAH H. PRATT, of Weymouth (son of VII. Cornelius), b. July 5, 1835; m. Lizzie Beals, April 30, 1861, dau. of Elias S. and Betsey T.; she b. Dec. 3, 1839.

Child:

JAMES HUMPHREY, b. Oct. 9, 1875.

---

33 (VIII.) BENJAMIN F. PRATT, of Weymouth (son of VII. Cornelius), b. June 28, 1824; m. Dec. 13, 1845, Eleanor Emerson French, dau. of Isaac and Susan.

He served in the War of the Rebellion, going out as captain of a Weymouth company; he was wounded, and for meritorious service was made a general.

Children:

1 ELLEN MARIA, b. Nov. 4, 1846; d. Oct. 8, 1849.

34    2 FRANKLIN C., b. Feb. 1, 1856.

---

35 (IX.) FRANKLIN C. PRATT, of Weymouth (son of VIII. Benjamin F.), b. Feb. 1, 1856; m. May 29, 1882, Edith E. Percival, of Boston.

Children:

1 CLARENCE LORIMER, b. March 30, 1883.

1 CHARLES ECKERT, b. May 2, 1885.

---

36 (VII.) ASA PRATT, of Weymouth (son of VI. Asa and Sarah Lovell), b. June 20, 1794; m. Dorcas ——, b. 1800; d. June 19, 1826.

Children:

1 ELEANOR W., b. May 3, 1821.

2 GEORGE L., b. June 25, 1824.

1128 1137 (VII.) COTTON PRATT (son of VI. Asa), b. April 1, 1805; d.
        Jan. 3, 1876; m. Sarah ——.   He was a sea-captain.

        Children:
    1  SARAH.
    2  MARIA.
    3  LAURA.
    4  EMMA.
    5  COTTON LOVELL.

# INDEX.

CPSIA information can be obtained at www.ICGtesting.com
Printed in the USA
BVOW04s1144250615

405674BV00017B/24/P